Machado de Assis

Studies in Violence, Mimesis, and Culture

Machado de Assis

TOWARD A POETICS OF EMULATION

João Cezar de Castro Rocha

Translated by Flora Thomson-DeVeaux

Michigan State University Press · *East Lansing*

♾ The paper used in this publication meets the minimum requirements of ANSI/NISO Z39.48-1992 (R 1997) (Permanence of Paper).

 Michigan State University Press
East Lansing, Michigan 48823-5245

Printed and bound in the United States of America.

21 20 19 18 17 16 15   1 2 3 4 5 6 7 8 9 10

LIBRARY OF CONGRESS CONTROL NUMBER: 2015931786
ISBN: 978-1-61186-181-5 (pbk.)
ISBN: 978-1-60917-468-2 (ebook: PDF)
ISBN: 978-1-62895-240-7 (ebook: ePub)
ISBN: 978-1-62896-240-6 (ebook: Kindle)

Book design by Charlie Sharp, Sharp Des!gns, Lansing, Michigan
Cover design by David Drummond, Salamander Design, www.salamanderhill.com.
Cover photograph of Machado de Assis's chess set is by Guilherme Gonçalves and is used courtesy of Academia Brasileira de Letras. All rights reserved.

g green press INITIATIVE Michigan State University Press is a member of the Green Press Initiative and is committed to developing and encouraging ecologically responsible publishing practices. For more information about the Green Press Initiative and the use of recycled paper in book publishing, please visit *www.greenpressinitiative.org*.

Visit Michigan State University Press at *www.msupress.org*

Contents

Translator's Note

In this new portrait of the author, João Cezar de Castro Rocha sets out on what he calls a journey around the whole of Machado de Assis's oeuvre: beginning with his earliest published pieces, sailing through faltering and then masterful short stories, novels, reviews, newspaper columns, and even dashes of poetry and theater. The circumnavigation is both broad and deep, with the strategy being a "deliberate effort to return to the text."

While preparing this translation I was lucky enough to discuss my concerns, confusions, and comments with João Cezar at length. This luxury, however, was sadly out of reach in the case of the Wizard of Cosme Velho.

Taking João Cezar's lead, I have sought my own deliberate return to the text, attempting to listen to Machado as if for the first time. Phrases and passages that were once daringly innovative have now become old friends to the Brazilian ear; and this has had its consequences, namely in the regrettable tendency to normalize strange turns of phrase, dulling the nib of Brás Cubas's "pen of mirth." In this respect, I would like to take a page from Benjamin Moser's book in his campaign to restore the strange novelty of Clarice Lispector's texts to their corresponding translations, as in *The Hour of the Star*.

It is no small task to reconcile the choices of even a single translator, let alone more than a handful over the course of decades. Given the variety of

English-language translations of Machado, my initial instinct was to favor existing translations whenever possible; after all, the translator of an entire novel or story will certainly be better positioned to make stylistic decisions than the translator of selected passages. But every translation has its own voice, and I soon realized that cobbling together such a patchwork would make Machado's work appear even more heterogeneous than the book's thesis might suggest. The oeuvre is quite varied, to be sure; but, as Machado put it when introducing the stories in *Papéis Avulsos*, we might consider his works, if not siblings, then "relatives sitting at the same table."

With that in mind, I have opted to cite consistently from selected translations of just a few novels, ones that I believe would fit in comfortably around such a table. The rest of the translations, whenever not noted otherwise, are my own—I can only hope that they will pull up a seat and start a conversation with their cousins. In more than one case I have resorted to my own translations not because of any stylistic deficiency in a published alternative, but in response to João Cezar's intense engagement with Machado's diction and syntax, his eye for unusual vocabulary and striking phrases, where it becomes indispensable that the translation run as close to the original phrasing as possible.

As for the translations that were incorporated into the text, minor adaptations have been made when necessary. For example, when proper names were Anglicized by a translator, I have restored the original spelling without comment so as to maintain consistency with other references to the same work. In the case of works in languages other than Spanish and Portuguese, I have sought out English translations when available and resignedly played Telephone and translated from the Portuguese when they were not. Published translations are cited throughout; when the title of a work appears in the original language, then the translation is mine.

I have refrained from peppering the text with my own footnotes and italics, not wishing to compete with João Cezar. As for key Portuguese-language terms that I felt would be unnecessarily stripped of nuance in a simple translation, I have defined them at their first appearance and let them be in later instances. Throughout, I have sought to move carefully and tread lightly when bringing a study on Machado into the English language; the penalties for betrayals are severe around these parts, and not just for translators, as Capitu can tell you.

Preface

T he most economical introduction to the project framing this book may be to examine a series of exhibitions, whose common thread may be interpreted through a mimetic lens.

The groundbreaking exhibition *Matisse Picasso* was put together in 2002. The intense and troubling connection strung between the two artists seems practically tailored to shed light on the elective affinities between *mimetic theory* and the array of aesthetic and intellectual procedures that I shall refer to as the *poetics of emulation*—a new theoretical framework proposed in this text.

In the words of John Golding on the importance of *Matisse Picasso:* "This exhibition tells one of the most compelling and rewarding stories in the entire history of art."[1]

Indeed.

Golding's statement is true in part because this exhibition brings out the circuit that, whether openly or not, has shaped Western culture's conception of art. I am referring to the aesthetic devices of *imitatio* and *aemulatio,* a pair of concepts, and above all a set of procedures, that rose to prominence through Latin culture, given the challenge of assimilating the techniques and works of Greek culture and the whole of the Hellenistic legacy. In this unique register, we are constantly wrestling with the triangular nature of mimetic desire, as identified by René Girard in *Mensonge romantique et vérité romanesque* (1961).

I shall briefly discuss the dynamics of mimetic desire, which is Girard's theoretical jumping-off point. Human desire, he suggests, is the product of the presence of a mediator. We do not desire directly, but indirectly, and the target of our desire is determined less by ourselves than by the networks woven by the mediations that surround us. Desire implies mediation between the *subject*, the *object*, and, of course, the mediator—being the *model* adopted for defining desire, which inevitably rests on a triangular relationship. As Girard himself put it, "The spatial metaphor which expresses this triple relationship is obviously the triangle."[2] From this perspective, the study of mediation is crucial, as the subject will tend to struggle with the model for control of the object, the desire for which having been awoken by the mediator—hence the element of conflict in the mimetic circuit. Here lies the true originality of Girard's system, which identifies the rise of structural violence in the seemingly neutral gesture of imitation.

Girard identified two forms of mediation:

> We shall speak of *external mediation* when the distance is sufficient to eliminate any contact between the two spheres of *possibilities* of which the mediator and the subject occupy the respective centers. We shall speak of *internal mediation* when this same distance is sufficiently reduced to allow these two spheres to penetrate each other more or less profoundly (9).

Internal mediation is the stage for potential conflicts, given the proximity between subject and model. The same is true for the aesthetic realm. Let us see: the new artist (*subject*), seeking to produce a work (*object*), must first calibrate his or her understanding of tradition as a whole, or of the work of a given artist—generally a renowned contemporary, and hence a *model*. Just as mimetic desire gives rise to rivalries and an eventual escalation of physical violence, intellectual and artistic rivalries also tend toward a high level of symbolic violence—as anyone who happens to be familiar with the art world or with the university system knows too well . . .

It thus comes as no surprise that, in terms of contact between Picasso and Matisse, "the two men had become the most important fixed points in each other's artistic lives."[3] In March 1906, the two painters met for the first time. Matisse, at age thirty-seven, was already a chef d'école. Picasso, twelve years his junior, had yet to acquire the airs of a master. In this first encounter, naturally, the Spaniard greedily drank in the French painter's lessons. Very soon thereafter, however—the next year, as a matter of fact—Picasso reinvented himself with *Les demoiselles d'Avignon*, the impact of which is, of course, extremely well known. Interestingly, but also predictably from a mimetic perspective, Matisse began to observe his colleague's work with redoubled attention. Productive tension set in, as Picasso later recalled: "You have got to be able to picture side by side everything Matisse and I were doing at that time. No one has ever looked at Matisse's paintings more carefully than I; and no one has looked at mine more carefully than he" (13).

It would not be overreaching, then, to suppose that one of the decisive chapters in the history of modern art was traced with decidedly mimetic brushstrokes.

A second exhibition extended this concept to the whole of the Spanish artist's works. This was *Picasso et les maîtres,* organized in 2008. Once again, the painter showed himself to be fully conscious of the process:

> It is we, the painters, the true heirs, who keep on painting. We are the heirs to Rembrandt, Velázquez, Cézanne, and Matisse. A painter always has a father and a mother; he is not born of nothing."[4]

It is not by chance that we are dealing with painting, after all. In the nineteenth century, even after the emergence of Romanticism and the subsequent obliteration of both rhetorical models and the centrality of the technique of *imitatio* and *aemulatio* in artistic practice, apprentices in painting schools still started out by *copying* traditional masterpieces, an act that fostered the *appropriation* of models—an indispensable part of invention. This was precisely the sort of formal education that Picasso undertook in Málaga, the city of his birth.

Marie-Laure Bernadac summed up the painter's process: "His relationship with the painters of the past has more of cannibalism, of iconophagy, than of pastiche or paraphrase. This is not only a matter of a relationship of canvas to canvas, but a dialogue between painters, of true identification, almost on an emotional level, with the artists that he admired and who made up his artistic pantheon."[5]

Picasso's case is exemplary in a potentially productive and not wholly disquieting understanding of mimetic desire—at least, in the aesthetic realm. In this sense, to put it in Girardian terms, one must transform the rivalry with the model into energy to pour into the work, thus bringing about the return of the object.[6]

Picasso et les maîtres included a special show focused on Picasso's obsession with Manet's classic painting *Le déjeuner sur l'herbe*, which had its debut in 1863 at the Salon des Refusés and was received with an authentic "succès de scandale."

When a Manet retrospective was organized in 1932, Picasso felt himself particularly challenged by the painting. A little over two decades later, in 1954, he began appropriating elements of the work through sketches and drawings that took into account, above all, the distribution of volumes and colors in the French artist's composition. Next, the procedure took on a fascinating form of concentration: "Picasso takes over Manet's work: its composition, its characters, and the relationship between them, which he had already made evolve. *He copies and interprets at the same time.*"[7]

(A consummate master, Picasso invented a gaze that brought *imitatio* and *aemulatio* together in a single act!)

After many a sketch and drawing, the Spaniard finally recreated Manet's painting with his own brushstrokes in 1960—for the first of countless times, once he (re)painted Manet's canvas obsessively. Finally, in 1962, Picasso produced three-dimensional models of the characters in *Le déjeuner*, transforming their shapes on the canvas into ideal projections into space. Inspired by this work, Carl Nesjar created sculptures that now stand outside the Moderna Museet in Stockholm. This surprising mimetic circle, from Manet's painting to Picasso's obsession, was closed, resulting in the materiality of multiple outdoor sandblasted concrete sculptures.

I hadn't even mentioned that Manet, for his part, saw his painting as a reinterpretation of a Titian painting and a Marcantonio Raimondi engraving. And as if that weren't enough, Raimondi took his inspiration from a work by Raphael. . . . The mimetic circle only intensifies, "through the exercise of the copier who is copied" (20).

Clearly, we are a long way away from W. Jackson Bate's idea of the "burden of the past,"[8] or Harold Bloom's notion of the "anxiety of influence."[9] On the contrary, the poetics of emulation, in dialogue with some assumptions of mimetic theory, allows us to imagine a "productivity of influence." Tradition thus becomes less of a burden, emerging rather as an unavoidable jumping-off point, since the centrality of the other is fully recognized.

As in the realm of *ars combinatoria*, the existence of rules is a necessary precondition for freedom.

As in jazz, improvisation demands rigorous discipline.

Another exhibition may help to further clarify my point.

Turner and the Masters was put together in 2009. The title itself pays tribute to the importance of mimetic procedures, whether in nineteenth-century England or twentieth-century France.

Just as would be the case with Picasso, Turner's career consisted of a series of appropriations of masterpieces, driven by ongoing rivalries with his colleagues. In other words, the technique of *imitatio* and *aemulatio* provided the compass for the "Painter of Light" to produce his work. David Solkin has a colorful take on the painter's ethos: "By the late 1790s, his reputation as a prodigy in the medium of watercolor was beginning to be eclipsed by the rising star of his good friend Thomas Girtin.... Unfortunately, his rival's premature death in 1802 brought this productive competition to an end almost before it had fully began."[10]

This unhappy circumstance, however, did nothing to diminish the centrality of emulation in Turner's artistic practice. On the contrary, it shaped his understanding of the art system, with pride of place reserved for seventeenth-century French painter Claude Lorrain.

This was a delicate topic: after all, while the public may see the hallmark of Turner's style residing in the intensity of the light that seems to spill out from the canvas toward the viewer, Claude's main contribution to the history of art was precisely the development of the technique of creating "an integrated imagery that addressed both the eye *and* the mind"[11] whose effect was the vivid impression that light came from the paiting itself. Far before Turner would merit the title of "Painter of Light," his French colleague had inaugurated the model.

Turner, then, could do nothing more than "comprehend Claude's mental and artistic procedures so he could not just replicate them in formal terms, but also assimilate and modernize the classical ideal" (59). In yet another case, mimetic rivalry gives rise to artistic fecundity.

Obsessed with the parallel, Turner left the British government a special bequest: two paintings by Claude and two of his own paintings, to be hung in the National Gallery. The painter stipulated only one thing: Claude's works, *Landscape with the Marriage of Isaac and Rebecca* (1648) and *Seaport with the Embarkation of the Queen of Sheba* (1648), had to be placed side by side with his own paintings, *Sun Rising through Vapour* (1807) and *Dido Building Carthage* (1815).

Turner wished to both lay bare his dialogue with Claude and underscore the success of his emulation.[12] The complexity of this gesture led to a new exhibition in 2012—*Turner Inspired: In the Light of Claude.*

At this point, two observations emerge.

First, the two exhibitions have the same title and exactly the same approach, suggesting a structural affinity that allows for a link between Girardian thought and aesthetic reflection: *Picasso et les maîtres; Turner and the Masters.*

Second, a decisive aspect should be highlighted here. The weight that Turner gave to emulation stemmed at least partially from the fact that, in the European art system, British painting never held a canonical spot. Hence the urgent need to face down the hegemonic models of his time: the Italian, Dutch, and French pictorial traditions. As would any intellectual or artist from a nonhegemonic context, Turner had to measure his talent and skills with those of hegemonic models.

David Solkin keenly intuited the association between emulation and rivalry in Turner's art; ultimately, in this book, I wish to offer up a new portrait of Machado de Assis, driven precisely by his complex relationship with Eça de Queirós. Another exhibition would also emphasize this theme, this one put together in 2009—*Titian, Tintoretto, Veronese: Rivals in Renaissance Venice.* In the revealing words of the curator:

> The Cinquecento, or sixteenth century, was an era of artistic rivalry in Venice. The best painters thrived in this context of ambition, envy, and pressure. The history of the time is littered with anecdotes and turns of phrase that make clear that painters, their patrons, and their audiences all

understood that competition, and a flourishing demand for pictures, often brought out the best in artists, making Venice a hub not only of commerce but also of painting.[13]

Venice became the stage for a vigorous internal system of emulation, anticipating the *Matisse Picasso* duel by centuries. This passage points to the potentially positive side of mimetic desire, via the "good internal meditation" proposed by Fornari. In mimetic relations, subject and model generally become so wrapped up in a spiral of rivalry that they wind up losing sight of the object of their desire. The artistic procedure that defines emulation, however, implies the possibility of the return of the object; the rivalry, after all, only makes sense if it results in the production of a new work.

And that's not all.

The Italian sixteenth century gave rise to a struggle between the Roman and Venetian schools—to wit, between, respectively, the meticulous primacy of drawing and the relative autonomy of color in composition, or the clash between Raphael and Titian. This was emulation turned on its head, of course, as the two artists took different paths, but were no less competitive for it.

A look at the rivalry between Italian schools allows us to bring a key name into the discussion for later development of the theoretical framework inaugurated by the poetics of emulation: El Greco. The epithet lent to Cretan native Domenikos Theotokopoulos, for that matter, evokes an involuntary metonymy of his trajectory.

At the time, Crete was a Venetian colony. It comes as no surprise, then, that El Greco would have traveled to the metropolis to broaden the horizons of his work. And, like a true "wheeling stranger of here and everywhere,"[14] he stayed in the city long enough to master the new Venetian style. The next leg took the Cretan to Rome, where he remained for approximately five years. Once again, he assimilated the contributions of Raphael's school, while still preserving elements of both the Byzantine tradition and Venetian painting.

Ever a wanderer, given to an omnivorous appetite when assimilating artistic procedures and aesthetic principles, El Greco stayed a short while in Madrid before finally settling down in Toledo.

This was a symbolic place, the stage for the first definitively multicultural experiment in European civilization, the highest point of which remains the

Toledo School of Translators. In the twelfth and thirteenth centuries, Arab, Jewish, and Christian scholars worked together in an exemplary process of trilingual translation and retranslation. They thus preserved the legacy of classical Greek culture, greatly broadening Europe's future humanistic repertoire. Toledo became a true bridge city between the cultural traditions of the East and the West.

For that reason, El Greco could hardly have imagined a better place to close out his career and create some of his most famous canvases; after all, he and the city of Toledo are two sides to the same coin, its circulation fixed from the very start of its journey. In the words of John H. Elliott:

> The Mediterranean world of the sixteenth century—the world of El Greco—was a world in which three civilisations coexisted, interacted and clashed: the Latin West; the Greek Orthodox East; and the civilisation of Islam. As a Cretan, and hence a subject of the Republic of Venice, Domenikos Theotokopoulos, known as El Greco (1541–1614), belonged both to the Greek East and to Latin Christendom. He and his generation lived much of their lives in the shadow of confrontation between Christendom and Islam.[15]

The poetics of emulation seeks to offer a theoretical framework able to tackle the circumstances sprung from the intersection of cultures, traditions, and aesthetic choices.

(In today's world, poetics must be transformed into cultural politics—a need that grows by the day.)

Acknowledgments

First, and without the slightest deference for protocol, I would like to thank the editor of the Brazilian edition, the writer and critic Evando Nascimento, for the patience with which he awaited the manuscripts; and, above all, for the critical gaze with which he pointed out imprecisions and suggested refinements. A more perfect combination of friendship, intellectual rigor, and generosity could not be found.

Second, I want to wholeheartedly thank William Johnsen for his interest in publishing my book in this series, and, above all, for a productive dialogue over the years, especially concerning our common interest in René Girard's mimetic theory.

Let me also mention the fundamental support given by Imitatio, which made the translation of this book possible.

Special recognition is due to the countless readers who gave me comments on the first version of this book. I owe much to the intelligence with which they critiqued me. They are, in alphabetical order: Adriana Lunardi, Alexandre Agnolon, André Carneiro Ramos, Carola Saavedra, David Toscana, Marcus Vinicius Nogueira Soares, María Teresa Atrián Pineda, Thomaz Amorim Neto, Valdir Prigol, Victoria Saramago, Victor K. Mendes, and Wanderlei Barreiro Lemos.

The National Council for Scientific and Technological Development (CNPq) fellowship for productivity in research was fundamental in carrying out the project that gave rise to this book. Rio de Janeiro State University's "Prociência" research fellowship played the same role.

I completed the first version of the second chapter thanks to the Hélio and Amélia Pedroso / Luso-American Foundation Endowed Chair in Portuguese Studies, granted by the Center for Portuguese Studies at the University of Massachusetts–Dartmouth. My thanks to Frank F. Sousa and Victor K. Mendes for their constant dialogue over the course of more than a decade.

I presented the first summary of the "poetics of emulation" while serving in the Cátedra de Estudios Latinoamericanos Machado de Assis–Universidad del Claustro Sor Juana / Embajada de Brasil en México. My thanks to Valquíria Wey, Sandra Lorenzano, and Paolo Pagliai for the opportunity to discuss my ideas. And to Alberto Ruy-Sánchez for an intense dialogue.

At the Colegio de México, thanks to an invitation from Guillermo de Jesús Palacios and Elena Gutiérrez de Velasco, I first discussed the possibility of broadening the concept of a "poetics of emulation" to include the whole of Latin American culture.

Thanks to María Luisa Armendáriz, I kept up a monthly column in the Mexican magazine *Nueva Era*, sketching out some of the ideas developed here.

Last but not least, a special acknowledgment is due to the Academia Brasileira de Letras (ABL). Its president, Dr. Geraldo Holanda Cavalcanti, generously allowed the reproduction of Machado de Assis's chess set on the cover of this book. I also want to thank the academic and poet Antonio Carlos Secchin and the librarian of the ABL, Luiz Antônio de Souza, for their support.

The Paradox
of the Ur-Author

This bring us to the central issue, that of the peculiar greatness of the great writer from a "small culture." The great writer is aware that his environment is a terrible conditioning factor, a factor which is even more appreciable where there are no conditions for confident prestige and an intense intellectual and literary life, both qualitatively and quantitatively, though that is no less the case with any other field. The great writer has, therefore, to exact from himself what his environment would not demand on such a scale. He will also have, or try to have, a cultural awareness and critical lucidity which are lacking, in comparable terms, in his contemporaries of the great cultures.

—Jorge de Sena, "Machado de Assis and His Carioca Quintet"

It is about time that Machado de Assis's works began to be comprehended as a coherently organized whole by perceiving that certain primary and principal structures are dismantled and rearticulated in the form of different, more complex, and more sophisticated structures, in accordance with the chronological order of his texts.

—Silviano Santiago, "The Rhetoric of Verisimilitude"

The second lesson I drew from my reading of *Casa Velha* was that, in order
to obtain a broader and more profound reading of Machado's works, one
must examine his (supposedly) lesser works, such as, for example, those
that the author himself did not republish.

—John Gledson, *Por um novo Machado de Assis*

In his crônicas,[1] Machado rehearsed the topic of "Um homem célebre"
[A Celebrated Man]. He rehearsed not only the topic, but also the tone,
injecting much of crônica's polka into the chamber piece that is the story, à
la a "concert for cello and machete."[2]

—José Miguel Wisnik, "Machado maxixe"

In the Middle of the Way

In one of his memorable series of talks, *Historia de nuestra idea del mundo*,
José Gaos, a Spanish philosopher who settled in Mexico after the triumph of
Francoism, laid out the possibilities inherent in a good introduction.[3]

On one hand, it allows the reader to orient herself from the start, following the author's reasoning step by step. (Gaos, however, was referring to those
who listened to his lectures; I will thus make the necessary adaptations.) On
the other hand—and here lies the greater advantage—a good introduction
allows the reader to simply close the book and turn to more fruitful tasks.

I aim to offer an alternative explanation for one of the core dilemmas
of Brazilian literary criticism: the "midlife crisis" that Machado de Assis
underwent from 1878 to 1880 and that resulted in his writing the *Memórias
Póstumas de Brás Cubas* [The Posthumous Memoirs of Brás Cubas], as well
as the remarkable production of his mature years. In the first chapter, I study
Machado's novels and short stories produced prior to 1880, using the contrast
to signal the revolution set off by the prose of the deceased author.

At the center of this alternative explanation, I situate the fallout from
the success enjoyed by Eça de Queirós, rereading the harsh articles produced
by Machado regarding *Primo Basílio* [Cousin Bazilio]. The novel is released
in February 1878, and, in April of the same year, Machado publishes two
long texts condemning both the Portuguese author's aesthetic choices as
well as the structure of his narrative. This severe analysis is considered one of

the high points of his critical work. I try to show instead that this appraisal reminds one of David Hume's critique of causality: it depends on customs alone, and not on a critical inquiry. Indeed, around this period Machado's perspective had been both aesthetically traditional and morally conservative. It is as if Machado, the author of *Posthumous Memoirs*, only became possible after he could overcome the narrow-minded principles of Machadinho ["Little Machado"],[4] the reader of *Cousin Bazilio*. I argue for this rereading in the second chapter.

From this, I derive the key hypothesis of this essay: an unforeseen consequence of Machado's reaction to Eça's novel was a return to the classical notion of *aemulatio*, which led him to develop the *poetics of emulation*. In the third chapter I introduce this idea, though it is already briefly mentioned in the second. I do not intend on offering a theoretical contribution to the study of *aemulatio*, a topic more fit for classical studies than Machadian criticism. The poetics of emulation equates to the modern reclaiming of rhetorical practices that were progressively abandoned after the advent of romanticism. I thus differentiate *aemulatio*—the defining technique of the pre-Romantic literary and artistic system—from the *poetics of emulation*—a deliberately anachronistic undertaking and a hallmark of Machadian literature.

"Deliberate anachronism" is here employed in the sense made famous by Jorge Luis Borges's short story, "Pierre Menard, Author of the *Quixote*." Machado, however, seemed to have already defined it in a crônica from the series *História de 15 dias* [Story of Fifteen Days], released on January 1, 1877: "But this is a tired curiosity, a deceased bit of news. Let us turn to the very newest thing, since it is quite ancient; rather, very ancient, since it is quite new" (III, 355).[5] Passages such as these are common, as I demonstrate in the last two chapters, dedicated precisely to reclaiming the semantic field of *aemulatio* in Machado's works. Machado often seems to reflect on the strangeness provoked by the updating of pre-Romantic literary practices in a post-Romantic environment—and the consequences of this shift are striking, in terms of cultural politics.

Thus, I address the effects of the *poetics of emulation* in the Brás Cubas rupture, in which the semantic field associated with *aemulatio* became one of the pillars of the Machadian oeuvre.

In the last two chapters, I map the vocabulary and the procedures of the techniques of *imitatio* and *aemulatio* across all literary genres and during the five decades in which Machado was writing. I argue for a crosscutting reading of the Machadian oeuvre as a whole, identifying its rhythms and its transformations.

Of course, this introduction is not the appropriate place to discuss the concept of *aemulatio*. I might as well say now that the practice of emulation implies a specific concept of a literary system, privileging the act of reading as an eminently inventive gesture. After all, in *imitating* a model considered the *authority* in a given genre, one seeks to *emulate that model*, producing a difference in relation to it. At the end of the fifth chapter and in the conclusion, I address the political potential in the poetics of emulation.

Having clarified the structure of the book, I will return to the topic at hand.

The success of *O crime do padre Amaro* [The Crime of Father Amaro] (1875) and *Cousin Bazilio* (1878) did not go unnoticed by the Brazilian author. They represented a powerful spur goading the solicitous Machadinho to risk it all and transform himself into the Machado admired across the world. This is not a "psychological" issue but one of the author's dissatisfaction with his own work—a dilemma exacerbated by the appearance of the young Portuguese novelist.

The argument is potentially controversial, I acknowledge, as it highlights literary rivalry as a relevant factor in Machado's transformation. This aspect contradicts the dominant image of the author of "A Causa Secreta" [The Secret Cause]: a perennially cordial Machado who abhorred controversy. I ask the reader to follow the chapters that comprise this essay as if they were pieces of a jigsaw, the assembly of which will depend on his or her cooperation.

In no sense do I consider the appearance of Queirós's novel as the *cause* of the Machadian metamorphosis. This is not a simple phenomenon, subject to an elementary explanation, but rather a process of great complexity, the raison d'être of Machado de Assis as a writer.

Such prudence is insufficient, as it skirts what really matters: the Machadian text.

(This essay represents a deliberate effort to *return to the text*, in order to map the *Machado de Assis literary system*.)

It would be naive to suppose that the novel, with the 1880 publication of *The Posthumous Memoirs of Brás Cubas*, and the short story, with the

1882 appearance of *Papéis avulsos* [Loose Papers], were suddenly and completely transformed. The Machadian rhythm was a slow one. *Cousin Bazilio* catalyzed textual forces that Machado had already harnessed here and there, although in a sporadic and sometimes a timid fashion. Rather than an absolute novelty, the writing of the *Posthumous Memoirs* represented the gathering of heteroclite resources, previously tested out in crônicas and stories.

This is why I dub my explanation for the Machadian existential and artistic crisis an *alternative* one. While I do not boil down the many dimensions of the problem to the breadth of my hypothesis, I strive to unveil a new angle from which it may be understood.

A Hypothesis

A memorable scene from *Citizen Kane*, by Orson Welles, presents one of the most incisive criticisms of the idea of interpretation as the art of revealing the truth—whether in understanding a person or reading a text. With a subtle movement of the camera, which progressively moves out to expose the plethora of pieces collected by the millionaire, the screen becomes the image of an unexpected museum in search of a curator. The key to the enigma of Charles Foster Kane may have resided in the meticulous examination of the pieces of art, the endless curiosities, the myriad of artifacts he gathered over the course of his life. The accumulation of information might just help decrypt the mystery: the meaning of the word "Rosebud," proffered by the press magnate in his final hour.

Meanwhile, in a final motion, the camera becomes an accomplice to the viewer, allowing her to move toward the fireplace, where worthless objects are being destroyed. Among so many pieces, one childhood relic stands out: a simple sled, apparently meaningless, although it appeared at the beginning of the film when the boy Kane was sent away by his parents in order to receive an education befitting his mother's recently acquired fortune. Bit by bit, the flames devouring the sled obliterate the name: "Rosebud." Like the purloined letter in the story by Edgar Allan Poe, the answer to the problem lies before the viewer's eyes—albeit not for long.

This scene discourages any mechanical interpretations. If the reporter in charge of producing the documentary had sought out the correct "clues," the meaning of the word "Rosebud" would be revealed, and would thus clarify

the central thread of Charles Foster Kane's life. So does the meticulous literary critic seek out the hidden phrase, the secret word, the oblique reference
capable of driving the hermeneutic circle at whose center all questions would
be answered, establishing the perfect link between Machadian text and historical context. In the last scene, the reporter recognizes the illusion that he
has been chasing: no life can be fully explained. Even if he had discovered
the meaning of "Rosebud," the reconstruction would be just that: a partial
assembly whose totality can never be reached. Did that total meaning ever
exist, we might ask, even for Kane himself?

The critical gaze is always anachronistic, teasing out current
preoccupations in the objects of any age. Such an inversion occurs in the
story "Uma visita de Alcibíades" [A Visit from Alcibiades], originally
published in the *Jornal das Famílias* in 1876 and included in *Loose Papers*
(1882). In it, the narrator, though he feels a true "Greek's devotion; devotion
or mania" (II, 352), when faced with the illustrious Athenian, he limits
himself to defending the fashion of his own time. At the same time, upon
being introduced to the clothing of the nineteenth century, the celebrated
orator dies "a second time" (II, 357), as he cannot, nor does he wish to,
abandon his classic values. That is why the narrator's words make the Attic
lose his sense of proportion:

> "My good sir," I said to him, "you may certainly demand that Olympic
> Jupiter be the eternal emblem of majesty: he is the mastery of the ideal,
> selfless art, superior to the passing times and the men who go along with
> them. But the art of dressing is something else entirely. This which seems
> absurd or ungainly is perfectly rational and beautiful—beautiful in our
> fashion, we who, as we walk along, do not hear the rhapsodes reciting their
> verses, nor the orators and their discourses, nor the philosophers and their
> philosophies. You yourself, if you become accustomed to seeing us, will
> find yourself taken with us, because . . ."
>
> "Wretch!" he bellowed, throwing himself upon me. (II, 356)

The narrator's reflection hews quite closely to Baudelaire's definition of
"modernity": a balance between the ephemeral and the eternal.[6] One possible reading of this dilemma would negate the hermeneutic exercise, since
everything becomes a pretext for the interpreter's obsessions. It is as if the

critic were to negate the possibility of literature at the moment in which he opened the book; after all, he would only be seeking to confirm previously formulated hypotheses. Within this alchemy—a failed one, because it is inevitably successful—there is one alternative: to become anachronistic in relation to oneself, and, like the reporter in *Citizen Kane*, denounce the illusion of a definitive answer. Anachronism is thus not a self-centered ruin, but rather the basis for all human action: no historical period was (or is) contemporaneous to itself.

The dilemma posed by Orson Welles hid an implacable critique, both of press magnate William Randolph Hearst and the traditional structure of Hollywood narrative, whose happy ending brings with it the unfailing solution to all its problems. Any object that "casually" appears on screen, just like all of the situations presented in the plot, snaps into place like the pieces of a jigsaw puzzle, and the final picture never disappoints the viewer.

Orson Welles's dilemma may be of particular interest for scholars of authors as complex as the creator of Quincas Borba—both the fortunate dog and the frustrated philosopher. If we adopt the free form of his corrosive humor, might we not associate the emblematic scene from the film with a recurring attitude in Machadian criticism?

With the publication of *The Posthumous Memoirs of Brás Cubas* in 1880 and *Loose Papers* two years later, Machado set off a revolution without precedent in Brazilian literature. This is an attempt to understand the internal motivation that might have led to such a radical experiment: how to understand the "midlife crisis" and the new diction of his prose? This question favored the sprouting of hypotheses as fruitful as they are often contradictory.

The eternal recurrence of the question inspires a provocation: to what extent is this a case of begging the question? In the Aristotelian definition, this is a logical problem that consists of using a point that ought to be proved at the end of the process of argumentation as the very premise of the argument. *Petitio principii* is thus fed by the very engine of investigation, as concentrating on the novels' flows into the eternal recurrence. After all, between the first four titles and the last five there opens a radically new horizon— often, it is true, constituted by the efficient combination of previously tested procedures, particularly the various types of narrators, exhaustively tested in stories and crônicas.

However, some constant characteristics are visible as early as *Ressur-reição* [Resurrection], the author's first novel, published in 1872, and even in short stories from the 1860s. A number of themes, for example—principally, the study of the condition of the agregado[7] and the pathology of jealousy; character sketches (especially of women); metaphorical series (a highlight being the series concerned with gaze); and textual procedures (particularly the explicit vision of the act of reading as an authorial gesture, of writing with one's eyes before picking up a pen). Even so, one cannot deny that the publication of the *Posthumous Memoirs* blazed paths that were new even to Machado. The very presence of constant characteristics serves as counterevidence: while there are undeniably common elements, their treatment reveals an unequivocal difference.

This supposition allows us to extend the deceased author's rupture to the realm of short stories, establishing a parallel between *Posthumous Memoirs* and *Loose Papers*. This is not an unproblematic artifice. Some of the stories included in the collection were published before *Iaiá Garcia*, the last novel from the so-called first phase, released in 1878. "A chinela turca" [The Turkish Slipper] is from 1875; "A Visit from Alcibiades," from 1876.

A story such as "Miss Dollar," from 1870, published in the first collection of this sort (*Contos fluminenses* [Tales from Rio], released the same year), provides an extremely rich take on the role of the reader. The text discusses a number of forms of reception; hence the constant, provocative descriptors: "superficial reader" (II, 28), and even "grave reader" (II, 32), later to be enshrined in the *Posthumous Memoirs*' "Note to the Reader."

This appeal to the reader may also be found in the narrative poem "Pálida Elvira" [Pallid Elvira], published in *Falenas* [Phalaenae] in 1870. The opening verses declare:

When, *my lady reader*, in the west
Appears the swooning, thoughtful dusk; (III, 69; italics mine)

Shortly thereafter, we see "my reader," who, being "a prudent man / Tranquilly closes my roman" (III, 71); the "reader my friend" (III, 47); and the "curious lady reader" (III, 76). To say nothing of the countless exhortations punctuating the poem, the structure of which depends on staging the act of reading the verses themselves:

And she? If you had but once in your life,
Dear reader, been sick with love, saintly delirium;
. . . .
Note that I do not speak of that bond
Of a night of dancing or conversation; (III, 80)

A similar move may be found, although in a fairly rudimentary form, in "Confissões de uma viúva moça" [Confessions of a Young Widow], a story published in the *Jornal das Famílias* in 1865 and also reproduced in *Tales from Rio*. Here is how the narrator braces herself against a vulgar suitor: "This man . . . is nothing more than a bad reader of realist novels" (II, 107–8). However, as the young widow does let herself be seduced, one concludes that she is an even less competent reader of romantic novels. The story dramatizes the act of reading serial publications: "My letters will proceed every eight days, so that the narrative may strike you with the effect of a weekly feuilleton in the newspaper" (II, 100). A renewed reading ought to explore this dramatization, emphasizing the dialogue with the reader without neglecting the conventional, "edifying" nature of the plot.

However, the parallelism between *Posthumous Memoirs* and *Loose Papers* has a powerful argument on its side: the most famous stories in the collection only appeared after 1880. This is the case with "O alienista" [The Alienist] (1881), "Teoria do Medalhão" [Stuffed-Shirt Theory] (1881), "O Espelho" [The Mirror] (1882), and "A Sereníssima República" [The Most Serene Republic] (1882).

This brings us to a working hypothesis: what would be the result of a cross-referenced reading of the novels of the second phase with the novels, stories, crônicas, poems, plays, and critical articles preceding the publication of the *Posthumous Memoirs*? Would such a crosscutting reading of the whole of Machado's literature allow us to imagine an alternative explanation for the existential and artistic crisis of the author of *Resurrection*? If the elements that structure the deceased author's prose are already scattered around here and there, what might have inspired their combination? This cannot be a linear explanation, much less one with a single cause, but must rather be a process of comings and goings, whose interpretation demands a new perspective.

Let me reiterate what I have said: the spectacular success of *Cousin

Bazilio may have led the formerly cautious author to risk everything in crafting *The Posthumous Memoirs of Brás Cubas.*

Intersection of Readings and Genres

Recall the story "Três Tesouros Perdidos" [Three Lost Treasures], released in *A Marmota* on January 5, 1858, and never republished by the author. It was the year of his debut as a short story writer, at a tender eighteen years. The tale is brief and conventional; it begins with a tense situation, which disguises a mistake soon to be clarified: the deceived husband, Mr. F., although he is naturally the last to know, ought to have been the first to suspect—as his wife, Mrs. E., abandons him and flees with his best friend. Nevertheless, Mr. F. imagines that his wife's lover is one Mr. X. He resolutely goes to meet the man, offering him a heroic choice: leave the city, or die. Mr. X. being unprepared for such a sudden journey, the husband, Mr. F., valiantly offers him two *contos* to defray his expenses. The tension is diluted into a comic resolution, moving the story closer to the realm of a light crônica, almost an anecdote. Upon returning home, Mr. F. realizes that he has been mistaken:

> When he came to himself, he was mad . . . raving mad!
>
> These days, when someone visits him, he says, in doleful tones, "I lost three treasures at once: a wife without equal, a tried-and-true friend, and a lovely wallet full of enchanting bills . . . that might very well warm my pockets!"
>
> As for this last point, the madman is correct, and seems to be a sane madman at that.(I, 65)[8]

We are faced with a naive sketch. However, from the very beginning, the triangle has been the quintessential Machadian geometric figure, an element developed in a number of texts and resulting in the sphinxlike novel *Dom Casmurro.*

Let us turn to a more detailed examination of this simple Machadian debut—precisely in the genre that would later enshrine him as an author.

The first paragraph of the story presents a structure that a more mature Machado would certainly modify: "One day, *it was four o'clock*, Mr. X. . . . was returning to *his* home *to dine*. The appetite that drove him did not make him notice a carriage stopped before *his* door" (I, 63; italics mine). In this excerpt, the use of the possessive pronoun establishes a relationship of "confirmation," referring to Mr. X.'s home, although the reader would be unlikely to consider an alternative. An interesting proposition would be to follow the progressive abandonment of such reiterative effects so as to increase the potential ambiguity of the phrase: a trademark of Machadian style. The specificities of "it was four o'clock" and "to dine" fill the same "confirming" role, revealing an author in training, concerned with the correctness of the text, as if he were an eager student striving for straight As. One does not need a particularly inspired critical imagination to envision the Machadian rewriting of the sentence: "One afternoon, Mr. X . . . was returning home. The appetite that drove him did not make him notice a carriage stopped before the door."

In "Folha rota" [Tattered Leaf], for example, from 1878, printed in the *Jornal das Famílias* and never republished by the author, the fact is no longer pure information, but rather a flicker to spark the reader's imagination: "The two hands found each other once more and were bound together. A few minutes, *three or four*, passed in this fashion" (II, 866; italics mine). This is not an example of chronological precision, but rather an emphasis on the psychological duration of the episode, suggesting the scene's discreet eroticism.

However, even in the simple novice's effort that is "Three Lost Treasures," one may note themes that will return frequently in Machado's prose.

On one hand, the presence of the "raving mad" husband who becomes a "sane madman" indicates the intersection between insanity and lucidity, one of the key elements in the Machadian gaze, the masterpiece in this vein being "The Alienist." Even the cartoonish figure of the deceived husband who goes insane when he discovers his wife's infidelity will return in a much better-constructed story, "O machete" [The Machete], published in the *Jornal das Famílias* in 1878, but also left out of Machado's short story collections.

On the other hand, the theme of jealousy, while only drawn with light brushstrokes, returns in the "posthumous doubts" of Félix, a character in *Resurrection* (I, 195), finally reaching maximum ambiguity in the unfettered imagination of Bento Santiago, in *Dom Casmurro*. I am not saying that "Three Lost Treasures" is anything more than a mere sketch, but it remains relevant in order to confirm that certain themes and procedures were already present in the Machadian oeuvre.

This observation reinforces my theory: in this essay, I wish to take a radical turn in the methodological procedure of taking a crosscutting look at Machado's work. The hypothesis of a possible interrelation between the literary genres at hand makes it possible to combine questions that have been proposed by other researchers in isolation. Instead of adding to the ranks of studies of the novel, we will identify thematic and textual elements present across the various genres wielded by the author of *Esaú e Jacó* [Esau and Jacob]. The writer of crônicas, far before the finger-flicks of Brás Cubas, had turned irreverence into the very way he related to the hasty newspaper reader. In the stories published before 1880 we may observe a laboratory of ideas, narrative experiments, and textual procedures resuscitated by the deceased author. In the history of literature, similar paths are hardly rare. Finally, critical writing opens an important path to understanding Machado's prose, as it covers all genres, constituting his particular form of examining the world. I am referring, however, to the possibility of rereading his criticism in an attempt to investigate whether or not its criteria for evaluation reveal the obsessions that staked out his specific place in the family of authors who know themselves to be readers above all. In his appreciation of others' literature, what is the role of valuing the act of reading as one of invention? In the exercise of critical activity, were these criteria already clearly defined as part of a Machadian hermeneutics, and only later incorporated into his fiction?

Such questions allow us to forge a new literary profile. To this end, I turn to the metaphor of the author as laborer, proposed by Machado in the preface to *Resurrection*. This metaphor circumscribes the Machadian oeuvre to a mastery of technique and discipline, moving toward a perfection of the vocation.

Let me reiterate my methodology: the simultaneous rereading of the stories, crônicas, novels, plays, poems, and critical pieces by the author of *Memorial de Aires* [Counselor Ayres' Memorial]. This is not an attempt to deny the obvious difference between the texts that follow the *Posthumous Memoirs* and those from the "first phase" of his production; for that matter, Machado himself would label it as such on more than one occasion. The difference is inescapable, and I seek to understand it through the concept of the poetics of emulation.

In other words, I am not looking to reinvent the wheel! If it is possible to confirm the significance of procedures and themes characteristic of the author's second phase in works prior to the *Posthumous Memoirs*, then a new question emerges. Instead of investigating the *cause* of the 1880 rupture, we may speculate as to the reason why the elements that *potentially* already coexisted in Machadian texts *took so long to fuse into the Brás Cubas compound*—an extremely successful discursive poultice. If certain elements had been developed separately across multiple literary genres, why did it take until 1880 for them to come together in a single work? Was some external push needed to ensure this alchemy's success?

Once again, I am not looking to reinvent the wheel, but rather inquire as to why it did not complete a full revolution earlier. If the hypothesis that I seek to find in reading the Machadian oeuvre holds up, that is.

This is the test to which I will put myself.

Ur-Author

Time to illuminate my path through Machado's texts, guided by a reflection on the ur-author (*autor-matriz*): a concept I present for the reader's perusal.

The ur-author is that whose work, by merit of its very complexity, legitimizes a plurality of critical readings; various elements in the text spur different theoretical approaches. Yet contradictory elements, which coexist creatively in essays, poetry, or fiction, have a habit of digging trenches in the field of criticism. Given the richness of such texts, which translates into a multiplicity of interpretive possibilities, the ur-author leads to the emergence of hermeneutical and methodological squabbles. An intellectual system needs this fuel to remain active. At the same time, this is the best way to preserve the vitality of a work, guaranteeing a dialogue with the concerns of the present day. This principle was laid out by Machado himself. Let us recall a crônica from January 15, 1877, from the series *A Story of Fifteen Days*: "Every age has its *Iliad*, these various *Iliads* forming the epic of the human spirit" (III, 357).

The centrality of reading is an essential figure in the move inaugurated by the *Posthumous Memoirs*. Being a systematic reader of tradition, Machado was able to become the ur-author par excellence of Brazilian literature. This is not to be confused with the concept of a canonical author; rather, what defines the ur-author is the semantic plurality of his or her text, rather than his or her relative place in literary history. Gonçalves de Magalhães, for instance, is an unsurpassable canonical author in the development of Brazilian literature—nevertheless, his writing is ultimately defined by a monotone thick with national zeal. If we turn to the Machadian oeuvre, *Iaiá Garcia*, for example, is not a typical text from an ur-author! The concept refers to potential textual power, not an absolute, hierarchical placement.

The essential ambiguity of the Machadian gaze—examining the things of its time and place, but carefully inserted into the literary tradition of many other places and times—drove heated polemics that enliven university classrooms to this day. In such cases, the ur-author is often used as a pretext for the defense of institutional positions. Hence the paradox: the more stimulating the ur-author is, the less legible the oeuvre becomes. Instead of intensely engaging with the text, debaters circumscribe their interests on the margins of critical squabbles. With every paragraph not examined, but held up as "evidence," fashionable concepts emerge. At every neglected subtlety, there appear diametrically opposed critical fronts that attack each other while ignoring one another, in a quarrel so monotonous it would bother even the most byzantine of polemicists.

This is the model of "reading as consultation," designed to build up an archive of quotations that confirm the critic's vision. Paradoxically, this style of reading is fed by the plurality inherent in the ur-author: the richness of the texts means that one can always find what one is looking for . . .

Method

How to escape the paradox of the ur-author?

A methodological proposal: the literature of the ur-author ought to be thought via the method of "thick description,"[9] developed by anthropologist Clifford Geertz and inspired by a concept from philosopher Gilbert Ryle.

Ryle reflected on the difference between two seemingly identical movements: an involuntary movement of the eyelid—a twitch—and the same movement when made deliberately—a wink. A "thin description" would simply observe the mechanics of both acts without perceiving any relevant distinction between the two. Thick description, meanwhile, would seek to understand them through their immersion in a given context, reconstructing a web of meanings able to produce significant differences. The mechanical movement thus becomes an interpretable gesture.

Here, I might recall the story "A chave" [The Key], published in *A Estação* in two installments between December 1879 and February 1880, where everything flows into deciphering the different meanings of Major Caldas's "wink."

The major supports young Luís Bastinhos's bid to marry his daughter, Marcelina. With the engagement on shaky ground, the father reveals himself a consummate amateur ethnographer:

> Caldas, who knew his daughter, said nothing more. When the suitor asked him, shortly thereafter, if he ought to consider himself happy, he resorted to a wholly enigmatic tack: *he winked*. Luís Bastinhos became radiant; he was lifted up to the clouds on the wings of happiness. (II, 883; italics mine)

The beau soon comes back to earth, as the daughter's reaction belies the promises in the father's wink. Might it simply have been a twitch? Over the course of the night, Luís Bastinhos shows himself to be an extraordinary dancer, which attracts the reluctant Marcelina's attention—as any reader of René Girard's mimetic theory would immediately suspect. The major returns to the task:

> "That's it . . . a talent that God reserved for a few . . . a very few . . . Yes, sir; you may believe yourself the king of my party."
> And he grasped his hands firmly, *winking*. By this time Luís Bastinhos had lost all faith in this gesture of the major's, and received it coldly. (II, 884; italics mine)

Now the meaning of the gesture has changed: slighted because the youth only dances with her cousin, Marcelina decides to switch roles, inviting Luís Bastinhos to dance. Needless to say, the couple is never again parted: from the dance to the altar, they go on waltzing. The impromptu ethnographer also persists in his peculiar hermeneutics. Machado concludes the story thusly:

> Luís Bastinhos shook his head smilingly; the major, supposing that they were whispering his praises, *winked*. (II, 885; italics mine)

The anthropologist's task, of course, lies in identifying the codes that allow her to assign meaning to the gestures that make up the cultural fabric; after all, no action can be understood without a clarification of its ties to other actions and social actors.

This methodology makes it possible to valorize the gesture considered both in isolation and in its context, seen as an environment that stimulates possible meanings. Thick description thus moves to overcome outmoded dichotomies between form and content, text and context. Hence the importance of Geertz's theory in the formulation of the assumptions behind New Historicism, notably in Stephen Greenblatt's work. He coined the phrase "poetics of culture" in order to characterize the analysis of William Shakespeare's theater and the Elizabethan era, and the fecundity of his investigations demonstrates thick reading's potential for literary and cultural studies.

For my part, in order to examine the complexities of certain authors—ur-authors, especially—I imagine a different experiment in appropriating Geertz's method. From this angle, the first question would be, why not consider Machado's work as a literary system in and of itself, driven by internal dynamics and with a logic that demands to be investigated on its own terms? Born in 1839, Machado began publishing at a very young age, in 1855, and continued until the year of his death in 1908: over five decades of prolific production, spread across a variety of literary genres. Why not study the presence of recurring themes, as well as the transformation in how they are employed? Why not identify metaphorical series that structure the author's worldview? Are there dominant semantic fields to be found across five decades of writing, forming a nucleus of key words used by the author of "The Metaphysics of Style"? Do the narrators of his stories and novels remain the same, or are there ruptures that ought to be identified and understood?

These questions demand a thick description of the Machadian oeuvre. In this essay, I plan to tease out the internal logic of the transformation that turned the timid author of *A mão e a luva* [The Hand and the Glove] into the irreverent reader of the *Posthumous Memoirs of Brás Cubas*. At the same time, a plunge into the Machadian textual corpus sheds light on important aspects of the condition of the Brazilian writer, born of nonhegemonic circumstances.

Thick description presupposes the technique of close reading but is broader than this practice, which generally limits itself to the meticulous study of a given text. I am thinking of the reconstruction of an entire literary system, comprising the author's works as a whole—to say nothing of his readings of a number of different traditions. Reading across literary genres is the most adequate method for a thick description of the literature of an ur-author, literature that evokes the image of a mosaic or a kaleidoscope as a compositional principle.

Hence, my proposal—let me be the first to recognize it—implies a drawback: blotting out the subtle relationships between Machado's texts and their historical context. I have no desire to return to the polemic over cosmopolitanism versus localism. The discussion no longer makes sense, as it was satisfactorily resolved by the work of Roberto Schwarz. The contributions from the author of *A Master on the Periphery of Capitalism* did away with the usefulness of a critical tradition that insisted on highlighting Machado's supposed absenteeism as a mark of his worldview and his literature. Schwarz's work sheds light on the predicaments of Brazilian society found between the lines of Machado's texts, and even in their deeper structure. As a consequence, and given the very richness of his work, I seek to explore another vein; and my method thus has a clear limit, bounded by a voyage around the author's library.

The *Machado de Assis literary system*, and this is a crucial point, cannot be reconstructed with an exclusive focus on his "visible" works. As in the case of Borges's "Pierre Menard, Author of the *Quixote*," there is also an "invisible" oeuvre, essential for interpreting the author of "O imortal" [The Immortal]. One must also consider his readings and his appropriations of tradition and contemporary literature, in part because the development of the poetics of emulation calls for a specific act of reading.

This is an effort to compose a new sketch of the author of *Quincas Borba*, drawing principally on his literary palette. In this essay, the reader will find a sort of textual collage of Machado's works. The only exception will be the third chapter, in which I discuss the idea of emulation, mainly by referring to other authors' texts. There is nothing more appropriate to present the practice of emulation than falling back on others' work in the process of affirming one's one voice.

The Machadian oeuvre will take center stage: even in bringing other authors to the discussion, the pivot of the analysis will always be the texts from the author of *Casa Velha* [The Old House]. References to theorists and critics will be concentrated in the epigraphs that open the chapters. I enthusiastically recommend a consultation of their books, as I would not be able to understand Machadian literature without the aid of their interpretations. At no point do I claim that *the text speaks for itself* or that *theory and criticism are mere pastimes* and ultimately a hindrance. I hope that I will not be accused of such naïveté.

Even so, I dare to embark on a different experiment: drawing a new portrait of Machado de Assis. For a brush and paint, his words. If the exercise should fail, at least there will remain the consolation of a systematic voyage around Machado's work.

CHAPTER 1

The Shipwreck of Illusions

To this day, while not considering that the better part of his youthful texts were not known, they were studied with an eye to what Machado de Assis would come to be. The history of his life was read back to front. Here we will attempt to study his youth for its own sake.

—Jean-Michel Massa, *A juventude de Machado de Assis*

The discontinuity between the *Posthumous Memoirs* and the somewhat colorless fiction of Machado's first phase is undeniable, unless we wish to ignore the facts of quality, which after all are the very reason for the existence of literary criticism. However, there is also a strict continuity, which is, moreover, more difficult to establish.

—Roberto Schwarz, *A Master on the Periphery of Capitalism: Machado de Assis*

The mature narratives of Machado de Assis do not present us with open-and-shut stories that might appeal for their intrigue, as is the case with the first phase. Nor do they explicitly lay out the problem they are addressing or the conclusion at which they arrive. Their meaning will always depend on the reader's interpretation.

—Ivan Teixeira, *Apresentação de Machado de Assis*

1

There are good motives to suppose that the Machado of the first phase may have harbored ambivalent feelings about paternalism, a protective but humiliating regime that demanded a heavy dose of cunning and hypocrisy from its dependents. As for the worthy, they shall live on the margins or perish.

—Alfredo Bosi, "Brás Cubas em três versões"

While there was no concession in the sense of condescension, a violation of personal convictions or the cheapening of ideas, it seems undeniable that Machado de Assis gave in to the tastes and expectations of the reading public that he imagined and/or desired for his works, and that this attention and sensitivity to the public may be one of the pillars of the grandeur of that same work.

—Hélio de Seixas Guimarães, *Os leitores de Machado de Assis*

A Year Like Any Other?

The year 1878 was not an easy one for the writer Machado de Assis.

However, everything seemed to indicate otherwise.

In January, he began publishing *Iaiá Garcia*, his fourth novel, in *O Cruzeiro*. First released as a serial, the plot kept audiences entertained from January 1 to March 2 in near-daily installments. Ironically, the last sentence of the novel might well describe the dilemma faced by its author: "Something escapes the shipwreck of illusions" (I, 509). In the book, the narrator is applauding the sincere grief of Estela, the widow of Luís Garcia—father to Iaiá Garcia, the character who lends her name to the title. In the case of the writer's life, the unexpected approached while he marched steadily down the path he had laid out for himself, enjoying growing renown and apparently immune to the vicissitudes of literary life.

Iaiá Garcia was the fourth novel of a sequence whose rhythm reveals the author's discipline and determination. The first of the series, *Resurrection*, came to light in 1872. In the preface, a solicitous Machado forged the image of the writer as laborer; an image, one might add, crucial for the interpretation I propose. Let us listen to his words:

I do not know what I ought to think of this book; above all, I am ignorant of what the reader will think of it. The benevolence with which a volume of short stories and novellas, which I published two years ago, was received, encouraged me to write it. It is an essay. It will be delivered unassumingly to the hands of critics and the public, who will treat it with whatever justice it deserves. . . .

My idea in writing this book was to place into action that thought of Shakespeare's:

Our doubts are traitors,
And make us lose the good we oft might win,
By fearing to attempt.

I did not wish to write a novel of manners; I attempted to sketch a situation and the contrast between two characters; with these simple elements I sought out the thrust of the book. The critics will decide whether the work corresponds to the aim, and, above all, if the laborer is suited for it.

This is what I ask, with heart in hand. (I, 116)

Machado was referring to the collection *Tales from Rio*. The year 1870 also saw the publication of a book of poems, *Falenas*, which included "Flor da Mocidade" [Flower of Youth]. The poem's final verses advise:

When the earth is more jovial
All good seems to us eternal
To harvest, before the advent of evil
To harvest, before the coming of winter. (III, 41)

The winter took almost a decade to arrive: in February 1878, it announced itself to the author of *Dom Casmurro*. As for the poem, Machado added a revealing note to it in 1901, in the edition he prepared of his *Poesias Completas* [Complete Poetry].

The classic French poets often used this form, which they called *triolet*. After long disuse, some poets of this century have resuscitated the triolet,

without scorning the older models. I do not believe that it has been used in
Portuguese, nor may it merit the transfer. The form, meanwhile, is elegant
and finds no obstacles in our language, in my opinion. (III, 181)

Two elements of my reading of Machado's work stand out here: the reference to Shakespeare, and the reference to the *resurrection* of classical forms,
without scorning the older models. The omnipresence of the English dramatist
and the reclaiming of literary practices, *after long disuse*, are two sides of
the same coin and afford a new understanding of this decisive moment for
Machado de Assis as a writer, the moment in which he reinvents himself in
writing *The Posthumous Memoirs of Brás Cubas.* I refer to the literary technique of *aemulatio*.

In order to allow the reader to follow the discussion, I ought to clarify the
term straightaway. The standing artistic practice prior to the Romantic explosion, *aemulatio* implied the adoption of models enshrined by tradition, and
even the deliberate imitation of a given aspect of a masterpiece. Nevertheless,
artists always sought to add elements to the model that had been lacking;
to emulate tradition, not simply perpetuate it. If I am not wrong, Machado
ends up inventing the voice of the deceased author after assiduously visiting
this discursive territory of the past—a deliberately anachronistic visit, all the
same, which produces significant differences from the model at hand.

Back to the project of the writer as laborer.

These were not idle words set down merely to seduce the public and
entice critical complacence. The fledgling novelist took the metaphor of a
worker of letters seriously, and, with enviable constancy, published a new
title every two years. In 1874, he released *The Hand and the Glove*; in 1876,
Helena; finally, in 1878, *Iaiá Garcia*.

Nor should you imagine that the laborer limited himself to writing
novels. He worked across all genres: from criticism to crônicas, from poetry
to theater, from short stories to novels, from political commentary to translations, from prefaces to speeches, from crônicas in verse to fantasy, from paraphrasing to imitations, from apologies to dialogues, from correspondence to
the reports he wrote as a theater censor for the Conservatório Dramático.[1]
In all these genres, he debuted with the modesty befitting the apprentice
preparing himself to surmount his limits.

It would not be unjust to say that, with the exception of literary criticism, Machado's debut efforts were somewhat fumbling.

His first stories are simply interesting exercises—promising, no doubt, but often tinged by a moralizing tone that would certainly surprise the reader of *The Posthumous Memoirs of Brás Cubas*.

The first books of poetry are not much more than training in literary technique, an effort to try out the various forms of linguistic expression. One should note, however, that they were the first to garner any acclaim for Machado.

The plays never managed to excite his contemporaries; nor are future Machadians attracted to his dramatizations.

The first crônicas echo a light tone, "as the pen runs," in Almeida Garret and José de Alencar's words. Machadinho would define the stories published in *Histórias da meia-noite* [Midnight Stories] (1873) thus: "A few narratives are collected here, written as the pen runs, with no other pretension than to occupy some measure of the reader's precious time." Shortly thereafter, he transforms the note to the reader into a page of acknowledgments, referring to the esteem garnered by the writer-laborer: "I shall take the opportunity to thank the critics and the public for the generosity with which they received my first novel, brought forth some time ago" (II, 160).

Indeed: even past age thirty, he was affectionately called Machadinho.

From his very first articles, however, his critical gaze was clearly promising, revealing a shrewd reader bent on acquiring a knowledge of tradition: the two sides of the coin that would cement the writer's posthumous fame.

Let us examine the nineteen-year-old who publishes the essay "The Past, Present, and Future of Literature" in two installments in *A Marmota*, during the month of April 1858. The study fulfills conventional formalities. Machadinho reviews Brazilian colonial literature, identifying its gravest flaw: in rigorously following a European mold, "literature became enslaved instead of creating a style of its own, so that it might later weigh in the literary balance of America" (III, 785). This balance would also call for a study of the classics, not merely flashes of local color:

> But after the political fiat ought to come a literary fiat, the emancipation of
> the intellectual world, faltering under the influential action of a literature

from overseas. But how? It is easier to renew a nation than a literature. *For this, there are no declarations of independence*; modifications come about gradually; *and no result is achieved in the space of a moment*. (III, 787; italics mine)

As if announcing his own rhythm, the youth analyzes the "present," which he beholds with some reservations—"Today's society is surely not compassionate, [and] does not welcome talent as it ought to" (III, 787)—and analyzes the future, which he envisions as a task—"While part of the nation is still shackled to old ideas, it falls to talent to educate them" (III, 789). This oscillation between conventional criteria, which guaranteed Machadinho's insertion in society, and flashes of criticism, which would be developed by the Machado of the *Posthumous Memoirs*, would long fetter the prose and the vision of the young writer—which also reduced the reach of his critical work. The critical vocation may only win out when one frees oneself from the obligation of fulfilling what is expected of a respectable man of letters. Only then can the deceased author be brought forth.

After all, *no result is achieved in the space of a moment*.

Recalling the words of Mário de Alencar: he believed Machado gave up literary criticism because of the risk involved in the task, a considerable one in a timid intellectual environment such as that of Brazil during the imperial court.[2]

Most likely.

In his review of *Mãe*, a play by José de Alencar, the author himself confirms such misgivings. The text was published in *Revista Dramática* on March 29, 1860:

Writing criticism and theater criticism is not only a difficult task, but also a perilous business.

The reason is simple. On the day when the pen, faithful to the precept of censure, touches on a blot and momentarily neglects a laudatory stanza, enmities rise up all at once, armed with calumnies. (III, 837)

In the frequently quoted "The Critic's Ideal," an article published in the *Diário do Rio de Janeiro* in October 1865, the subject returns, with slightly more refined diction:

With such principles, *I understand that it is difficult to make a living*; but criticism is not a rosy profession, and if it is, it is so only as regards the intimate satisfaction derived from telling the truth. (III, 799; italics mine)

Mário de Alencar was right, at least in part.

The young writer's path was not an easy one. Mulatto, born in quite humble circumstances, an agregado during his childhood and adolescence, he went to work at Paula Brito's typography shop at age fifteen and became a typographer's apprentice at the National Press at age seventeen, a position he held for two years. He would later become an exemplary public servant, under the monarchy as well as the republic. Given Machado's beginnings, any chance of literary or social success in the slaveholding, patriarchal Brazil of the nineteenth century would have seemed an extravagant, romantic fiction.

The burden of his humble circumstances, however, should not be exaggerated; that is only fitting for panegyrics. Thanks to Jean-Michel Massa's study, *A juventude de Machado de Assis, 1839–1870*, we have learned that his difficulties were no greater than those of other talented mulattoes in nineteenth-century Brazil, some of poor extraction, who were also able to ascend socially. After all, this was the century of college graduates and mulattoes, as Gilberto Freyre declares in *The Mansions and the Shanties*.[3]

Recognizing this is important in order to avoid the shallow repetition of clichés about Machado's existential journey. However, going from one extreme to the other is hardly productive. In the end, the obstacles tied to the condition of the agregado (which were sometimes insuperable) form a dominant theme in Machado's works, omnipresent in the novels up to *Iaiá Garcia*. Moreover, the worldview of a senator's son—the case of José de Alencar and Joaquim Nabuco, for example—necessarily differs from the perspective of the son of a mulatto housepainter.

Mário de Alencar was right, in part: why should he risk himself *even more*? In any case, one may as well ask: rather than abandoning criticism, didn't Machado channel it into his fiction, especially after the *Posthumous Memoirs*? In doing this, he began to overcome his obstacles as a writer—clear limitations in the first group of novels, which were perfectly punctilious but nothing more, culminating with the innocuous *Iaiá Garcia*.

The reader will likely object: despite what I promised in the introduction, I just declared that Machado's beginnings were faltering without analyzing a single line from the author of *Esau and Jacob*, except for a few brief passages of literary criticism. I strung together a veritable necklace of adjectives, but I did not put myself to the true test of critical activity: examining the author's texts.

I accept the objection and correct the course of my prose, undertaking a somewhat formal study of Machado's first four novels, to then contrast them with his production posterior to the *Posthumous Memoirs*. The force of the transformation in Machado's work will thus be clarified.

The Key to the Writing

Machado's first novels have conventional conclusions, which clarify the driving theme of the plot and address all of the reader's doubts. The narrator even offers edifying conclusions, showing himself to be perfectly in step with the precepts of the time—good manners and high morals, to put it bluntly. In terms of form as well as content, what stands out is the excessively cautious, even conservative bent of the author-laborer in his first efforts.

It is important to consider this hypothesis. Nothing hobbles the understanding of Machado's existential and artistic crisis more than a comfortable hagiography incapable of recognizing the obvious limits that Machadinho imposed on his work for at least two decades.

The texts from the so-called second phase, meanwhile, contain enigmas that remain unresolved at the end of the story, provoking endless discussions that stimulate generation after generation of readers. Formal ambiguity and a critical vision of the world fade into one; in both cases, the dominant note is one of uncertainty.

I may put this in explicit terms by analyzing the endings of the first four novels, demonstrating concisely the rupture that explodes in Machado's work after the watershed year of 1878.

In the last paragraph of *Resurrection*, the reader is presented with a summary of the narrative, with a moralizing maxim to boot:

> Blessed with all the means that might make him fortunate, in society's estimation, Felix is essentially *infelicitous*. Nature placed him in that class of cowardly and visionary men befitting that reflection from the poet: they

"lose the good they oft might win," by fearing to attempt. Not content with the exterior happiness that surrounds him, he yearns for that other happiness of intimate, lasting, and consoling affections. This he will never attain, because his heart, while it reappeared for a few days, had forgotten in its grave the feeling of trust and the memory of illusions. (I, 195)

One need not say much more. This is the effect of the passage: there is little else to say. The simple sentence, "*Felix* is essentially *infelicitous*," involves such a trite pun that the mature Machado would be hard-pressed to employ. And that is not all; the narrator patiently lays out the cause of Felix's misfortune, even explaining the title of the novel. "Resurrection" referred to the character's chance to love again—which does not happen because he would suffer even in the absence of any confirmation of his beloved's infidelity. "The doctor's love suffered *posthumous doubts*" (I, 195; italics mine). The expression is striking, but is lost among the paragraph's edifying, trivial diction.

These "posthumous" doubts would never allow him to reconcile love with constant suspicion. (The more unfounded these notions, the clearer they would seem to the unhappy character—after all, how to disprove a chimera?) Here lies the structural relationship between jealousy and a certain concept of literature, one uninterested in offering definitive answers. In both cases, we are dealing with discursive forms that allude to the impossibility of finding the evidence that one never ceases to seek out. Every jealous figure is a potential fabulist; in the absence of "proof," the only recourse left is one's imagination. The dilemma reappears in the story of Bento Santiago, and in countless stories. The reader of *Dom Casmurro* cannot know if Capitu and Escobar were lovers or not: in a sense, it is as if Machado had produced a text in which the indeterminacy of jealousy had contaminated the very act of reading.

In the next novel, *The Hand and the Glove*, the novel's finishing touch once more ties the title of the book to its denouement in a perfect symmetry, imposing the ultimate meaning of the text:

Destiny ought not lie, and did not lie as to Luís Alves' ambition. Guiomar had been right; he was that strong man. After a month of marriage, as they were chatting about what newlyweds chat about, which is themselves, and recalling the brief campaign of the courtship, Guiomar confessed to her husband that on that occasion she had seen the full power of his will.

"I saw that you were a resolute man," the young woman told Luís Alves, who listened to her as he sat.

"Resolute and ambitious," Luís Alves added smilingly; "you must have noticed that I am both things."

"Ambition is no flaw."

"On the contrary, it is a virtue; I feel that I have it, and that I shall follow it through. I am not simply trusting in my youth and moral force; I am also trusting in you, who will be a new strength for me."

"Oh! yes!" exclaimed Guiomar.

And in a charming tone, she went on:

"But what will you give me by way of payment? A place in the Chamber? A minister's post?"

"The luster of my name," he replied.

Guiomar, who had been standing before him with her hands clasped in his, let herself fall slowly over her husband's knees, and the two ambitions exchanged a fraternal kiss. Each was fit for the other, as if that glove had been made for that hand. (I, 270)

The adjective "fraternal" removes all eroticism from the kiss, making it almost a signature on a contract that favors both parties. The marriage, however, is recent, insinuating that the union between Luís Alves and Guiomar is driven more by precise calculations than by sentimental raptures. The former agregada's ambition has met its match in the solidity of the future public figure. The reader closes the book and may leave it there: how to discover "posthumous doubts" in a plot that, in concluding its narrative, returns to the very title of the book in an effort to bring it home? The irony implicit in the "fraternal kiss" ought to blush before the conventional diction of the text.

Once again, we see the same oscillation identified in the literary criticism: the discovery of the "posthumous doubts" and the derision of the "fraternal kiss" are drowned out by the tone of the overwhelmingly prim prose. Hence the central impediment of this period, during which talent is hostage to the need to obey the conventions of the age.

In *Helena*, the procedure changes somewhat. The reader is now forced to make a small effort, but nothing on par with the snares laid by Bentinho during the story of his misfortune, or the irreverence that Brás Cubas reserves for his readers. Recall the last sentence of the novel:

> Alone with Estacio, the chaplain looked at him a long time, then lifted his eyes to the counselor's portrait, smiled a melancholy smile, turned back to Estacio, raised him, and embraced him with tender affection. "Courage, my son!" he said.
>
> "All is ruined, Reverend Father, I have lost everything."
>
> Meanwhile, at the house in Rio Comprido, Estacio's bride, horrified by Helena's death and depressed by the gloomy, somber ceremony, sadly retired to her bedroom. On the threshold she received her father's third kiss. (Caldwell 197)

The third kiss is a simple mystery, which the reader, pleased with his shrewdness, may solve with little trouble. This is a resource used extensively by Charles Dickens, for example: one need only sprinkle the narrative with simple enigmas, the certain decoding of which will guarantee the author's success with his public. To understand the last sentence of *Helena*, we must simply turn to the passage from chapter 14 on Eugênia's uneasiness:

> She was awakened from this dream by her father's imprinting on her forehead his second kiss. The first, as the reader will recall, was given her on the night after the counselor's death. The third would probably be bestowed on her wedding day. (Caldwell 93)

Eugênia would attain her goal without greater obstacles. After all, the narrator has given the perfect cue—*as the reader will recall.* The novel may be finished without the slightest concern for Estácio's apparent despair. His marriage to Dr. Camargo's willful daughter will allow him to overcome his sorrow at Helena's death. To return to the main effect of this kind of writing: the end of the plot addresses all of the reader's doubts, much like the Hollywood plots mentioned in the introduction. The conservative tone of the narrative and the traditional tack of the prose melt together, as they spring from the same cautious fundament.

On the first anniversary of Luís Garcia's death, Iaiá went with her husband to the cemetery, to leave a wreath of flowers on her father's tomb. Another wreath had been placed there, with a ribbon which bore these words: "To my husband." Iaiá ardently kissed the simple dedication, as she would kiss her stepmother if she were to appear just then. The widow's grief was sincere. Something escapes the shipwreck of illusions. (I, 509)

First, we are told that the widow's grief—being *sincere*, as the narrator insists on underlining—has escaped from the shipwreck of illusions. The reader is thus directed to two passages from the previous chapter that seem to prepare the eloquent ending. In the first, Estela turns to sealing Iaiá Garcia's union with Jorge, although without hearing harsh, even accusatory words from the girl:

I shall say nothing; that word explains it all. If you love him, as I believe, it is your happiness that I bring to you—I shall not say that it is in exchange for mine, because that would be to throw my sacrifice in your face, but *in exchange for an illusion, and nothing more.* Do not think that I wish you ill; I cannot wish misfortune on a person who has or had some affection for me and was a worthy substitute for my mother. If I wished you ill, I should likely not have done what I did. (I, 501; italics mine)

Estela needed to turn things around quickly and convince Iaiá Garcia to accept the proposal, instead of insisting on a refusal that would stain her reputation, given that the widow had been involved with the young girl's suitor. She opts for a risky gambit; however, certain of her success, she plays her trump card. The Balzacian theme of lost illusions returns discreetly, albeit with a revealing twist:

All the joys of marriage, I found at your father's side. We did not marry for love; it was a reasoned choice, and thus the right one. *We had no illusions*; we could be happy without disenchantment. Your father did not share my feelings; he was more timid than proud. (I, 504; italics mine)

Estela, more sober than a character out of Balzac, does not see the shipwreck of her illusions; she never encouraged them to begin with. The task of tying together illusions and disillusions in order to peacefully wrap up the novel is not a difficult one. The narrator maintains absolute control over the plot, as well as its interpretive possibilities. A pedagogical, decorous figure, he seeks to instruct as well as entertain, faithfully respecting the Horatian principle, as I will show in my study of the story "Confessions of a Young Widow." Thus, while the author sets up a modest puzzle, he always offers the key to its assembly. This idea is laid out explicitly in chapter 13, in the scene in which Jorge receives a letter from Procópio Dias. Here is the decisive passage:

> Jorge found that night, in his home, a letter from Buenos Aires. Procópio Dias narrated the voyage and its first steps and said he had every hope of tarrying only a short while. All this was a third of the letter. The other two-thirds were longing, protests, expressions of feeling, and a name at the end, a single name, which was *the key to the writing*. (I, 471; italics mine)

Iaiá Garcia's name brings the aging businessman's unrequited love for Luís Garcia's daughter to the surface of the text. Nothing escapes the pan-optical gaze of the first-phase narrator; the reader may simply admire his omniscience. Hence the idea of the *key to the writing*, where decoding the text depends on the narrator's capacities of observation. In "A parasita azul" [The Blue Parasite], a story published in 1872 in the *Jornal das Famílias* and rereleased the next year in *Midnight Stories*, the same ability is praised, albeit in less solemn tones:

> There are no mysteries for an author who can investigate all the corners of the heart. While the people of Santa Luzia produce a thousand conjectures as to the true cause of the indifference displayed by the lovely Isabel up to this point, *I am equipped to tell the impatient reader* that she is in love. (II, 182; italics mine)

In the first four novels, the stability of the interpretive act is always preserved by an extremely well-behaved text. Without great difficulty, the reader may find the *key to the writing*, tying the work's title to the close of the narrative. The impression is thus of a reasonably unambiguous conclusion. Starting with *The Posthumous Memoirs of Brás Cubas*, however, the

Machadian text becomes increasingly enigmatic, and is less easily reduced to the interpretation suggested by the narrator; in extreme cases, the narrator does not even suggest it. In this sense, the deceased author's writing seems to find itself halfway between the hermeneutic tranquility of the first phase and the semantic indetermination of the second. While the last chapter is filled with "negatives," the meaning of the absence is still explained, albeit ironically.

> This last chapter is all negatives. I didn't attain fame with my poultice, I wasn't a minister, I wasn't a caliph, I didn't come to know marriage. The truth is that, alongside these lacks, I was granted the good fortune of not buying my bread with the sweat of my brow. More than that; I didn't suffer Dona Plácida's death, nor Quincas Borba's semidementia. Summing up a few things and others, anyone might imagine that there was neither want nor surplus, and, consequently, that I came out even with life. And they will imagine wrongly; because upon arriving on this other side of the mystery, I found myself with a small sum, which is the final negative in this chapter of negatives: I had no children; I did not bequeath to any creature the legacy of our misery. (I, 639)

The clearly ironic diction sets this ending apart from the pattern of previous novels. In any case, the deceased author still provides us with coordinates for our reading. It is true that his cynicism calls his very declarations into question; it is also true that the irony of the text as a whole destabilizes the act of interpretation. A comparison to the ending of *Quincas Borba* helps us understand the radicalization of Machado's process of composition in terms of what we might refer to as "resistance to interpretation," a defining characteristic of his texts after the late 1870s. This trait favors fiction that may be read innovatively; now it is the reader's task to come up with alternatives instead of waiting for the diligent narrator to present her with the *key to the writing*. The brief final chapter in Rubião's saga is the very model of hermeneutic ambiguity, ringing in a form of literature that leaves no room for comfortable, stable interpretations:

> I wished to speak here of the end of Quincas Borba, who fell ill, whined eternally, fled madly in search of his owner, and showed up dead in the

street, three days later. But, seeing the dog's death narrated in its own chapter, you will likely ask me if it is he or his deceased homonym who gives
the book its title, and why one rather than another—*a question pregnant
with questions, which would carry us far along. . . .* Come now! Weep for the
two newly dead, if you have tears. If you only have laughter, then laugh! It's
all the same. The Southern Cross, which beautiful Sofia refused to behold
as Rubião asked, is high enough that it can't make out the laughter or the
tears of men. (I, 806; italics mine)

Hermeneutical ambiguity, double meanings, impossible to conclude:
the interpretive act becomes a puzzle where the key piece can never be
found. The backward secret of the Machadian text, after the inventions of
the *Posthumous Memoirs*, is that the key piece does not exist: this is the polar
opposite of the setup of *Iaiá Garcia*. This procedure is what truly drives *Dom
Casmurro*. In this sense, a skeptical reading of the final passage of *Quincas
Borba* is reasonable; however, if it is to be understood as a vade mecum, it
appears quite unproductive. This is not a matter of placing all one's chips
on the equivalence drawn between laughter and tears, operating off boiler-
plate skepticism. "It's the same thing" because there are no clear criteria for
discerning the ultimate force behind human actions. This is not an attempt
to imprison the resistance to interpretation inside a theory that makes the
world *necessarily* the realm of endless ambiguity; in this case, paradoxically,
we know at least one thing with absolute certainty.

I am reminded of the title of the poem published in 1886 in *A Semana*,
later included in *Ocidentais* [Westerners] (1901): "Questions with No
Answer." Machadian literature learns to walk in this direction, and the final
verses of the poem still echo the last chapter of *Quincas Borba*:

Venus, however, Venus brilliant and beautiful,
Who heard nothing, gave no reply,
Lets [sic] *laugh or cry* from her window
          Pale Maria. (III, 159; italics mine)

Another detail ought to be pointed out. As in the first novels, the last
chapter of the unfortunate sage of Rubião once again invokes the title of the
book. However, the reference no longer produces the ultimate meaning of

the story; rather, it presents the reader with *questions with no answer*, meant to spawn new doubts: *a question pregnant with questions that would take us far along* . . . "Quincas Borba": the philosopher or the dog? Or: "Quincas Borba": the dog or the philosopher? The order of the elements changes nothing, as no result may be defined precisely. The reader is obliged to go out on a limb and produce his own interpretation.

♦   ♦   ♦

The hermeneutic tranquility of the first translations of Machado's work into English is symptomatic—it is as if the author had not taken the leap of the *Posthumous Memoirs*.

Brás Cubas's novel was released in 1952 in a translation by William L. Grossman, entitled *Epitaph of a Small Winner*. The title alludes to the well-known passage in the last chapter: *I found myself with a small balance*. Oddly enough, in the translation, the title of the book and the conclusion of the narrative come together once again.

The case of *Quincas Borba* is even more revealing.

In Clotilde Wilson's translation, the novel came out in the United States in 1954, with the title *Philosopher or Dog?*, hence splashing the *question pregnant with questions that would take us far along* . . . across the book's cover. Nevertheless, at least the dilemma remains a *question without an answer*. Then, the same translation was released in England in the same year, with the clarifying title *The Heritage of Quincas Borba*! The *philosopher*'s heritage, then, to leave no doubts.

The greatest legacy of the deceased author's literature stands out, by contrast, in the disorientation of his first translators.

♦   ♦   ♦

I had said that the resistance to interpretation begins to take a radical turn in the writing of *Quincas Borba*. A bit farther along, we find the intrinsically ambiguous structure of *Dom Casmurro*. In order to go straight to the point, I will continue with the same expository concision, simply transcribing the last chapter of the novel of Bentinho's misadventures. This is a particularly problematic chapter, starting with the title—"Well, and the Rest?" The question, apparently an idle one, poses an enigma that has occupied readers to this day:

Now, why is it that none of these capricious creatures made me forget the first love of my heart? Perhaps because none had her undertow eyes, nor her sly, oblique, gypsy look. But this is not really what remains of this book. What remains to know is if the Capitu of Glória beach was already in the girl of Matacavalos, or if the latter had been changed into the former because of some intervening incident. Jesus, son of Sirach, had he known of my first fits of jealousy, would have said to me, as in his Chapter IX, verse I: "Be not jealous of thy wife, lest she deceive thee with arts she learned of thee." But I think not, and that you will agree with me; if you remember Capitu as a girl, you will recognize that the one was in the other, like the fruit inside its rind.

And anyway, whatever the solution, one thing is left, and is the sum total, or the total residue, to wit, that my first love and my best friend, both so affectionate and beloved—destiny willed it that they ended up joining together and deceiving me. . . . May the earth rest lightly on them! On to the *History of the Suburbs*! (Gledson 244)

This cunning passage is one of the most treacherous in all of Machado's oeuvre. Its analysis has fascinated generations of exegetes.

First, the narrator seeks to persuade the reader: "But I think not, and that you will agree with me." However, the reader may recall a declaration from José Dias; in this case, the discrepancy will be glaring. The agregado uses an image similar to the narrator's, but comes to the opposite conclusion: "Years ago, I thought differently; I confused her childish ways with expressions of character, and didn't see that that mischievous girl, already with her thoughtful eyes, was the capricious bloom which would produce such a sweet, wholesome fruit" (Gledson 176). Hence, even as the narrator announces his final condemnation of Capitu, his hesitation undermines the declaration—"And anyway, *whatever the solution*, one thing is left." Now, the *solution* is precisely the one thing that cannot be *whatever* explanation; it must explain definitive certainty as to Capitu's "guilt." If not, then *nothing is left*, much less any certainty of adultery. Moreover, the last sentence will refer the reader to the second chapter, when a project was announced and chiefly abandoned: "Then I thought I might write a *History of the Suburbs* . . . a modest undertaking, but it required documents and dates as preliminaries, all of which would be boring and time-consuming" (Gledson 6). The narrator's instability and the erratic bent of his decisions undermine the conclusion he seeks to draw. This *History of the Suburbs* will likely never be written, remaining one of the many projects of the legions of unrealized geniuses who dominate literary life at any latitude. However, if this is so, the narrative of *Dom Casmurro* may be seen as a story that claims to be true, but which is lacking precisely *documents and dates*! In this case, how to arrive at a secure verdict?

In other words, the reader must arm herself with undertow eyes in order to survive the shipwreck of Bentinho's illusions.[4]

For my part, I hope that the world that opens up between the first four novels and what follows the *Posthumous Memoirs* comes into focus.

Let me return to the hypothesis sketched out in the introduction: the rupture has a pivotal event in February 1878. I do not claim that this was the *determinant*, much less the only element at play, but rather invoke a *catalyzing effect* that allowed the author of *Iaiá Garcia* to overcome his own limits and reinvent his literature.

Gazes and Lighthouses

Having already dealt with *Dom Casmurro*, I shall open this brief interpretive exercise by identifying a semantic field, which, by running through all the novels, reinforces my analysis. Moreover, a return to the defining vocabulary of Machado's oeuvre is one of the aims of this book.

(Semantic fields are the pigments with which I will trace this new portrait of the author.)

I refer to the group of metaphors and allusions related to the gaze, which would produce the classic analogy of the eyes as "windows to the soul." A prosaic formulation, much like the dominant Machadian treatment of the subject back in *Iaiá Garcia*. On the contrary, as we have just seen, Bentinho condemns himself before the enigma of Capitu's gaze: "Now, why is it that none of these capricious creatures made me forget the first love of my heart? Perhaps because none had *her undertow eyes, nor her sly, oblique, gypsy look.*"

In the first four novels, virtually any gaze could be translated with the simplest interpretive gesture.

Let us examine two or three passages.

I begin with a poem, "Books and Flowers," published in *Phalaenae* (1870). Here the decisive equivalence stands out:

> *Your eyes are my books*
> What book could be better,
> Where one could better *read*
> The page of love? (III, 51; italics mine)

The simplicity of the verses anticipates a recurring usage in the first four novels, dominated by an association between the noun and the verb: the eyes are always reading, or being read. And they decipher situations, messages, and people—with invariable success.

In *Resurrection*, Meneses is comforted by the apparently inconsolable Felix. The cultivator of "posthumous doubts" could think of nothing better to say to his friend than "I wish it were not so! But I am *reading on your face* that the only way to console you for this shipwreck is to give you another ship" (I, 135; italics mine). The reader, meanwhile, is never shipwrecked, as the eyes, the face, the smallest gestures, and virtually *all intentions* are decipherable through a careful reading, laid out in the first chapter of *Iaiá Garcia*:

> At the moment when this narrative begins, Luís Garcia was forty-one years old. He was tall and thin, starting to bald, clean-shaven, with a circumspect air. His manner was cold, modest, and courteous; his aspect, slightly sad. *A keen observer could divine* beyond that apparent or withdrawn impassivity the ruins of a disillusioned heart. So it was; experience, come before its time, had produced in Luís Garcia a state of apathy and skepticism with smatterings of disdain. (I, 393; italics mine)

"So it was"—and it could not be otherwise. How to contest the authority of the narrator, who deciphers gazes and identifies the intentions that lie beneath gestures and tones of voice? After all, the *key to the writing* never escapes him. In this passage, even before the action begins, the narrator reveals Luís Garcia's complete psychological profile, which will remain unaltered: during the reading, no surprise will alter the full-body portrait we have of the character. The same technique stands for our introduction to Estela:

"She was pallid, but without any hint of aesthetic melancholy. She had large, dark, eyes with an impression of moral strength, which gave Estela's physical beauty its defining characteristic" (I, 409). Once again, the eyes reveal the entirety of a personality that will remain identical over the course of the novel. These marble characters from the first Machado are almost always one-dimensional. Or is it the narrator who, in his quest to maintain absolutely everything under strict surveillance, winds up transforming all the landscapes into monotonous plains? Here you have the fully realized figure of the panoptical narrator, still leagues away from the drunkard author of the *Posthumous Memoirs*.[5]

In *Helena*, Dr. Camargo has the difficult task of conveying the contents of Counselor Vale's surprising will to Estácio and Dona Úrsula. The document reveals the existence of an illegitimate daughter, the heroine who gives her name to the book's title. As the plot unfolds, the reader discovers that Helena is not actually the counselor's daughter; but, in the first chapters, nobody knows this. Thus, although son and aunt disguise their feelings, the narrator easily identifies the prevailing sentiment before the proclamation of their relative's last wishes: "Their curiosity, however, was natural and *he read it in their eyes* but said nothing" (Caldwell 7; italics mine).

A similar measure is used by Luís Alves, a character in *The Hand and the Glove*. In order to confirm the effect produced by a particular attitude, he falls back on the hermeneutic that prevails in Machado's first novels: "Luís Alves *gazed at length* at Guiomar, as if looking to *see in her face* all the antecedents of the baroness's resolution" (I, 244; italics mine).

In these novels, there are a number of scenes that recall a game of chess, in which looks are exchanged like moves on the chessboard of conscience: long periods of observation, set off by even longer-lasting periods of dissimulations and misinterpretations. Earlier in *The Hand and the Glove*, Guiomar strolls through the gardens at the baroness's house, holding a tellingly closed book—a suggestive metaphor, which paves the way for the narrator's conclusion: "If she felt any yearning, *it could not be read on her face*, which was indeed quiet and pensive, but without the slightest shadow of pity or sadness" (I, 209; italics mine). Doubtless a closed book to Estêvão, a romantic out of place who is never able to understand the heroine's motives. A closed book, *ma non troppo*, as the narrator may flip through her pages, finding a number of keys with which to decipher her; and, even if her face is turned inward, he glimpses what he needs to know: *without the slightest shadow of pity or sadness.*

The narrators and characters after the invention of Brás Cubas, however, seem to gradually lose control of the interpretation, anticipating the process that should ideally take place within the reader, given the growing complexity of Machado's fictional techniques. Thus, while the panoptical narrator fits with a relatively smooth reading, the deceased author or the casmurrian narrator[6] provide an unpredictable act of reading.

For this very reason, Rubião was definitively lost at the moment in which "he came across those luxuriant eyes, which seemed to repeat the exhortation of the prophet: every one that thirsteth, come ye to the waters" (I, 644). Rubião, the ignoramus, does not realize that Sofia's gaze is laying the way for the moral undertow of a character yet to come—Capitu, of course. The thirst, in this case, was both that of the country teacher for the lavish silhouette of the wife of Cristiano Palha, and that of the seductive lady's husband for Rubião's unexpected windfall.

A few pages later, Quincas Borba the philosopher has his eccentric character defined in a revealing fashion: "He had another air now: his eyes, turned inward, saw his brain thinking" (I, 646). These thoughts are never revealed to the reader. Might the narrator have had access to the logic of the creator of Humanitism? With such eyes, the windows to the soul are permanently closed: this, incidentally, is one of the definitions of madness. Rubião is, symptomatically, introduced in the opposite fashion: "He listened, *with his soul in his eyes*, sincerely wishing to understand" (I, 648; italics mine). In the war of gazes, Rubião will never come out with the potatoes—as you recall, the motto of Quincas Borbas's Humanitism was "to the victor, the potatoes." The transparency with which he announces his aims facilitates the work of flatterers and adversaries. The contrast in their attitudes is an essay in itself, the decisive paragraph being written with the help of the famous characterizations of Capitu. José Dias' original assessment, in dialogue with young Bentinho: "Capitu, in spite of those eyes that the devil gave her . . . Have you noticed her eyes? They're a bit like a gypsy's, oblique and sly" (Gledson 48). It falls to the casmurrian narrator to put the final touches on the portrait:

Lovers' language, lend me an exact and poetic comparison in order to say
what those eyes of Capitu were like. No image comes to mind that doesn't
offend against the rules of good style, to say what they were and what they
did to me. Undertow eyes? Why not? Undertow. That's the notion that the
new expression put in my head. *They held some kind of mysterious, active
fluid*, a force that dragged one in, like the undertow of a wave retreating
from the shore on stormy days. (Gledson 63)

The same undertow causes the death of his friend Escobar, and will continue to haunt the casmurrian narrator. He believes he has found out in those
same mysterious, active—and, I might add, enigmatic—eyes *the key to the
writing*, the indisputable hermeneutic:

> There was general confusion. In the midst of it, Capitu looked for some
> moments at the body with such a fixed gaze, with such a passionately fixed
> gaze, that it's small wonder that into her eyes *there came a few silent tears....*
>   Mine stopped immediately. I stood looking at hers; Capitu wiped
> them hastily, looking sidelong at the people in the room. She redoubled
> her caresses for her friend, and tried to take her away; but it seems that the
> body held her back, too. *There was a moment when Capitu's eyes fixed on
> the body, like those of the widow* though without her tears or cries, but large
> and wide open, like the waves on the sea out there, as if she too wanted to
> swallow up that morning's swimmer. (Gledson 211–12; italics mine)

An emblematic scene: the crossing of gazes will decide the fate of the narrative. The *few* tears become, above all, *silent*; that is, "evidence" of adultery,
now undeniable—clearly understood, in Bentinho's eyes. The dynamic of
the scene is decisive: Bentinho observes Capitu while she gazes at Escobar's
cadaver. But who observes Bentinho as he observes Capitu gazing on the
body of her friend? Or, shall I say: who observes Bentinho observe Capitu
gazing on the body of her lover? Friend or lover: how to know? Quite unlike
the first four novels, *Dom Casmurro* leaves doubt as its legacy.
    I recall the second scene of the third act of *Hamlet*. Wishing to find out
if the specter is truly his father's ghost, the prince of Denmark concocts a
stratagem; in fact, Shakespeare turns to a device previously used by Thomas
Kyd in *The Spanish Tragedy*.

(Appropriating both tradition—the classics, that is—as well as the ingenuity of contemporaries is a mark of Shakespearean genius. Here is one of the principal lessons that Machado owes to Shakespeare. This is the foundation of the poetics of emulation, especially in its anachronistic recuperation of tradition.)

The Hamletian artifice: in order to test the veracity of the specter's accusations, the prince of Denmark has a play put on, *The Murder of Gonzago*. However, he adds a scene not present in the original text, representing the circumstances of his father's death—poisoned as he slept. Obsessed by the desire to obtain a precise interpretation free of any misgivings, Hamlet engineers a complex triangulation of gazes: while Claudius, his uncle, now king and stepfather, watches the play, Hamlet observes his reactions to the plot unfolding on the improvised stage; finally, Horatio, the prince's faithful friend, also observes the king's expression. Only then does Hamlet accept the version of his father's murder, when he compares his impressions with those of his friend:

> HAMLET: O good Horatio, I'll take the ghost's word for a thousand pound! Didst perceive?
> HORATIO: Very well, my lord.
> HAMLET: Upon the talk of the poisoning?
> HORATIO: I did very well note him. (3.2.260–64)[7]

In the case of Bento Santiago, *this very triangulation is lacking*. The narrator is quickly satisfied with his own observations, and does not even consider consulting a third party. The narrative is the effort to reconstitute the lost triangulation through the figure of the reader, who, like Horatio, must confirm his suspicions: *you will agree with me; if you remember Capitu as a girl*... The casmurrian narrator had nothing of the serenity of Counselor Ayres:

> That silence of Fidélia's, in contrast to her chattiness a short time before, seemed to me to indicate that she believed the work was falling behind. Or perhaps the love of art now had a tighter grip on her than at the start, provoking this exclusive dedication to painting. *The secret cause of an act*

often escapes keen eyes, to say nothing of my own, which lost their natural sharpness with age; but I believe that it was one of those two, *and there is no reason to disbelieve that it was not both in succession.* (I, 1167; italics mine)

Nevertheless, as if they were a perfect boomerang, Capitu's enigmatic eyes return in the last chapter of the novel, clarifying the fascination they continued to exert over Bento Santiago. Everything occurs as if Machado's characters moved from the all-revealing "gaze" that may be comprehended to the dulled "gaze" that escapes from even the narrator's control, turning the act of reading into a peculiar form of the "posthumous doubts" that tormented Felix in *Resurrection.*

Here I close the first cycle of the formal analysis of Machado's first works, in contrast with the texts that follow the *Posthumous Memoirs.*

Before taking the next step, I shall note what has been addressed thus far: I sought to show how Machado's first four novels are cast in quite a traditional mold, as the study of the semantic field of the gaze ought to have emphasized.

Now I begin a new cycle, dedicated to studying the conservative, even moralizing content of the first productions from the author of *Tales from Rio.*

Jealousy and Literature

Tales from Rio, released in 1870, included a selection of previously published texts. So that the reader is able to appreciate their thematic transformation, I shall indicate the original publication dates of the stories. All of them, incidentally, were first published in the *Jornal das Famílias*: "Frei Simão" [Brother Simão] in June 1864; "Confessions of a Young Widow" in April 1865; "Linha reta e linha curva" [Straight Line and Curved Line] in a number of installments between 1865 and 1866; "A mulher de preto" [The Woman in Black] in April and May 1868; "O segredo de Augusta" [Augusta's Secret] in July and August 1868; "Luís Soares" in January 1869. "Miss Dollar" was the only story to be published first in the book itself.

I will also discuss texts published over the course of the 1870s and 1880s, to show how the approach to the topics of jealousy, adultery, vanity, and

dissembling undergoes a metamorphosis similar to the formal transformation seen in the novels. There is, however, one important difference: these
transformations occur before 1880. In the short stories and the crônicas as
well, the wheel seems to have spun before the Brás Cubas revolution. In this
sense, while one must highlight the internal transformations in the *Machado
de Assis literary system*, it is equally important to emphasize the complex lines
of continuity.

Let us begin with the dominant theme in the Machadian oeuvre: jealousy.

In *Resurrection*, Felix, the protagonist, gives up on marrying Livia, a
young and beautiful widow entirely given over to her own fancies. As we
have seen, Felix's behavior is explained in a terse phrase: "The doctor's love
suffered posthumous doubts" (I, 195). A malicious anonymous letter, clearly
false at that, was enough to cloud the couple's future. Though the widow's
fidelity was proven, the doctor could not free his spirit from the *likelihood*
of a future betrayal: "As the years passed, the veracity of the letter that had
impeded their wedding struck him as not only possible, but even probable"
(I, 195).

Infidelity, whether real or virtual, is the theme of the plot—that is to
say, the specter of adultery structures the novel. But here lies the double-
edged wit of the future author of *Dom Casmurro*: an invented infidelity is
the imaginary effect of a man's unfounded jealousy. This is the topic that
really matters, casting an inescapable shadow over one's knowledge: to know
or not to know, that is the dilemma of the jealous. Jealousy and adultery had
taken over Machado since his first texts, as in his first short story, "Three Lost
Treasures" (1858). However, it is imperative to distinguish between the two,
as an author such as Machado also suggests the existence of a "literature of
adultery," in addition to the already-mentioned "literature of jealousy."

Adultery is a close relative of the successful investigation, of the kind
found in an easily resolved detective novel; there is no doubt about the "facts"
of the event. After all, in this case, there is always a body on the scene—in
fact, at least two bodies . . .

As the *Oxford English Dictionary* tells us, adultery is the "voluntary
sexual intercourse between a married person and another who is not his
or her spouse."[8] Since adultery has actually taken place, the writer's central
problem becomes an examination of the reaction of the "victim," as well as an
analysis of the motives of the "sinner." Of course, I am thinking of *Madame*

Bovary, by Gustave Flaubert, published in 1857, and in its radical rewriting, *Cousin Bazilio*, by Eça de Queirós, released in 1878—*February 1878*, I might add. Investigating Charles's or Jorge's reactions and understanding Emma's and Luísa's motives: this is the heart of these novels.

Jealousy, meanwhile, as the same dictionary puts it, is defined by the "fear of being supplanted in the affection, or distrust of the fidelity, of a beloved person," and "vigilance in guarding a possession from loss or damage."[9] Jealousy has another, far more unsettling dimension—which, while neglected by the dictionary, is revealed by literature. The jealous figure never has direct proof of the infidelity. He cannot know; if he knows, he is no longer jealous. That is to say that, in theory, the jealous figure only conjures up evidence and never proves the betrayal. To repeat: if he has "proof," he is no longer "jealous," he is "betrayed"—the reader will be able to substitute the elegant term for a more common, far more expressive turn of phrase.

The jealous figure is a possessive type with a powerful imagination, a frustrated fabulist who produces not books, but rather fantasies of adultery. In the absence of the definitive "proof" of betrayal, the jealous figure concocts likelihoods, creating plots that favor the hypothesis of adultery. The texts that deal with jealousy even display a common structure. First there comes a doubt, whether reasonable or not. As confirmation will always escape the jealous figure, he is obliged to fabricate evidence that, while invented, paradoxically feeds the initial suspicion and serves as definitive proof. From then on, the jealous figure moves into a self-centered discourse, the circular logic of which is presented as the confirmation of its own terms, in a vicious cycle that is extremely difficult to break.

For his part, Machado scratched the surface of the topic in *Resurrection*, definitively developing it in *Dom Casmurro*. The narrator himself reveals the deeper structure of the problem:

> Talking of this, it's natural for you to ask me if, having been so jealous of her, I didn't go on being so in spite of my son and the passing years. Yes, sir, I did. I went on being so, to such a point that the least gesture alarmed me, the tiniest word, any kind of insistence on a point; often mere indifference was enough. *I came to be jealous of everything and everyone.* A neighbor, a waltz partner, any man, young or old, filled me with terror or mistrust. (Gledson 196; italics mine)

This sentiment, associated with an uncontrollable fantasy, leads to a predictable result: the certainty of the other's guilt, a conviction exacerbated precisely by the absence of concrete proof. In Bento Santiago's words, "My imagination was a great Iberian mare; the least breeze brought forth a foal, and that foal soon turned into Alexander's horse" (Gledson 78). A predictable result, but a paradoxical one, as this means forming a conviction in the necessary absence of definitive fact. The etymology of *evidence* is revealing. The jealous figure is not content with circumstantial clues; a voyeur of his misfortune, he must witness the "irrefutable" proof of his betrayal. It is unlikely that anyone has ever put it as emphatically as Othello:

> OTHELLO: Villain, be sure thou prove my love a whore,
> Be sure of it; give me the *ocular proof*:
> Or by the worth of man's eternal soul,
> Thou hadst been better have been born a dog
> Than answer my waked wrath!

> IAGO: Is't come to this?

> OTHELLO: *Make me to see't*; or, at the least, so prove it,
> That the probation bear no hinge nor loop
> To hang a doubt on; or woe upon thy life! (3.3.360–67)[10]

A novel like *Dom Casmurro* also lacks "ocular proof," nor does it reveal "evidence." The "literature of jealousy" is thus a discourse fed by doubt, by the impossibility of knowing the ultimate "truth" of the world. An investigation into the changes in the approach to the topic of jealousy implies mapping fundamental modifications in the Machadian conception of literature. In this sense, *Dom Casmurro* is a powerful paean to the force of fiction, to the idea of literature as a machine for producing *questions with no answer*. There is no way to know if Capitu was unfaithful, although she doubtless could have been; and in this lesson lies the superiority of Machado's literature.[11]

In the following texts that I study, with an emphasis on those in *Tales of Rio*, the reader will accompany the slow transformation wrought on the subject in the veritable laboratory of forms and ideas that these stories constitute.

This journey clarifies the defining trait of Machado's first phase: conventional structure in the novel and conservative content in the short story—and vice versa, as the terms are perfectly interchangeable here.

Decorum, Above All

At the beginning of his trajectory, Machado cultivated a prim style, especially in regards to the treatment given topics considered sensitive for a nineteenth-century audience. In "The Woman in Black" (1868), adultery is not only condemned, but also simply doesn't happen; the accusation is the result of a misunderstanding. A friend of Madalena's leaves a portrait and a letter in her care, under the condition that she never reveal the name of the objects' owner. Madalena's husband, suspecting that he has been betrayed, demands that she come forward. When his wife refuses, he simply abandons her. She, in turn, lives as if she were a widow, always dressed appropriately in black. The narrator hastily moves to calm the reader: "Yet Madalena was no *criminal*; her *crime* was an appearance; she was condemned for her loyalty to honor. The letter and the portrait did not belong to her; they were merely an imprudent and ruinous deposit" (II, 76; italics mine). The supposed infidelity reveals, on the contrary, a noble gesture born of an exemplary character—although, let us not forget, the deposit was *imprudent and ruinous*. While Estêvão is in love with the "widow," it falls to him to reveal the truth to Meneses, the obstinate husband. In triumphal tones, the altruistic friend anticipates the vocabulary of resurrection—in this case, of the trust between husband and wife:

> My intention is not only to resuscitate the past; it is to repair it, restore it in all its splendor, with all the legitimacy it is due; my aim is to tell you, my dear friend, that the *condemned woman* is an *innocent woman*. (II, 78; italics mine)

Note the vocabulary employed here, and the weight of its use: *criminal*, *crime*, *condemned woman*, *innocent woman*. After reading similar passages, labeling this a possible flash of Machadian irony would be denying the obvious. One must acknowledge the conservative bent of the form and content produced by Machadinho in order to appreciate the irreverence of the future author of the *Posthumous Memoirs*.

In "Confessions of a Young Widow" (1865), adultery is a, shall we say, "spiritual" occurrence. For that matter, young Machado shows a certain aversion to direct references to the body and eroticism—as I show in the following chapter, this is one of the reasons for his severe criticism of *Cousin Bazilio*. In this story, a married woman allows a cheap seducer to court her; but the young wife decides to resist. After receiving a letter from Emílio confessing his love, her behavior is impeccable. Machadinho was always concerned with the image and the propriety of his female characters. The future widow resorts to a measure that might have been definitive: "I burned the letter that burned my hands and my head" (II, 104). I will ignore the dubious taste of the sentence and concentrate on the sequence of the action. The wife, seeing her "fall" is imminent, seeks to brace herself, and moves closer to her husband:

> I made a spontaneous movement: I threw myself into his arms.
>
> He embraced me with some astonishment.
>
> And when my embrace grew long, I felt that he repelled me softly, saying:
>
> "That's well enough, you're suffocating me!"
>
> I fell back.
>
> I was saddened to see that that man, who *could and ought to save me*, did not understand, not even instinctually, that if I embraced him so tightly it was as if I were clinging to the *idea of duty*. (II, 104; italics mine)

The husband's indifference—pay attention, readers, don't miss the lesson here!—merely sets off the events. And, as it should be, punishment arrives at a gallop. After the husband unexpectedly dies, the handsome beau naturally abandons the widow; he had no intention of becoming seriously involved with any one woman, limiting himself to compromising the seriousness of many. The moralizing bent of the story is clear, especially at the end. The narrator is the widow herself, young and disillusioned: "In exchange for my love, my first love, I thus received ingratitude and scorn. It was just: *that guilty love* could have had no happy end; I was *punished* by the very consequences of my *crime*" (II, 117; italics mine). Once again, the chosen vocabulary is telling. In the story, the betrayal is not even consummated; there is no concrete physical act, but the young wife's consent to contact with a stranger, that alone, is enough to stigmatize her. In this case it hardly matters if the narrator's voice is feminine, as she joins in the chorus of society's dominant values.

In this short story, Machado also problematizes the model of serial publications and the specific ways in which they are received, making "Confessions of a Young Widow" a relevant text in the history of his experimentations with narrative voices and acts of reading. Nevertheless, the edifying angle hampers the full development of this potential, as the pedagogical narrator comes to dominate the text. We have only to look to the translation that the widow proposes of the Horatian principle, *docere et delectare*—"I give you my word that you will *enjoy* and *learn*" (II, 100; italics mine). It is curious that the narrator inverts the order of the terms in Horace's formula; for the young widow, *delectare* seems to take priority over *docere*.[12]

A relevant change comes into play during the 1870s, starting in the short stories and crônicas—likely in these two genres because of the frequency with which they were produced, as well as the immediate response from readers, to say nothing of the reduced length of these texts, which favors more daring experiments, above all in terms of narrative voice.

In "Ernesto de Tal" [Ernesto Something], published in the *Jornal das Famílias* in March and April 1873 and reproduced the same year in *Midnight Stories*, the topic and the text's approach to it see a decisive shift: not only is the adultery real, but the narrative also imagines the "forgiveness" of the betrayed figure. Moreover, there is space for the reader to form a separate interpretation: the model of the "key to the writing" is finally being set aside. The Ernesto in question has fallen for Rosina, a flirtatious girl accustomed to corresponding with a number of suitors at the same time. On one occasion, the names on the list of beaus include Ernesto and another youth, introduced as "the young man with the long nose" (II, 207). Even after he discovers the romantic triangle drawn around him, Ernesto forgives Rosina and strikes up a relationship with his old rival—a purely commercial relationship, one might add. Or perhaps not. Turning to the end of the story:

> This is not to say that the friendship between the two faded. On the contrary, Ernesto's rival showed certain magnanimity, drawing tighter the ties that had bound them since the peculiar circumstance that brought them

together. But there was more; two years after Ernesto's marriage, we see the two as business partners in a shop, with the most tranquil intimacy prevailing between them. The young man with the long nose is godfather to one of Ernesto's sons.

"Why don't you marry?" Ernesto occasionally asks his associate, friend, and his son's godfather.

"No chance, my friend," the other responds, "by now I'll die a bachelor." (II, 220)

A bachelor, but not necessarily unaccompanied, as the reader may guess. Ernesto Something—a sort of "eternal husband" à la Dostoyevsky—prefers to keep his eyes firmly shut. The text insinuates continued infidelity under the guise of a happy marriage.

This situation would appear in Eça de Queirós' posthumous novel *Alves & Cia* [Alves & Co], released in 1925. Godofredo da Conceição Alves and Ludovina, a respectable couple, have their routine disrupted by the appearance of Machado, an associate of Alves's and an eloquent admirer of the charms of his friend's spouse. After a threat of retaliation, which is never carried through on, and a (temporary) separation, all is well again and the two resume business together. They continue to prosper, reinforcing the irony of the title: *Alves & Co.* The close of the narrative suggests it all. Alves says to his associate:

"And to think we nearly fought a duel, Machado! Young people are so rash! And over what, friend Machado? Why, nothing at all!"

And Machado, in turn, claps him on the back and answers, smiling:

"Quite right, friend Alves, nothing at all!"[13]

Machado would produce some of his best short stories on the topic. In "Noite de almirante" [Admiral's Night], released in the *Gazeta de Notícias* on February 10, 1884, and reproduced that same year in *Histórias sem data* [Stories without a Date], the relationship between the sailor Deolindo and the young and excitable Genoveva could double as a treatise on psychology. The couple's time together is inaugurated by a true case of love at first sight. However, after three idyllic months, the sailor is forced to depart. The journey would not be a short one:

He'd be eight or ten months away. To commit themselves, they thought they should swear an oath of fidelity.

"I swear by God in heaven. And you?"

"Me too."

"Say out loud then."

"I swear by God in heaven; may the light fail me at the hour of death."

The pact was sworn, but not necessarily signed with equal conviction by both parties; perhaps that was why Deolindo demanded that his love repeat her oath, in a subtle preview of the story's development. Despite their promise of eternal love, which Deolindo respected with shocking rigor for a sailor, Genoveva swiftly fell in love and went to live with the peddler José Diogo. After all, sailors and peddlers are always traveling: the latter on land, the former on the high seas. Amid so many uncertainties, why not seek out some form of stability? When asked about her oath of love, the girl "from up-country, twenty years old, with *mischievous black eyes*" (Gledson 97; italics mine), disarms the sailor with her answer: "Yes, Deolindo, it was true. When I swore it, it was true" (102). In this case, it is as if the adultery merited immediate forgiveness: in the realm of the ephemeral, how to demand that one remain true to absolute values? This is no longer a matter of a "crime," but rather of an ordinary circumstance; it happened to Genoveva, of course, but how to be sure that it will not happen to the reader?

In this difference lies the progressive elaboration of the topic of adultery. Where the severe judge's eye reigned, now we begin to work with a keen observer of the radical instability of human relations.

As for jealousy, this also undergoes a significant transformation.

"O relógio de ouro" [The Gold Watch], published in the *Jornal das Famílias* in April and May 1873 and reproduced later the same year in *Midnight Stories*, presents a simple anecdote that serves to herald the complexity of future approaches to the subject. All revolves around an innocent suspicion, which is resolved easily: the man's watch found by zealous Luís Negreiros was no proof of infidelity, but a birthday present from his wife herself. This is the same structure as "The Woman in Black"; but here Machado allows himself to play around with the absurdity of the situation. After the wife's refusal to reveal the owner of the ill-fated watch, the story's ending must have made readers smile with the innocence of the plot:

A cloud came over Luís Negreiros' eyes. The tormented husband threw his hands into his wife's lap and roared:

"Answer me, you devil, or die!"

Clarinha cried out.

"Wait!" she said.

Luís Negreiros drew back.

"Kill me," she said, "but read this first. When this letter arrived at your office, you were no longer there: that's what the messenger told me."

Luís Negreiros took the letter, brought it to the lamp, and read these lines with utter stupefaction:

> *My darling husband. I know that your birthday is tomorrow; I have sent you this gift.*
> *Your wife.*

And thus ended the story of the gold watch. (II, 240)

Later on, Machado would become interested in the impossibility of eliminating doubt, rather than dismissing it with easy tricks. In doing so, he reinvented his literature.

In "Uns braços" [A Pair of Arms], published in the *Gazeta de Notícias* on November 5, 1885, and reproduced in *Várias histórias* [Several Stories] (1896), the strength of the text lies in young Inácio's uncertainty as to Dona Severina. To recall the plot: Inácio, scribe to the pitiless Borges, lives in his employer's house, alongside Dona Severina, the lawyer's wife. The suggestive description of the youth is as follows:

> He was fifteen, and looked every bit of it. The head was handsome, with its disheveled hair and the dreamy, inquisitive eyes of a lad who questions, searches, and never quite finds—all this crowning a body not without charm, even if it was badly dressed. (Gledson 182)

If we put the lad alongside the arms that give the story its title, the stage is set:

> It was, truly, Dona Severina's fault, going around with them bare all the time. All her indoor dresses had short sleeves, which stopped a few inches

below her shoulder; from that point on her arms were on show. They really were lovely and rounded, in harmony with the lady herself, more plump than she was thin. (Gledson 182)

The eroticism in the narrative springs from the virtual impossibility that anything concrete might happen, given the invariably rude and unfortunately constant presence of the lawyer, until one day, with Inácio dozing and dreaming of Dona Severina, she came cautiously over and "gave him a kiss on the mouth" (Gledson 191). Her fear that the boy might have simply been pretending to sleep subsequently drives her to change her attitude and, above all, begin covering her arms with an impertinent shawl. Shortly thereafter, Inácio returns to his father's house and will spend years without discovering what truly happened. For him, it had been "a dream! No more than a dream!" (193). Here lies a demonstration of the tone of the Machadian text in its second phase: nothing can be known with absolute certainty.

The effect is refined in "Missa do galo" [Midnight Mass], published in *A Semana* on May 12, 1894, and reproduced in *Páginas recolhidas* [Gathered Pages] (1899). Once again, the relationship between a seventeen-year-old student and a character straight from Balzac, Conceição, is marked by mystery and ambiguity, the trademarks of the mature phase's approach to jealousy and adultery. In the half-light, amid a dialogue between the future narrator and the wife of the notary Meneses (a man notorious for indiscreet extramarital affairs), the woman weaves a subtle web of enchantment. The opening of the story displays all the force of Machado's best writing: "*I've never been able to understand* the conversation I had with a lady, many years ago" (Gledson 231). The narrator is the youth, now aged and probably beginning to understand his dialogue with Conceição. The text is one of the most erotic in Machado's vast oeuvre. Paragraph by paragraph, the experienced woman's seduction offers a thousand and one opportunities for the student to try his luck; but nothing happens, as he barely understands the situation. Not even when everything seems—well, if not clear, then at least suggested with certain emphasis:

Conceição listened to me with her head leaning on the back of the chair, her eyes peeping between half-shut lids, fixed on me. From time to time she passed her tongue over her lips, to wet them. When I stopped talking

she said nothing to me; we stayed that way for a few seconds. Then I saw
her lift her head, entwine her fingers and rest her chin on them, with her
elbows on the arms of the chair, all this without taking her big sharp eyes
off me. (Gledson 234)

As the seventeen-year-old saw it, Meneses's wife couldn't sleep; and, for
lack of anything better to do, she was chatting with him. The close of the
story, however, sheds a retrospective light—not on what happened, but on
what might have happened: "The notary had died of apoplexy. Conceição
was living in Engenho Novo, but I didn't go to visit, nor did I happen to
see her. Later, I heard she'd married her late husband's apprenticed clerk"
(Gledson 240). Indeed, perhaps the clerk in question took a different interpretation of the wife's Balzacian insomnia. The couple would live in the very
neighborhood where Bento Santiago came to write not the *History of the
Suburbs*, but rather *Dom Casmurro*.

Dissembling and Vanity

Similarly, Machado began by systematically condemning both dissemblers
and the vain.

We might look to the story "Luís Soares," published in the *Jornal das
Famílias* in 1869 and republished in *Tales from Rio* the next year. The titular
character, having frittered away his inheritance, has two options: being supported by a rich uncle, or setting up a fortuitous marriage. Here we have yet
another take on the tactic employed by the agregado, a typical social passport
in nineteenth-century Brazil that Machado would analyze to the point of
exhaustion—this being a sort of autobiographical expiation, as the author
had intimate experience with the dilemmas of the position. Fortune will
smile on this bohemian, however, and two ways out appear to him at the
same time and in the same place: he will marry his cousin, who is already
under his uncle's protection. The cousin had always been in love with him,
though the rogue had never paid her any attention.

Nevertheless, Luís Soares's entirely false comportment will lead him to
ruin just as he is about to triumph. In a rocambolesque turnaround—a typical feature of Machado's early stories and novels—a fantastical will appears.

Bento, Adelaide's father, had left his daughter a fortune of 300 *contos de réis*, a considerable sum at the time. There was only one condition: she was obliged to marry her cousin. It all seemed perfect, but for the young man's evident opportunism. As soon as he heard of his cousin's newfound wealth, he fell in love with her in the blink of an eye! In this case, there is no need to resort to thick description to differentiate a twitch from a wink: Luís Soares plans to seize his cousin's fortune. The narrator holds nothing back in evaluating his attitude, commenting on the niece's decision to refuse the match even at the risk of losing her inheritance: "The major listened to the girl attentively, seeking to defend his nephew, but deep down he believed that Soares was a bad character" (II, 58). Just like that: *bad character*, completely unironic and in keeping with the moral values of the period. At the story's end, the punishment is complete, verging on melodramatic: even without marrying, Adelaide receives the 300 *contos* and prepares for a luxurious journey to Europe, naturally without her cousin's company. The cruelest punishment in nineteenth-century Brazil, apparently! Luís Soares leaves his uncle's house; impoverished and with no other alternatives, he commits suicide. And as if that weren't enough, the narrator adds a final punishment: he is quickly forgotten by his friends. Indeed, they prefer to

> hum the song from *Barbe-Bleue*.
>   Luís Soares received no other funeral oration from his closest friends.
> (II, 59)

"Augusta's Secret," meanwhile, is a screed against vanity. The short story was published in the *Jornal das Famílias* in July and August 1868 and included by the author in *Tales from Rio*. Here Augusta—another beautiful thirty-year-old woman—is confronted with an apparently impossible dilemma. Her daughter Adelaide has just turned fifteen; according to the customs of the time, this is the age at which she should marry, just as her mother did. Vasconcelos, the girl's father, has even chosen a suitor. However, Augusta rejects the match with such obstinacy that her husband begins to suspect her motives: might she have a secret relationship with the future groom? The simple mystery is solved when the husband overhears a conversation between Augusta and a friend. The latter, not understanding Augusta's firm refusal, argued incredulously:

"What I can't understand," Carlota said, "is your insistence. Sooner or later, Adelaide must be married."

"Oh! As late as possible," said Augusta.

There was a silence.

Vasconcelos was impatient.

"Ah!" Augusta went on, "if you knew the fear that the idea of Adelaide's marrying strikes into me . . ."

"But why on earth?"

"Why, Carlota? You have thought of every thing but one. I am afraid because her children will be my grandchildren! The idea of being a grandmother is wretched, Carlota." (II, 98)

The husband is relieved; and through his voice, the narrator unhesitatingly reveals the dark side of vanity: "I heard the cause of her fears. I had never thought that the love of one's own beauty could lead to such egotism" (II, 98). However, one should clarify, rather egotism than betrayal—at least as far as Vasconcelos is concerned.

As the years went by, Machado's vision underwent an appreciable transformation. The author came to see dissembling and vanity with new eyes.

In "Galeria póstuma" [Posthumous Gallery], published in the *Gazeta de Notícias* on August 2, 1883, and reproduced the same year in *Stories without a Date*, the true protagonist of the story is the diary kept by Joaquim Fidélis, a respectable, universally admired man living in Engenho Velho, if we are to take the narrator at his word: "As dear as he was, with his handsome ways, able to speak with everyone; educated with the educated, ignorant with the ignorant, a lad with the lads, and even a girl with the girls" (II, 396). The ideal friend, the neighbor of one's dreams, a true Zelig *avant la lettre*.

However, a bitter surprise is in store for his nephew Benjamim, who discovers a secret diary kept by his uncle; after reading edifying evaluations of public men and accurate analyses of the direction of national politics, he begins to flip through more compromising pages. The cordial gentleman had sketched out honest profiles of his best friends, not even sparing his nephew. In his uncle's evaluation: "Discreet, loyal, and good—so good as to be gullible. As firm in his affections as variable in his opinions. Superficial, given to novelties, drawn to the vocabulary and the formulas of law" (II, 400). Even harsher evaluations were reserved for old friends. An unexpected Janus of the suburbs, Joaquim Fidélis had learned to dissemble as if it were a sort of artificial respiration. This time the narrator does not condemn the diarist, as composing the journal reveals the mask that we are obliged to use in everyday life; after all, socializing with Joaquim Fidélis would hardly be appealing if he revealed all of his honest impressions.

(A fable in a minor key, might not "Posthumous Gallery" remind us of the author's personal trajectory? Machadinho, solicitous and socializing agreeably; and Machado, discreet, but composing a single and multifaceted "diary of Joaquim Fidélis," revealing the blemishes of Brazilian society and the predicaments of the human condition.)

In terms of Machado's novels, a slight semantic slide is set off, leading from hypocrisy to dissembling.

Let us look at two examples.

In *The Hand and the Glove* (1874), at the key point of the plot, Guiomar is obliged to choose her future husband. In theory, she is free to decide between Luís Alves and Jorge; but in practice, the baroness expects Guiomar to opt for her nephew. The astute girl makes use of a little trick:

"I choose . . . Jorge," murmured Guiomar after a few moments. The baroness started.

"Are you quite serious? I can't believe it; this is not what your heart feels."

The reader sees that the awaited word, the word that the girl felt come from her heart to her lips and strain to break through them, was not proffered by her but by her godmother; *and if he has read attentively* what came above he will see that this is precisely what she wanted. But why did Jorge's name brush her lips? The girl did not wish to deceive the baroness, but rather produce an unfaithful translation of her heart's voice, so that her godmother might compare the translation with the original for herself. *In this there was a bit of half-indirectness, of strategy, of affectation, I am on the verge of saying hypocrisy, if the term would not be taken badly.* (I, 265; italics mine)

The narrator stumbles, hesitates, and almost gives up on the vocabulary of hypocrisy, resorting to what amounts to linguistic circumnavigation: *In this there was a bit of half-indirectness, of strategy, of affectation.* However, if dissembling is an unavoidable part of day-to-day living, how to declare plainly what one really thinks, all the time? How to ease the task of social living without daily, crucial doses of merciful lying?

This understanding will broaden Machado's horizons. In *Counselor Ayres' Memorial* (1908), when it is announced that Tristão will leave for Portugal, Dona Carmo attempts to console herself by imagining that Fidelia, at least, will stay with the Aguiars. Her husband also wants to believe that the young woman will stay: "Aguiar would share his wife's sentiments, *but the banking profession drives and accustoms one to dissembling.* And perhaps they had not yet spoken of Tristão's impending return; felicity rhymes with eternity, and just then they were in a state of felicity." Soon thereafter, the Counselor jots down his impressions of Tristão in the form of a maxim, as if he were some La Rochefoucauld living on Livramento Hill (the neighborhood where Machado was born): "Perhaps he has a measure of dissimulation, as well as other civilized defects, but *in this world imperfection is a necessity*" (I, 1165; italics mine).

As simple as that: no condemnations, edifying lessons, or narrative stuttering. Dissembling is part of the job of living in society.

"Uma senhora" [A Lady], published in the *Gazeta de Notícias* on November 27, 1883, and republished the next year in *Stories without a Date*, revisits the topic of "Augusta's Secret" (1868). The two stories mirror one another, clarifying Machado's rewriting of his own work. The main character, Dona Camila, suffers the same dilemma as Augusta. In the narrator's recollection: "The first time I saw her, she was thirty-six, but only looked thirty-two, seemingly not past twenty-nine" (II, 423). Dona Camila naturally attempts to delay her daughter's marriage as long as possible, for reasons that the reader will remember from Augusta's misfortunes. This time, however, the daughter's marriage goes forward, and the fruit is not long to follow: to put it simply, Dona Camila goes to bed a mother and wakes up a grandmother. The resolution of the story, however, is more good-humored than its previous incarnation:

> It was her grandson. She, however, was so close to the child, so careful, so often, without any another woman around, that she seemed more like a mother than a grandmother; and many people believed she was indeed

the mother. As for Dona Camila's intentions, I shall not swear to them ("But I say unto you, Swear not at all," Matthew 5:34). I shall simply say that no mother was more zealous than Dona Camila with her grandson; and attributing a baby son to her was the most likely thing in the world. (II, 429)

In order to seem younger, the grandmother begins to treat the grandson as if he were her child. Note the important point, which summarizes the meaning of this Machadian transformation: one does not *condemn* the action, one *understands* the motive.

In "Fulano" [So-and-So], released in the *Gazeta de Notícias* on January 4, 1884, and included in *Stories without a Date* later that year, the reader will find a curiously prescient vision of the culture of celebrity, based on the desire to be recognized and escape from the anonymity of modern urban life. Even the name of the main character is an ironic touch: Fulano [So-and-So] Beltrão, an individual with no importance whatsoever who, at the price of self-promotion, becomes somebody—at least in his own estimation. It all begins with an anonymous article praising him in the *Jornal do Comércio*. The idea of recognition completely changes our So-and-So's routine:

> *Until then he had been a perfect casmurro,*[14] who did not attend company meetings, did not vote in political elections, did not go to the theater, did nothing, absolutely nothing. In that same month of March, the twenty-second or the twenty-third, he gave the Santa Casa de Misericórdia a ticket from the great Spanish lottery and received a creditable letter from the director, thanking him in the name of the poor. He consulted his wife and friends as to whether he should publish the letter or store it away, feeling that not publishing it would be impolite. Indeed, the letter came to light on the twenty-sixth of March, in full, with one of the pages dedicated to comments elaborating on the donor's piety. (II, 437; italics mine)

As a rule, no casmurrism is immune to good publicity. All of Fulano Beltrão's energies were spent on simple calculations, their aim always being the favorable appearance of his name in the press. Returning to the important point here: vanity is not simply condemned, but rather understood as an unavoidable element of the complexity of human behavior. This So-and-So, clearly, becomes a caricature. However, is his personal translation of the Cartesian *cogito*—"I show myself, therefore I exist"—not rooted in our own daily gestures and habits?

Time, once again, to revisit the path taken so far: both from a formal perspective and in terms of the approach to sensitive topics, Machado's works undergo a notable transformation, sketched out in short stories from the 1870s and radicalized in the *Posthumous Memoirs of Brás Cubas.*

Winter Has Come

The Shakespearean epigraph that ushers in *Resurrection* was partially translated by Machado at the end of the novel. As it seems, some men "lose the good [they] oft might win / By fearing to attempt," as "our doubts are traitors." Yes, doubts betray us; above all, they betray our audacity, advising against risk-taking. However, how to construct a relevant work if one always moves the way the wind is blowing? In a note prefacing a new edition of the novel, published in 1905, the mature author rereads the novice's effort:

> This was my first novel, written many years ago. In this new edition, I have not altered its composition nor its style, simply substituting two or three words and correcting the spelling here or there. Like others that came later, and some short stories and novels of the time, it belongs to the *first phase of my literary life.* (I, 116; italics mine).

Machado was right to indicate two distinct phases in his trajectory. This is exactly what we have seen, in our comparative reading of his novels and short stories. As his first novels were released in new editions, Machado, tellingly, harped on the same note. In the 1907 preface to a new edition of *The Hand and the Glove,* he acknowledges:

> The thirty-odd years that have passed between the appearance of this novel and this reprinting seem to explain *the differences in composition and the manner of the author.* While the latter would not now give it the same general form, it is true that he did so at one time, and, in the end, all may serve to define the same person. (I, 198; italics mine)

Equally revealing is the note to the reader that Machado wrote for the republication of *Helena* in 1905:

> This new edition of *Helena* comes forth with various emendations of language and other things, which do not alter the book's general aspect. It is of the same date as when I composed and published it, *and thus different from what time has wrought of me since*; it corresponds to the chapter of my spiritual history for the year 1876.
>
> Do not blame me for anything romantic you may find in it. Of my writings from those days, this one is especially dear to me. Even now *that I have long since gone on to other works, of a different style*, I hear a faraway echo on rereading these pages, an echo of youth and ingenuous faith. It is clear that in no case would I take from them their former aspect; each work belongs to its own time. (Caldwell 4)

In a letter to José Veríssimo, sent on December 15, 1898, Machado thanks the critic for his comments on the new edition of *Iaiá Garcia*. His justification is revealing:

> What you call *my second style, I naturally find more admirable and complete than the previous one*, but it is sweet to find those who remember the latter, and who forgivingly dig down in it until they manage to salvage from it some roots of my present hedges. (III, 1044; italics mine)

Upon the publication of his *Complete Poetry* in 1901, Machado returns to the point:

> Of certain and other verses, I shall say nothing more than that I made them with love; and of the earliest of them, that I reread them with nostalgia. I have omitted a few pages from the first series. The rest suffice for the reader to *note the difference in age and in composition*. (III, 16; italics mine)

Identifying two phases in Machado's production, therefore, has nothing to do with the trite urge to name period styles or identify literary currents. This is not a matter of labeling, but rather of observing the internal logic of an oeuvre, which implies signaling substantial differences between clearly delineated—but not discontinuous—moments in a long trajectory.

I may now suggest a close to this chapter: Machadinho's most striking *work* was not his literature—not *yet*, or not *completely*—but rather his social ascension in the court of Pedro II. Machado had to wait for the opportune moment to make his appearance. This was likely less a chess-player's calculation and more a fortuitous move, its motive thus being less clear.

Did Machadinho need an impasse in order to lose his fear of taking risks?

The hindrance—or at least a decisive catalyzer—finally appeared.

In February 1878.

And it arrived by boat.

CHAPTER 2

In the Middle of the Way
There Was an Author

Only when he dove down to the depths of himself, in order to shed his illusions, did Machado manage to create a work worthy of his genius—or, if you prefer, his daemon, the *daimon* that stirred within him without his knowing, still in a fetal state or slumbering, but which after a certain point began pecking at the eggshell in order to come out here, in the light of day; after all, the sun shines on us all.

—Augusto Meyer, "De Machadinho a Brás Cubas"

The novelist of *Iaiá Garcia* was forty when he broke the last shackles of romanticism. His culture was by then utterly robust and complete. Imbued with the serene beauty of antiquity, he found in Hellenic art a perfect harmony with the disposition of his spirit. He was a Lucian of Samosata born and raised in the nineteenth century on Livramento Hill, in the neighborhood of the sailors and street vendors, the boatmen and the Negroes for hire.

—Alfredo Pujol, *Machado de Assis*

One of the points that stand out in the investigation is the striking fad for Eça de Queirós, a true national web of admiration that, I would argue, has stretched as far as my generation and even beyond it. Eça was so widely read and so beloved that [Gilberto Freyre] even places him among the ranks of those who contributed to Brazil's intellectual unity.

—Antonio Candido, "Eça de Queirós, passado e presente"

Literary re-creation has taken place over the centuries, through translating in verse or prose, paraphrasing, and adaptation of classic works such as those by Homer, Dante, or Virgil, to say nothing of biblical themes or legends such as those of the *One Thousand and One Nights.*

—Fernando Sabino, *Amor de Capitu*

Is *Cousin Bazilio* an imitation of *Madame Bovary*? Without a doubt, if we return to the classical sense of imitation as the adoption of a model that, in preserving, one manages to outdo. Choosing this vision means rejecting the Romantic lie of originality that has lingered across the centuries.

—Christopher Domínguez Michael, "Eçalatría"

The Triumph and the Shadow

This chapter's hypothesis is controversial, but I have no intention of entangling myself in sterile debates. I propose that, midway through an exemplary if monotonous trajectory, Machado de Assis stumbled over Eça de Queirós. The author of *Iaiá Garcia* was forced to deal with the impact of *The Crime of Father Amaro*; and, above all, with the success of *Cousin Bazilio.*

Thus, the Machadian winter would set in for good in 1878, the year that the Portuguese writer's second novel was released.

And it arrived by boat.

All the newspapers, magazines, books, and other novelties from Europe came in that way: they disembarked at customs and were immediately fought over by an avid public. Machado himself recalls the scene in a crônica in *A Semana*, from December 1, 1895:

Back then each new piece from Dumas, *fils* or Augier, to name just two masters, *came straightaway in print on the first packet boat.* The young lads would run to read it, translate it, and bring it to the theater, where the actors would study it and perform it before a keen and enthusiastic audience, which heard it ten, twenty, thirty times. (III, 687; italics mine)

Now, what was odd was that this novelty spoke Portuguese—rather than the usual model, which stuck to French or English. With this in mind, recall the telling introduction to this piece of Machadian criticism:

One of the great and lively talents of the current generation in Portugal, Sr. Eça de Queirós, has just published his second novel, *Cousin Bazilio.* The first, *The Crime of Father Amaro,* was certainly not his literary debut. On both sides of the Atlantic, we had long appreciated the vigorous and brilliant style from the collaborator of Sr. Ramalho Ortigão, in those *Farpas* [Barbs], in which, one might note, those two notable writers came together as one. It was, however, his debut in the novel, and such a sensational debut that critics and public alike joined hands and *from that moment on placed the author's name among the foremost gallery of contemporaries.* He was obliged to continue in the career he had begun; or, shall we say, *to reap the fruit of his triumph.* Which exists, and is complete and unquestionable.

But is this triumph *due solely to the author's true labors?* (III, 903; italics mine)

The diction of the piece declares Machado's surprise at Eça's immediate success; after all, when *Cousin Bazilio* was released in February 1878, Machado was publishing *Iaiá Garcia,* his fourth novel, in near-daily installments in the newspaper, following a model of unflinching discipline. Let me repeat: *his fourth novel,* despite not having tasted the glory of Queirosian acclaim; *critics and public alike joined hands,* paving Eça's path to enshrinement. The words cannot disguise his discomfort: *such a sensational debut; the author's name among the foremost gallery of contemporaries; reap the fruit of his triumph.* Hence, the rhetorical question that opens the second paragraph—but is this triumph *due solely to the author's true labors?*—is weighted with the malice typical of literary life, albeit surprising from cautious Machadinho. This malice betrays the displeasure of the author as laborer, he whose constant work has not brought the expected fruits.

It has become a cliché to consider the two articles on *Cousin Bazilio,* published in *O Cruzeiro* on April 16 and 30, 1878, as one of the utmost expressions of Machado's critical work. On the contrary—these are his least inspired pages. However, the aggressive tone of certain passages, hardly to be expected for a man who never cultivated controversy, may have been the catalyst that allowed the prim author of *The Hand and the Glove* to reinvent himself. And he was able to do it because in the middle of the way there was an author.

> ("In the middle of the way there was a stone. / There was a stone in the middle of the way"—to recall Carlos Drummond de Andrade's famous lines.)

Two writers, as a matter of fact.

On one hand, Eça and his success; on the other, the author that Machadinho was about to become.

In his articles on *Cousin Bazilio*, there emerges a new idea, almost a *new sensation*, although one as old as the classics: the idea of *aemulatio*. I will thus argue for a poetic-rhetorical reading of Machado's transformation. While referencing his rivalry with Eça, I do not understand it as a psychological trait, but rather a catalyst that unearthed Machado's dissatisfaction with his own technique.

Here, if I am not wrong, lies the turning point in his work.

A paradox appears in Machado's criticism of the Portuguese author's novels:

> Sr. Eça de Queirós is a *faithful and most severe disciple* of the realism propagated by the author of *Assommoir*. Had he been a *mere copyist*, the critic's duty would have been to leave him defenseless in the hands of blind enthusiasm, which would ultimately kill him; *but he is a man of talent*, who has just recently crossed the threshold of the *literary workshop*. (III, 904; italics mine)

One has only to underline the key words—*faithful and most severe disciple*; *copyist*; *man of talent*; *literary workshop*—in order to begin investigating the thread of Machado's reflections. In theory, a *faithful and most severe disciple*, possibly even a *copyist*, would never be considered a *man of talent*. In the model imposed by inflated notions of subjectivity and authorship, placing the terms together seems absolute nonsense. However, a more interesting way of understanding Machado's perspective rests on the notion of a *literary workshop*. This is a typical metaphor of the world of pre-Romantic artistic practices, associated to the techniques of *imitation* and *aemulatio*. In the articles on *Cousin Bazilio*, this world gradually becomes the decisive critical novelty, making the *pen of mirth* and the *ink of melancholy* possible.

The Itinerary

In an attempt to prepare the ground for my introduction of this possibility, I begin with the dilemma faced by every novelist in a peripheral country (that is, every country outside the hegemonic cultures): how to deal with the canon of the English and French traditions, which formed the modern novel in the eighteenth and nineteenth centuries? The understanding of Machado's reaction to *Cousin Bazilio* may shift, once inserted into this debate. Eça's triumph had made the equation more complex: after 1878, no author writing in Portuguese could ignore the impact of *Cousin Bazilio*. Writing novels in Portuguese now meant facing two Queirosian titles: *The Crime of Father Amaro* and *Cousin Bazilio*. By this time, Machado had already published four novels, none of which would be a candidate for obligatory reading in any literary tradition, even within the limited scope of Brazilian literature. *Cousin Bazilio*, although vastly different in its conception and style, was rubbing shoulders with Almeida Garrett's *Viagens na minha terra* [Travels in My Homeland], published in book form in 1846. Machado would only be admitted to this select group two years later, thanks to the prose of the deceased author.

The second step involves the careful reading of two of Machado's articles, with the aim of identifying the aesthetic criteria that made such a severe take on Queirós's work possible. Here, the reader may be taken aback: these criteria were aesthetically normative and morally conservative.

Finally, after a brief study of certain aspects of *Cousin Bazilio* that the Brazilian author preferred to ignore, I seek to observe, *using Machado's own text*, the emergence of the idea of emulation as a decisive criterion for judgment: still a faltering criterion, but present and responsible for the best moments in Machado's analysis of Queirós's work.

Here you have the itinerary for this chapter.

As we look back from the end of the path, it seems that the stone that was Eça de Queirós may have become the spur that drove Machadinho to finally take some risks. Machado stopped *losing the good we oft might win / By fearing to attempt.*

Centers and Peripheries

In a pioneering text, published in the *Jornal de Debates* on September 23, 1837, Pereira da Silva turned his column, "Literatura," to the topic that drives my argument. How to understand the ways in which nonhegemonic literatures and cultures develop strategies in order to affirm their values before hegemonic literatures and cultures?

◆   ◆   ◆

I have barely begun, and a digression beckons.

In this essay I do not deal with essences, but with strategies; I do not attribute a single value to the notion of a center, or of a hegemonic culture, nor do I confuse the concept with a specific geographical position. Similarly, I would not waste the reader's time on useless laments or unfounded jingoism spun around the peripheral, nonhegemonic condition. This is not a matter of fixed latitude, but rather the oscillation of relationships of power—here lies the decisive point. Every hegemonic culture contains peripheral pockets, while every nonhegemonic sphere includes islands of prosperity to rival the most central of centers; the redundancy is inevitable. I do not attribute an absolute meaning to given positions, rather indicating the dynamic nature of asymmetrical relationships—a fundamental point in reevaluating Machado's reaction to *Cousin Bazilio.*

I think, for example, of the revealing reflections of Catherine Morland, a character from Jane Austen's *Northanger Abbey.* At a dance in Bath, Catherine's partner scorns the city in comparison the capital of the empire. Catherine's answer is an essay in and of itself:

Well, other people must judge for themselves, and those who go to London may think nothing of Bath. But I, who live in a small retired village in the country, can never find greater sameness in such a place as this, than in my own home; for here are a variety of amusements, a variety of things to be seen and done all day long, which I can know nothing of there.[1]

Between a rural town and London, Bath stands at a bipolar position: an alternative center for the settlements around it, but an undeniable periphery for London. In the next century, the same triangulation will appear in Emma Bovary's aspirations, split between the province and fictitious Yonville, the dream of visiting Paris and the reality of Rouen; a true bridge-city, like Catherine Morland's Bath. These triangular relationships, meanwhile, would help mold Latin American cultures in the nineteenth century, constantly dealing with the London-Paris axis, albeit mediated by Lisbon and Madrid.

◆　◆　◆

In highlighting the tension between hegemonic and nonhegemonic cultures, I refer to the concrete existence of literatures favored by the particular historical circumstances, benefiting one language over another in the diffusion of works. The "universality" of this author or that one depends more on the language he or she writes in than on the intrinsic quality of his or her work. And so, while in the eighteenth and nineteenth centuries French was the lingua franca of the utopian republic of letters, in the twentieth and twenty-first centuries English has become the new lingua franca in the academic and digital world. Books produced in English or even French have a vastly broader ability to circulate than those published in, say, Danish or Swedish. Authors who write in those languages have a much greater chance of occupying the center of the canon, as they write in the language of a culture that occupies a central position in power relations—once again, the redundancy is inevitable.

In their study of Franz Kafka, Gilles Deleuze and Félix Guattari developed the concept of a "minor literature" in order to reflect on the conditions in which the noncanonical use of a hegemonic language may produce destabilizing effects within a code that still remains dominant. Thus, the deliberately understylized German employed by the author of *The Metamorphosis* literally becomes the terse language of the imperial administration. The dry, short phrases produce a mirror image of the ambivalence of the civilizing process, idealized in the notion of *Bildung* but embodied in the harsh hand of the everyday bureaucracy wielded by those in power.[2]

The situation may grow more complex still. How to reflect on the same array of problems when the language at hand has never been hegemonic—not the French of the Enlightenment, much less the German of philosophy, nor the English of the contemporary world, but the Portuguese of Machado de Assis and Eça de Queirós? How to produce noncanonical effects within a hegemonic code when the very language one is writing in demands a preliminary step: translation? The dilemma may grow even starker. How to *produce* under the conditions of nonhegemonic cultures without first *translating* the canons of the literatures considered to be central?

This same difficulty may be found at more distant latitudes; it is not an exclusively Latin American or Iberian stumbling block. On the contrary, a comparative analysis favors a renewed understanding of Machado's criticism of *Cousin Bazilio.*

On November 26, 1887, Danish critic Georg Brandes began a fascinating correspondence with Friedrich Nietzsche. In his first letter, hewing surprisingly close to the typical concerns of the best Latin American authors, Brandes permitted himself to ask:

> Have you read anything of mine? *I write almost exclusively in Danish and attempt to solve the greatest variety of problems.* I have not written in German for some time. I believe that my best readers may be found in the Slavic countries. For two years I gave conferences in French in Warsaw, and this year [I spoke] in Saint Petersburg and Moscow. This is how I seek to overcome the *agonizing bounds of the homeland.*[3]

An inevitable anxiety, especially when one writes *almost exclusively in Danish*—or in Portuguese, or Hungarian, or even Spanish, to a certain extent. During his short but intense exchange of letters with Nietzsche, from November 26, 1887, to January 4, 1889, the date that the last letter from the philosopher was posted, the subject returns obsessively, revealing the critic's efforts to overcome the barrier of language. Around this period, Nietzsche also felt isolated, an exile in his own land. Brandes resorted to a number of strategies—he wrote in German, gave talks in French, traveled to Moscow and St. Petersburg, and finally released a book in Polish—none of which may have been the most efficient in overcoming the isolation caused by the Danish language.

Brandes tirelessly recommends works key for the philosophical project of the author of *Ecce Homo*. However, the same obstacle crops up at every turn. In a letter sent on January 11, 1888, Brandes laments: "There is a Scandinavian thinker whose works would greatly interest you *if you could read them in some translation*: I am thinking of Søren Kierkegaard" (84; italics mine). The Danish critic articulated what might be labeled the "anxiety of illegibility" or the "translation imperative." Brandes never stops reminding Nietzsche how much he is missing by not reading Polish, Swedish, Icelandic, Danish—a step farther, and he might even demand that the philosopher also learn Spanish and Portuguese! In other words, rather than demonstrating the arrogance of a pedantic academic or the provincialism of an upstart intellectual, Brandes's repeated reading suggestions clarify his own anxiety. He found himself isolated, both in his language and in his environment. Take the letter sent in February 1888: "I imagine that you are enjoying a pleasant spring, while we in recent days have been buried under repugnant snows, *separated from Europe*" (88; italics mine).

This sentiment remains current, a century later. As Polish poet Czeslaw Milosz would confess: "*My corner of Europe*, owing to the extraordinary and lethal events that have been occurring there, comparable only to violent earthquakes, affords a peculiar perspective."[4] His reflections are shot through with the awareness of belonging to the periphery of Europe. Likewise, the author—who received the Nobel Prize for Literature in 1980—repeatedly laments that the best Polish poets are not translated, and thus remain virtually unknown. It is as if Brandes and Milosz belonged to the same period and not to different centuries. Well, Machado and Eça, in the key year of 1878, grappled with the same obstacles mentioned by the Danish critic.

In this chapter, I will discuss precisely the strategies developed around nonhegemonic literatures and cultures in order to affirm their values before hegemonic literatures and cultures. Here, the poetics of emulation sparks unexpected consequences on the level of cultural politics. As this possibility unfolds, it demands an approach that should not be limited to the Lusophone sphere, affording a broader comparative study.

The Centrality of Translation

Back to Pereira da Silva's text. In the article, "Modern Novels and Their Influence," he underlines the topic's relevance:

> Almost all literatures begin with their *novels*: the infancy of a culture is
> always rocked in the cradle of fiction, and of games of the imagination;
> moreover, the *fair sex*, which since the dawn of societies, strictly speaking,
> has dominated the world and dictated tastes, has allied itself to this literary
> *specialty.*[5]

The opening words of the article are more wishful than declarative. In
1836, Gonçalves de Magalhães released *Suspiros poéticos e saudades* [Poetic
Sighs and Longings], a volume of poetry that, alongside the publication of
Niterói: Revista brasiliense [Niterói: Brazilian Magazine], officially inaugurated romanticism in Brazil. Therefore, if "almost all literatures begin with
their *novels*," wouldn't it be high time for Brazilian *novels* to show themselves?
According to Pereira da Silva, however, the absence of *Brazilian* novelists
was no impediment to the formation of a faithful public of *female readers*.
After emphasizing the importance of Sir Walter Scott, seen as "the man who
entirely changed the form of the novel," he laments that Brazilian representatives of the *fair sex* "still have not read the novels of this Scottish Homer, *as
they have yet to be translated into the Portuguese language*, one so crowded
with bad novels and wretched novellas" (45; italics mine).

This paradoxical absence of novelists is easily understood: the reading
public in Brazil was formed around novels, novellas, and stories, *narratives
primarily read in translation*, although some readers had access to texts in
French; even novels written in other languages were read in translation to
the language of Montaigne. Hence the "translation imperative" in the case of
nonhegemonic languages. This was how Nietzsche could finally read one of
the authors recommended by Brandes, as he reported in a letter on November 20, 1888: "The day before yesterday, I read with great pleasure *Getting
Married*, by Mr. August Strindberg, as if I were at home. I sincerely admire
him. And I would admire him more if I did not have the impression that, in
him, I admire something of myself" (115).

Here lies the key point in reevaluating the scale of the leap from

Machadinho to Machado, as well as spurring the poetics of emulation's unexpected shift into active cultural politics. On a formal level, how to make the precedence of *reading* over *writing*, of the *translation* over the *original*, productive? How to cast secondary (*secundidade*) as a principle for invention? Might one consider this position a feature of Lusophone literature—or, to put it more generally, a defining element of nonhegemonic literatures? Yes: a position brought to light in the resentful tang of Eça's affirmation in the harsh reply, which would only be published posthumously, to Machado's equally severe criticism of *Cousin Bazilio*. To recall his tart reaction to the Brazilian's allegations of imitation:

> Of the two books, criticism certainly came to find *The Crime of Father Amaro* first; and when, one day, it stumbled upon an advertisement for *Faute de l'Abbé Mouret* in a French newspaper or spotted it in a bookseller's window, it immediately applied a rule of threes, concluding that *Faute de l'Abbé Mouret* must be to *The Crime of Father Amaro* as France is to Portugal. Little effort was required to turn up the following unknown quantity: PLAGIARISM![6]

Here we have the simple but brutal arithmetic of nonhegemonic cultures: as Alfonso Reyes saw it, we are perennially late to the banquet of civilization. And one has to rush so as to not miss out on dessert. In another century, Oswald de Andrade confirmed the principle of the rule of threes. The product of the equation never favors us: "The labor of the futurist generation was cyclopean. Setting the imperial watch of the nation's literature."[7] As we know, the watch-hands of the Republic of Letters hew to a highly inflexible meridian. Hence Eça's emphasis on the French, English, and German models as products of the "three great thinking nations" (174).

Eça's unpublished text was a reply in kind to Machado's far-from-diplomatic verdict (I will repeat this quotation later on, but it must be introduced here):

> That Sr. Eça de Queirós is a disciple of the author of *Assommoir* is known to all. *The Crime of Father Amaro* itself is an *imitation* of the novel by Zola, *La Faute de L'Abbé Mouret*. An analogous situation, *the same* tendencies; a difference in the setting; difference in the denouement; *identical* style;

recollections of the other, such as in the chapter of the Mass, and others; finally, *the same title*. (III, 903–4; italics mine)

Here we have *a question pregnant with questions that would take us far along…*

The Crime of Father Amaro was first published in the *Revista Ocidental* in Lisbon, from February 15 to April 15, 1875. Eça would later reject this edition, calling it a rough draft. He prepared a second version, the first edition to be released as a book, which was published in 1876. This was practically a new book; in his words, the *definitive edition*. A third edition, the second in book form, would appear in 1880. Indeed, the 1876 version that Machado consulted for his critique bears clear marks of Zola's influence in the rewriting of the text, although it would hardly be accurate to characterize it as an *imitation*. Rather, this is a typical example of *aemulatio*, the same principle adopted by Eça in his reworking of motifs from *Madame Bovary*.

One might note that, even in the reply published in the preface to the third edition,[8] released in 1880—the same year that the *Posthumous Memoirs of Brás Cubas* was published—Eça was still on the defense: "Knowing the two books, *only corneal obtuseness or cynical bad faith*"[9] would make it possible to conflate the novels.

Machado preferred not to reply.

The problem of literary primogeniture, while clearly not exclusive to the nineteenth century, was suffered acutely by the writers of that period, one cause being the centrality of the printed text as a medium of mass communication. In this context, how could a Lusophone author help but "imitate" the "superior" model of *the three great thinking nations*? The Queirosian rule of threes imposes brutally strict limits. Moreover, the average taste of the Portuguese and Brazilian reading publics was formed through the translation of novels written in the languages of those nations. Note the bitterness in Eça's reply, which perfectly clarifies the weight that this tradition exerted on Portuguese-language authors, a weight exacerbated by the fact that they were part of a *domestic episode*, currying favor with audiences in Portugal and Brazil. In the Lusophone literary system—in other words, the nonhegemonic literary system—especially within the genre of the novel, translation brings a sweeping theoretical question in its wake: how to reflect on the conditions of literary creation when *translation* takes on the role of *tradition*? How to write novels in Portuguese in the shadow of the English and French works of the eighteenth and nineteenth centuries? Here I have even limited the scope of my reference to the two dominant models in the creation of the modern novel, leaving aside the German vein, its *Bildungsroman*, and the virtual omnipresence of Russian fiction in the nineteenth century—both, as a general rule, read in French translation, extremely liberal translations, one might note, which shamelessly adapted the original text to the Parisian reader's palate.

To put it bluntly: Machado's harsh reaction to the success of *Cousin Bazilio* and Eça's ill-mannered reply stem from an issue of cultural politics that evades resolution to this day. The Machadian criticism and the Queirosian rewriting of *Madame Bovary* offer a sketch of an answer. From this broader perspective, Machado's two articles may take on unexpected hues, ultimately spilling into the anachronistic return to the technique of *aemulatio*—an anachronism that serves as a checkmate in terms of cultural politics.

Emulation, as a technique, implies the conscious imitation of a previously established model with the aim of adding new elements to it. The deliberately anachronistic recovery of the arts of *imitatio* and *aemulatio* transforms the secondary of the peripheral condition into a *potentially* productive force.

The very source of the deceased author's malicious spark.

Machadian Criticism

I begin my rereading of the articles dedicated to *Cousin Bazilio* with a query as simple as it is unavoidable: what Machado is this, reading and criticizing the novel by Eça de Queirós so bitingly? The question may seem impertinent, but that impertinence is vital to establishing the accuracy of my hypothesis. The supposition behind this line of questioning is all-encompassing: we need to radically reread Machado's criticism, questioning his assumptions.

Machado's reading hits the target on strategic points, and may have been a factor in the Portuguese author's subsequent change in course. His next book, *O mandarim* [The Mandarin], would be a far cry from the first two, a stylistic leap comparable to Machado's producing the *Posthumous Memoirs of Brás Cubas*. This is precisely why I seek to clarify the critical assumptions of

Machado's argument—as Eça, at least at first, seems to have taken the blow to heart. Recall the friendly tone of the letter sent from England, on June 29, 1878:

> I hoped to delay no further in thanking you for your excellent article of the sixteenth. Although adverse to me, almost completely opposed, and inspired in a practically political hostility towards the realist school—the article, by virtue of its distinction and the talent with which it was composed, *honors my book, almost increasing its authority.*[10]

To this day, Machado's judgment is read as a manifestation of his critical talent. *Cousin Bazilio* was published in February 1878 to overwhelming success. The first print run of three thousand copies was sold out in a blink of an eye. A second edition revised by the author was released later that year. With telling speed, Machado writes a frankly contrary review of the novel on April 16; this is the article Eça mentions in his letter. Two weeks later—on April 30, to be precise—the author of *Iaiá Garcia* is back at it, clarifying specific points of his reading in an effort to respond to those who disagreed with the first article. Not a few had sprung to the defense of the author of *The Crime of Father Amaro*; it even appears plausible that Machado's attack helped to unite Eça's Brazilian admirers.

By now this Machadian analysis has become canonical; its study has been raised to the level of cliché, one difficult to dispute. But the reason for such enthusiasm, let alone unanimity, over this reading is far from clear. Machado's argument may be summarized in three points.

First of all, Machado condemns unconditional adherence to the "realism of Zola," as it implies a juggling act (in the naturalist model, no ingredient can be left out) that undermines the plausibility of the plot. He also points out structural flaws in the story, especially in the accidental nature of central events. Finally, Machado judges the characters insufficiently developed. Emphasis on his famous take on the heroine: "Luísa is a negative character, and, surrounded by the action conceived by the author, she is more a puppet than a moral person" (III, 905).

This cliché needs to be questioned.

My point of departure is very simple: the two articles on *Cousin Bazilio* were not written with the pen of mirth and the ink of melancholy belonging to the deceased author, whose birth certificate is dated 1880. In other words, the reader of *Cousin Bazilio* was the author of *Iaiá Garcia*, not the creator of the *Posthumous Memoirs of Brás Cubas*.

I move to restore chronology to the controversy, instead of retrospectively projecting the Machado of the *Posthumous Memoirs* onto the whole of his work. Unless I am mistaken, a hermeneutical mistake has become a common reading. To wit: the Machado who criticized *Cousin Bazilio* based his judgment on the very aesthetic criteria that a novel such as the *Posthumous Memoirs* would show to be out of date and practically cartoonish! The criteria of Machadinho, the reader of *Cousin Bazilio*, are not and could never be those of Machado, the author of the *Posthumous Memoirs*.

Hence the necessity of unearthing Machado's aesthetic criteria in evaluating the novel by Queirós.

First of all, his criteria are surprisingly moralistic—and not in the sense of the French moralism of the seventeenth century, which hewed close to Machado's own heart, but in the bourgeois vein satirized by Flaubert, attacked by Eça, and hung out to dry in the *Posthumous Memoirs*. This, for example, is how Machadinho describes the affair between Luísa and Bazilio: "This union of a few weeks, which is the initial and essential event of the plot, is nothing more than an *erotic incident with little importance, both repugnant and vulgar*" (III, 906; italics mine).

Why *repugnant* and *vulgar*? Simply because it is an *erotic incident*! Machado is thus forced to condemn the central "downfall of the works of Sr. Eça de Queirós—or, one might say, of his merciless realism: it is *physical sensation*. The examples pile up from page to page; to list them would be to form an agglomeration, thus exacerbating their raw, uncovered nature" (III, 908; italics mine). The Machado of 1878 is visibly discomfited by Eça's lack of ceremony in dealing with the body and erotic desire in his fiction, and goes so far as to attribute the book's success to the scandal raised by such liberty:

> Our language had not known such photographic and servile reproduction of the most *trifling, ignoble* things. For the first time, a book appeared in which suspect and—let us say the word straight out, as we are combating the doctrine, not the talent, much less the man—in which *suspect* and *base* matters were treated with painstaking care and related with all the preciseness of an inventory. (III, 904; italics mine)

Our language had not known: when read against the grain, the critique exposes the Achilles' heel of the author of *Helena*. The first four novels and the majority of the stories by Machadinho were, on the contrary, written in a style that *our language knew* (and quite well at that) . . . Eça's audacity may have made the author of *Resurrection* understand the epigraph to his first novel in a new light: those who fear risking themselves "lose the good we oft might win / By fearing to attempt" (I, 195). When transposed to the literary scene, the line seems to demand nothing less than the radical rethinking of compositional techniques and central themes.

Machado condemned *The Crime of Father Amaro*, but the proviso struck at *Cousin Bazilio* as well. This critic was closer to the prim author of *The Hand and the Glove*, a novel published in 1874, whose narrator— with a zeal that today strikes us as anti-Machadian—took it upon himself to explain the protagonist's daring behavior. Her actions are completely understandable, one might add: between a rock and a hard place, faced with one marriage that would perpetuate her status as a dependent and another that would open the door to an independent life, Guiomar opts for the latter. But she needs to act swiftly, as her fate depends on a quick decision from Luís Alves, a promising and ambitious young man. Pressured by the circumstances, Guiomar draws up a headstrong note urging her suitor to take the final step. The message was concise, containing only the essential: "The paper held a single phrase:—*Ask me*—written in the middle of the leaf in a fine, elegant, feminine hand" (I, 259). This resolute attitude gives a glimpse of the virility of the heroine,[11] whose calculating and artifices reveal her talent for politics—an elective affinity with her future husband, one might add. Yet here is how we must "justify" (the narrator uses this very word!) Guiomar's actions:

> From this observation, Luís Alves was struck by a quite natural thought. *The note, hardly appropriate in any other circumstance, was justified* by the declaration that he himself had made to the girl a few days earlier, when he asked her to get to know him first, and said that on the day she judged him worthy to be her husband, he would take heed and follow suit. But if this was true of the note, the same was not the case with the hour. What had driven the girl to toss that decisive paper, eloquent in its gravity, from her window at midnight?

Luís Alves concluded that there was some urgent reason, and thus that he must address the situation with the means at hand. (I, 270; italics mine)

Must we recall that back in 1857, through his perfection of free indirect discourse, Flaubert had already explored the rich possibilities of a narrator who, in becoming "invisible," forced the reader to draw his or her own conclusions? In the passage I have just transcribed, despite a laborious analytic effort, it seems that we have traveled back in time and found ourselves in the realm of the omniscient narrator, an absolute ruler always ready to "judge" the characters' actions in the name of decorum. 1874 found Portuguese-language literature on the threshold of the publication of *The Crime of Father Amaro,* which would be released a year later. Just before the passage cited above, the reader was treated to the following description of the protagonist's moral inclinations: "Guiomar was truly in love. But to what extent was that sentiment involuntary? Nearly to the extent of *tarnishing the chastity of our heroine's heart*" (I, 252; italics mine). A few details here are significant: *our heroine,* in an attempt to encourage the reader to identify with the plot and its characters. And this is a reassuring identification; after all, Guiomar keeps her emotions on a short leash. These are spontaneous emotions, undoubtedly—within such a pious imagination, a dissembling heroine would be an unacceptable paradox—but they are also tightly regulated, as *that sentiment,* if unbridled, might give way to compromising raptures. The exact compromise lies in the prim formula: *nearly to the extent.*

Machadinho needed to change his worldview, just as he needed to remake his conception of literature.

And he needed to do it quickly.

Especially after *February 1878.*

But the change was not easy, as we may glean from a letter sent to José Carlos Rodrigues on January 25, 1873. In it, Machado thanks the editor for the favorable review published of his first novel, *Resurrection*:

I clasp your hands in gratitude for your article in *Novo Mundo* regarding my novel. And I thank you not only for the obliging words, but also for your observations. . . . *I abhor the literature of scandal,* and I sought to steer away from that pitfall. If anything has escaped me, *I hope to amend it in my next composition.* (III, 1032; italics mine)

José Carlos Rodrigues founded the magazine *O Novo Mundo*, directing it from 1872 to 1879. In December 1872 he published the review to which Machado refers. The new novelist was quick to thank him; and, in March of the next year, the magazine would publish one of Machado's most important critical studies, "News of the Present Brazilian Literature: Instinct of Nationality." Machadinho was always able to forge powerful networks and opportune alliances. The severe judge condemned certain passages of *Resurrection*, leaning on the same moral foundation that would be evoked by the (equally rigid) reader of *Cousin Bazilio*:

> Unfortunately, the author describes certain scenes featuring Cecília, Félix, and Moreirinha in such vivid detail that we cannot conceive of a quantity of color sufficient to neutralize the tones in which he has painted them. The ending of page 47 is unpardonable; the statue at the end of page 41 might well have been omitted; and certain of Vianna's "urges" are horrible.[12]

While remaining true to the modesty of the writer-laborer, Machadinho was also concerned with the propriety of the content in his plots: certainly a model author in this respect. Under this category—and we must recognize this without flinching—the following passage from the celebrated critique of 1878 is undeniably pre-Flaubertian, and post-1880, we might call it decidedly anti-Machadian. In discussing Luísa's conjugal behavior, which becomes, shall we say, more creative after the affair with her cousin, Machado reacted thus:

> What does the author of this passage tell us? That Luísa was slightly ashamed of the way "she loved [her husband] ... sensing vaguely that such amorous violence was not dignified in a married woman; she was afraid it might be a mere *capricious fancy, and for her own husband!*"[13]
> *How awful! A capricious fancy for one's own husband!* (III, 911; italics mine)

Coming from the pen of the deceased author, these exclamations would have a deliciously cynical and even erotic tone, as is the case in the extraordinary chapter 55, "The Old Dialogue of Adam and Eve," in which the lovers' coitus is suggested by punctuation marks.[14] From the author of *Iaiá Garcia*, however, the exclamation points are to be taken seriously. Rio's high society and the illustrious representatives of the imperial court would probably read this summary condemnation of Luísa, the "criminal"—to recall the vocabulary used to refer to adultery during Machado's first phase—with a solemn shake of the head, tacitly falling in line with the author's elevated moral values.

But there's more.

In the celebrated critique of *Cousin Bazilio*, Machado echoed the opinion of Eça de Queirós' father, unwittingly, of course, which makes their coincidence particularly significant. In a letter sent to Eça in the heat of the moment, on February 26, 1878, his father praised the composition ("The novel is magnificent, and as a work of art I believe it superior to *Father Amaro*"),[15] but allowed himself one proviso: "From the point of view of the realist school that has you in its sway, the novel is a perfect work of art. I believe, however, that even within this school, there is *a point beyond which one ought not go*" (48; italics mine). We are already familiar with another formula: *nearly to the extent*. The difference is slight, and the moralizing principle is the same. But how to go about toeing a movable line, as limits in literature tend to be unstable? From the paternal point of view, nothing could be easier: "In whatever you write, I recommend that you avoid descriptions that ladies cannot read without blushing" (49). An infallible criterion, followed to the letter by the pedagogical narrator of *The Hand and the Glove*. This agreement between the Brazilian author and the father of the Portuguese novelist can hardly be chalked up as a point for Machado's critical sagacity. Rather, it suggests the extent to which the reader of *Cousin Bazilio* was in step with the conservative values of his time.

And there is more still.

In 1859, the young critic, then just twenty years old, published three articles in *O Espelho*, discussing his "Ideas on the Theater." December 25 saw the last of the series, entitled "The Dramatic Conservatory," in which Machado analyzed the scope and utility of the institution. From 1862 to 1864, as a censor—a member of the Brazilian Dramatic Conservatory, that is—he would author sixteen reports. Before even entering the institution, he had argued for its relevance:

> Dramatic literature, much like the people as a whole, has a *policing body, which provides it with censorship and punishment*: this is the conservatory.
>
> The aims of this institution are, or ought to be, twofold: moral and

intellectual. It fulfills the first in *correcting the less decent aspects of dramatic works*; the second is attained in analyzing and judging the literary merit of these same works.

With these targets, a dramatic conservatory is more than useful; it is necessary. *Official criticism, a court without appeal, guaranteed by the government* and sustained by public opinion, is the most fruitful of criticism, whenever ruled by reason and stripped of deaf stratagems. (III, 794–95; italics mine)

To head off the ill-considered anachronism—*policing body* should be understood through its etymology: *politia*, in the sense of government, custom, habit. The Conservatory would thus be a *policing body*, a group of people dedicated to "policing" the propriety of the plays to be translated and performed. This made it not merely *useful*, but *necessary*, as it guaranteed the emendation of *the less decent aspects of dramatic works*. This guarantee was solid, as a negative report would keep a text from being put on. The censor's voice served as an *official criticism, a court without appeal, guaranteed by the government*. The foolish anachronism is warded off, but we should not fall into any sort of critical hagiography: the words of this twenty-year-old would be fully endorsed by all the stuffed shirts of the Segundo Reinado.[16]

And by Eça's father . . .

Not that the mature author's opinions were much different. In one observation in the essay "News of the Present Brazilian Literature. Instinct of Nationality," Machado indicates the tenor of his critique of *Cousin Bazilio*:

> The *moral tendencies* of the Brazilian novel are good, on the whole. *Not all are irreproachable from beginning to end*; there will always be something *for a severe critique to point out and correct*. But the general tone is acceptable. *The books of a certain French school*, though widely read among us, have not *contaminated* Brazilian literature, nor do I see any tendency to adopt its doctrines, which is a notable merit in and of itself. The works I speak of were welcomed here, received warmly as guests, but neither allied themselves to the family *nor took command of the house*. (III, 805; italics mine)

Machado offers a tip of his hat to the editor of the magazine: the sentence "there will always be something *for a severe critique to point out and correct*" seems to allude to José Carlos Rodrigues's review of the debut novel from the writer who was now a collaborator at *O Novo Mundo*. Now, just five years after this text was composed, a book inspired by *a certain French school* was threatening to *contaminate Brazilian literature*: none other than *Cousin Bazilio*. The *severe critique* that Machado brandished had already been announced in the 1873 article. I ask the reader to note the vocabulary here, recalling the moralistic diction we saw in Machado's first stories: *moral tendencies*; *irreproachable*; *correct*.

There is still more.

Machado's first article on *Cousin Bazilio* provoked Eça's Brazilian partisans, and many wrote replies rebutting the negative verdict from the author of *Iaiá Garcia*. One harsh blow was delivered by Amenófis Efendi, the pen name of Ataliba Lopes de Gomensoro, who published the article "Eleazar and Eça de Queirós: A Critic of *Cousin Bazilio*" in the *Gazeta de Notícias* on April 24, 1878. In order to prove that the novel's eroticism was not gratuitous, Amenófis resorted to a theoretically bulletproof argument: he transcribed some of the more, shall we say, intense passages from Song of Songs, which compared breasts to "clusters of grapes." Who would turn down a glass of such wine? Not even the censor of *Cousin Bazilio*; after all, as Amenófis supposes, he "must know that the Song of Songs is a part of his sacred book—the Bible."[17]

Touché.

Machadinho, however, did not falter. In the second article in the series, he took the bait. Here is his reaction to the possibility of an overheated reading of the Scriptures: "You receive the book *as a Catholic should*, that is to say, in its mystical and superior sense, and in that case you cannot call it erotic" (III, 911; italics mine). Is there any need for extended commentary here? As if he were presenting the distinguished public with a certificate of good conduct, the critic supports an appropriately pious exegesis, fending off any parodic appropriation of the Bible. In just two years, this same reader of *Cousin Bazilio* would be transformed into the author of a novel whose first paragraph draws an irreverent parallel with those very same Scriptures. First defended with tooth and nail; now, digested and mulled over in the prose of Brás Cubas:

> I pondered for a time whether I ought to open these memoirs at the beginning or at the end—that is, if I would put first my birth or my death.

While the common practice would be to begin with one's birth, two considerations led me to adopt a different method: the first is that I am not quite an author deceased, but a deceased author, for whom the tomb was another cradle; the second is that this would make the writing more spirited, and fresher. Moses, who also told of his own death, did not put it in the opening but at the finish: a radical difference between this book and the Pentateuch. (I, 513)

The production of this *radical difference* demanded that he overcome a normative aesthetic, one packaged along with an omniscient narrator, the implacable judge of the moral actions of his characters, a perfect panoptical representative of social mores. Here we might recall the theoretical basis for Machado's central critique of the way the plot unfolds in *Cousin Bazilio*:

Take out the misplaced letters, and Jorge's house becomes a corner of *Paradise*; without this entirely accidental circumstance, the novel would end. Now, this substitution of the essential with the secondary, with all the actions of character and sentiment grafted onto an incident, a chance event, this is what struck me as incongruent and contrary to the laws of art. (III, 910)

The *laws of art*? Does this mean that the critic of *Cousin Bazilio* is arguing for a normative conception for the genre of the novel, a category precisely defined by its omnivorous, multifaceted nature? Novels were not even a part of the codification of genres, in the art of rhetoric. Moreover, the parodic element present in the assimilation of a broad variety of discourses points toward the Menippean satire, one of the keys in Machado's imminent leap, the diction that would enshrine the future *Posthumous Memoirs*. However, within the prêt-à-porter aesthetic of the reader of *Cousin Bazilio*, always keenly attuned to proper behavior and linguistic rectitude, any deviation from the norm ought to be condemned. Hence, following this logic, the perceptual criterion surfaces in an unmistakable reference: "The secondary cannot dominate the absolute; it is like Boileau's rhyme: *il ne doit qu'obéir*" (III, 910).

Machado is referring to the author of *The Art of Poetry*, a didactic poem from 1674 and a fundamental text in the codification of French classicism.

There is no discussion possible here: one must obey the rules! Brandishing Boileau as an *avant la lettre* theorist on the novel is inevitably an entertaining anachronism, and not a productive one; the genre would only be consolidated several decades after the author's death in 1711. Finally, Machado resorts to the coup de grâce for all normative aesthetics when he indignantly condemns "the language, allusions, episodes, and other parts of the book which I noted as the least befitting *literary decorum*" (III, 911; italics mine). Machado may well have been thinking of the famous scene from chapter 7, with its epigrammatic close:

> He respectfully kissed her knees; and then he murmured a request. She blushed and smiled and said: "No! No!" And when she emerged from her ecstasy, she covered her scarlet face with her hands, muttering reprovingly: "Oh, Bazilio!"
>
> He twirled his moustaches, very pleased with himself. He had taught her a *new sensation*; he had her in the palm of his hand! (Jull Costa 221)

The expression was the talk of Rio's newspapers. And with good reason: the *new sensation* referred to the scene of oral sex, a new experience for Luísa and certainly—at least literarily, in Portuguese—for the readers of novels like *The Hand and the Glove* and *Iaiá Garcia*. Machadinho thought the episode an example of extremely poor taste; after all, even besotted Guiomar was able to impose clear limits and preserve *the chastity of her heart*. And, much like Pamela, the hero of the eponymous 1740 novel by Samuel Richardson, Guiomar found her *virtue rewarded* with marriage. The English novel, a landmark in the genre, was subtitled with the phrase—Virtue Rewarded—which, incidentally, could stand in for a whole treatise on decorum. And like the ladies evoked by Eça's father, the readers of both Richardson and Machadinho were able to turn the pages of their novels without blushing. In the cruel but precise words of Augusto Meyer, "the celebrated author of *Helena* and *Iaiá Garcia*, masterpieces of 'touch-me-not' literature."[18] A style divorced from the body and sensuality—naturally.

Now I may cap off my hypothesis: the Machadinho of 1878 (the reader of *Cousin Bazilio*) would certainly condemn the Machado of 1880 (the author of *The Posthumous Memoirs of Brás Cubas*). The adventures of Brás Cubas would strike the moralizing critic of 1878 as unnecessarily erotic; the motives behind his actions would be judged as unclear; and above all, the normative critic of 1878 would condemn the extreme implausibility of a dead man writing his own book. To say nothing of the fundamental defect in its structure: what on earth does he mean by starting a story with its conclusion? And how to endorse a novel where the secondary always seems to dominate the essential, fed by endless digressions with an undeniable Sternian flavor? Machado-Boileau would certainly size up *The Posthumous Memoirs of Brás Cubas* as an indecent, poorly constructed work.

Likewise, the reader of *Cousin Bazilio* would condemn the author of *Quincas Borba* for showing a husband, Cristiano Palha, who does not shrink from using his spouse Sofia's generous physical endowments to lure in Rubião: *How awful! A capricious fancy for one's own husband!* And what to say of the author of stories like "A Pair of Arms," "Admiral's Night," and "Midnight Mass," with their stark erotic energy?

The normative perspective of his reading of *Cousin Bazilio* ought not to come as a surprise; what would be surprising, coming from Machadinho, would be an analysis divorced from the "application" of the "laws of art," masquerading as moral codes. By 1878, however, the aesthetic foundation behind both articles was already swimming against the tide of history. Oddly enough, Machado's stylistic leap would make this anachronism productive. Before then, however, the anachronism had to become a deliberate move, not an involuntary one. In achieving this, Machado would develop the poetics of emulation.

I seek to steer around the old mistake: reading Machado's *entire oeuvre* as if it had all been written by the author of *The Posthumous Memoirs of Brás Cubas*, the anthological stories of *Loose Papers*, the masterful lines of *Westerners*, and the impeccable crônicas mainly produced after the late 1870s.

This pious presumption may serve for a panegyric, but it is no help in understanding the internal logic that, according to Augusto Meyer, leads to "the transformation of Luís Garcia into Brás Cubas, or of Machadinho into Machadão" (410). Mere praise imprisons Machado within the timid profile of the founder of the Academia Brasileira de Letras, an exemplary worker, good friend, better husband, and unblemished citizen.

For better or for worse, he was all of those things.

However, he was also the author of novels that still challenge us today, the creator of stories that turned our certainties about Brazil, the world, and ourselves, on their heads, the writer of crônicas whose prose and wit have yet to find a rival.

How to understand the transition from one to the other?

To repeat my hypothesis: in order to bring about the Brás Cubas revolution, Machado the author needed to bid farewell to Machadinho, the reader of *Cousin Bazilio*. Machadian criticism has not been able to state this with the clarity demanded of it, because it is founded on the optimistic assumption that the reader of Eça's novel and the author of the *Posthumous Memoirs* are one and the same.

Flaubert

My outlook is based on the suggestion that between Machadinho and Machado there lies a garden of forking paths. This garden may have a name of its own. Rather: it may be possible to make out one of its main avenues.

Time to pose a difficult question: how could Machado not have seriously discussed the obvious presence of Flaubert in Queirós's work? Less astute critics had brought it up. To give one example: in an article published in the *Gazeta de Notícias* on April 23, 1878, Luiz de Andrade pointed out the parallel. "The other figures in the foreground, Luísa and Juliana, have great merit. The former, upright, fair, and photographically detailed, strikes us as [being as] sculptural as that of *Madame Bovary*. Juliana may be overloaded, but is splendidly drawn" (212).

Why did Machado reserve such space in his study to Balzac, and Zola in particular, when Flaubert's text lies just below the surface of *Cousin Bazilio*, insinuating itself in countless passages?

In countless *recyclings*.

Machado's critique also includes a touchingly naive part. In referring to the moment when the cousins' separation is compared to the plot of Balzac's novel *Eugénie Grandet*, published in 1833, Machado exclaims—apparently pleased with his own sharp wit—"Sr. Eça de Queirós took it upon himself to show us the train of his thought" (III, 905). In this passage from the novel,[19] Eça is simply trying to throw the reader off, as the major parallel in the work leads to *Madame Bovary*. In the next century, Jorge Luis Borges would unhesitatingly link the two novels:

The love of French literature would never leave him. He practiced Parnassian aesthetics, and, in his greatly varying novels, that of Flaubert as well. In *Cousin Bazilio* (1878) one can make out the tutelary shadow of *Madame Bovary*, although Émile Zola judged Eça superior to his undisputed archetype, adding these words to his judgment: "Here speaks a disciple of Flaubert."[20]

How to understand Machado's lapse?

To reframe the question: can we understand this from a purely formal point of view, related to the environment in which both *Cousin Bazilio* and *The Posthumous Memoirs of Brás Cubas* were composed?

Let me pose it once again: can we understand Machado's lapse within the scope of relationships of appropriation developed by writers from non-hegemonic cultures?

Naturally, I have no precise answer. And if I set out to find one, I would be locked up in the Casa Verde of literary criticism—the infamous madhouse of Machado's celebrated novella "The Alienist." I may content myself with a hypothesis, in an attempt to shed light on the crossroads set at the year 1878 within the Lusophone world. Portuguese-language writers, as we already know, had to consider the authors of the "three great thinking nations"—the French, English, and German—to which we ought to add the Russians, given the history of the nineteenth-century novel. Machado's critique revealed that, with the Queirosian novel's entry on to the scene, one novelist writing in Portuguese ought to be added to the list. Machado, we might well recall, would only attain the same status after the publication of the *Posthumous Memoirs*—that is, only after his visceral reading of *Cousin Bazilio*, and even then without the immediate prominence that his Portuguese colleague would attain.

Eça, Reader of *Madame Bovary*

How did Eça appropriate the works of Flaubert, *among other authors?*

On one hand, I seek to understand the specifically Queirosian method of recycling the Flaubertian novel, thus underscoring the systematic use of free indirect discourse in Portuguese.

On the other hand, I wish to compose a typology of forms of appropriation sprung from nonhegemonic areas, in their asymmetric trade with the literatures and artistic manifestations of the "great thinking nations"—always returning to that bitter, and thus revealing, turn of phrase from Eça.

Is it possible to go beyond a thematic analysis—an undeniably important, but, at least for my purposes, limited, approach? Can we identify any dominant formal element in the recreation of scenes from *Madame Bovary* in the text of *Cousin Bazilio?*

All hands on deck.

In the sixth chapter of the first part of *Madame Bovary*, the reader finds a psychological portrait of the protagonist:

> For six months, then, a fifteen-year-old Emma dirtied her hands with the greasy dust of old lending libraries. With Walter Scott, later she fell in love with historical events, dreamed of guardrooms, old oak chests and minstrels. She would have liked to live in some old manor-house, like those long-waisted chatelaines who, in the shade of pointed arches, spent their days leaning on the stone, chin in hand, watching a white-plumed knight galloping on his black horse from the distant fields.[21]

Flaubert goes on to name the Scotswoman Mary Stuart and a long list of figures from French history who sparked the fundamentally French imagination of his heroine—a point not without consequences.

In the first chapter of *Cousin Bazilio*, the reader also learns of the considerably less nationalistic reading preferences of Luísa, whom we find devouring a best seller of the period:

> The book was *The Lady of the Camellias*. She read a lot of novels; she had a monthly subscription with a shop in the Baixa. When she was eighteen and still single, she had been mad about Walter Scott and about Scotland; at the time, she had wanted to go and live in one of those Scottish castles which bore the clan's coat of arms over its pointed arches and which was furnished with Gothic chests and displays of weapons and hung with vast tapestries embroidered with heroic legends which the breeze from the loch would stir into life; and she had loved Evandale, Morton and Ivanhoe, all so grave and tender and all wearing an eagle's feather in their cap, pinned in

place with a brooch in the form of a Scottish thistle made out of emeralds and diamonds. But now she was captivated by the "modern": Paris and its furniture and its romantic novels. (Jull Costa 11–12)

Associating these passages has already become a cliché in Queirosian criticism; I am well aware that I'm not inventing the wheel here. I propose that Eça's form of rewriting the first text radicalizes the social criticism present in Flaubert. In *Madame Bovary*, Emma's readings and imagination are shackled to an idealized past: first a fling with Scotland, and then France, an excess of France. Take a look at the list of names that comes after the mention of the Scottish queen: "At this time she had a cult for Mary Stuart and enthusiastic veneration for illustrious or unhappy women. Joan of Arc, Héloïse, Agnès Sorel, the beautiful Ferronière, and Clémence Isaure." There follows an equally French list of male names: "St. Louis with his oak, the dying Bayard, some cruelties of Louis XI, a little of St. Bartholomew's, the plume of the Béarnais, and always the remembrance of the painted plates glorifying Louis XIV" (33).

It comes as no surprise that Emma never gets to see Paris: having come to know the city on paper, she would probably be disappointed by the metropolis in the flesh. Luísa's readings, meanwhile, bring about the odd approximation of very different and distant historical periods: there is the idealized past of Scott's fiction, but also the recent past in the heroine from Alexandre Dumas *fils*, followed by a reference to the *modern*, which Eça puts in italics. This Queirosian transcription features an extraordinary concentration of periods and historical cultures. Moreover, with a subtle touch, the Portuguese author reveals the foreign twist to Luísa's imagination; while Emma's daydreams share her accent, Luísa only conjures up visions of abroad. In this she presages the figure of Counselor Acácio, who can only state the obvious by resorting to quotations from elsewhere or another time—always justified as long as they are foreign.

In an attempt to underscore the idea of imitation, Machado noted a possible parallel for the famous character: "One need merely quote the long dinner held by Counselor Acácio (*a transcription of the character of Henri Monier*)" (III, 908; italics mine). Machado was thinking of Joseph Prudhomme, a symbol for the Parisian middle class, immortalized by Henry Monnier in his two-volume *Mémoires de Monsieur Joseph Prudhomme*, released in 1857—the same year as *Madame Bovary*, incidentally. Nor would it be incorrect to point out elements in Counselor Acácio similar to those of Homais the pharmacist, whose actions take on great importance in Flaubert's novel.

Let us take a look at another example.

In the ninth chapter of the second part—when Emma is about to cave to Rodolphe's advances, but has not even kissed her future lover yet—the reader finds the following passage: "It was the first time that Emma had heard such words addressed to her, and her pride unfolded languidly in the warmth of this language, like someone stretching in a hot bath" (125). Soon enough, the adultery becomes concrete; but we must wait six long pages to hear her joyful confession, Emma's *felix culpa*:

> But when she saw herself in the mirror she wondered at her face. Never had her eyes been so large, so black, nor so deep. Something subtle about her being transfigured her.
>
> She repeated: "I have a lover! a lover!" delighting at the idea as if a second puberty had come to her. So at last she was to know those joys of love, that fever of happiness of which she had despaired! She was entering upon a marvelous world where all would be passion, ecstasy, delirium. She felt herself surrounded by an endless rapture. A blue space surrounded her and ordinary existence appeared only intermittently between these heights, dark and far away beneath her. (131)

In the sixth chapter of *Cousin Bazilio*, Eça re-creates these scenes—rather, he fuses the two into one, in an effect of structural concentration that seems to define the way he reads *Madame Bovary*.

Luísa and Bazilio are already lovers, their first erotic encounter having happened in the previous chapter. Luísa's reaction is as follows:

> And Luísa had sighed and devoutly kissed the paper! It was the first time that anyone had written to her in such romantic terms, and her pride relaxed into the amorous warmth of these words, like a desiccated body sinking into a warm bath; she felt her self-esteem grow, and it seemed to her that she was finally entering a superior and more interesting existence, where each hour had a different charm, each step led to some new ecstasy,

and in which her soul was clothed in a splendor radiant with sensations!
(Jull Costa 171)

Note the slight shift: while for Emma it *was the first time she had heard
such words*, in Luísa's case it was *the first time that anyone had written to her
in such romantic terms*. The immediate experience of the lovers' physical
encounter is transformed into an experience mediated by writing and reading. Moreover, in Queirós's novel, the reader is not obliged to wait more than
a paragraph to find the confession from Luísa, dazzled by her own image,
newly adorned with beauty from another source, novel like the sensation
Bazilio will soon introduce her to:

> She went to look at herself in the mirror; her skin seemed clearer, fresher,
> and there was a tender gleam in her eyes. Was Leopoldina right when she
> said that there was nothing like a little mischief to make one prettier? She
> had a lover!
>
> And standing in the middle of the room, staring into space, her arms
> folded, she said again: "I have a lover!" She was remembering the previous
> night, the drawing room, the pointed flames of the candles, and certain
> extraordinary silences when it had seemed to her that life had stopped, while
> in the portrait of Jorge's mother's, dark eyes in a pale face watched from the
> wall with their fixed, painted gaze. Just at that moment, Juliana came in car-
> rying a basket of ironed clothes. It was time to get dressed. (Jull Costa 171)

In this passage, Eça attains a maximum level of concentration; not only
does he fuse two scenes from *Madame Bovary* into one in *Cousin Bazilio*,
but he also foreshadows the development of the plot in the allusion to Luísa's
husband—through the portrait of his mother, and then through Juliana's
entrance. This is the framework for Queirós' rewriting: accumulating elements in the search for the formal concentration at the core of his novel;
and these, as I discuss in the next chapter, are the defining techniques of the
poetics of emulation.

Similarly, Eça demonstrates his mastery of free indirect discourse; and
this is how we should read the juxtaposition of Emma's and Leopoldina's
voices. In the third chapter of the second part, just before giving birth, Emma
thinks to herself:

She hoped for a son; he would be strong and dark; she would call him George; and this idea of having a male child was like an unexpected revenge for all her impotence in the past. A man, at least, is free; he can explore all passions and all countries, overcome obstacles, taste of the most distant pleasures. But a woman is always hampered. Being inert as well as pliable, she has against her the weakness of the flesh and the inequity of the law. Like the veil held to her hat by a ribbon, her will flutters in every breeze; she is always drawn by some desire, restrained by some rule of conduct. (74)

She then gives birth to a daughter, naturally, and faints: her fate seems sealed. In the fifth chapter of *Cousin Bazilio*, Leopoldina is less eloquent, but still undergoes a moment of "*Madame Bovary, c'est moi*":

"Oh!" she exclaimed. "Men are so much more fortunate than we are! I was born to be a man! The things I would do!"

She got up and went over to the wing chair by the window where she sat down languidly. The tranquil evening was coming on; gathering behind the houses, beyond the empty lots, were round, yellowish clouds, edged with blood-red or orange.

And returning to the idea of action and independence, she said:

"A man can do anything! Nothing is barred to him! He can travel, have adventures . . . You know, I would love a cigarette."

The trouble was Juliana would smell it, and it would look bad.

"It's like a convent in here!" muttered Leopoldina. "Though, I must say, you do have a very comfortable prison!" (Jull Costa 160)

Once again, Eça re-creates a passage from *Madame Bovary*. However, instead of simply mentioning Luísa, he has two characters strike up a revealing dialogue, and then alludes once again to Juliana's controlling presence. Two birds with one stone: scenes are concentrated and Emma's voice is split between two characters. Leopoldina then affirms her desire for autonomy: "A woman with a child is useless, she's tied hand and foot! There's no pleasure left in life. She's just there to put up with them . . . Good lord! If it were me? God have mercy on me, but if I were to have that misfortune I think I'd pay a visit to the old woman over on Travessa da Palha!" (Jull Costa 160) This solution does not occur to Flaubert's protagonist, but Eça's character would readily employ it. Leopoldina is truly a Madame Bovary in miniature, albeit with clearly more efficient methods.

Queirós's scenes boast a concentration of elements, often in a dizzy succession, the collateral effect of which is the radicalization of the original social criticism. Leopoldina is reasonably successful in her plan for equality between the sexes, to judge by the number of lovers she has accumulated and by the way things turn out for her. In the last chapter, significantly enough, we are told that "Leopoldina was dancing at a soirée held at Cunha's house" (Jull Costa 436). Unaccustomed to dancing alone, she almost certainly spent the night in good company.

Eça rewrites *Madame Bovary* through a sort of concentration. His gaze thus cuts across a number of social spheres—and this is the decisive point.

The hypocrisy of Lisbon society is satirized without mercy in the cartoonish figure of Counselor Acácio; in public, a professional moralist, at home, "cozying up with the maid" (I, 863).

The limited and limiting status imposed on women becomes evident in the plurality of female characters in the novel, a much richer cast than the landscape provided us in *Madame Bovary*. Luísa is indeed a puppet, but in this helplessness lies the strength of the critique, exposing the extremely slim options of a young woman in provincial nineteenth-century Lisbon. Machado pointed this out but could not understand its consequences. On the verge of his departure, Jorge recognizes the same thing, asking his friend Sebastião to be sure to visit his wife—that is, to remember to watch over her: "She doesn't have it in her: her hands start to shake, her mouth goes all dry . . . She's a woman, very much a woman. You won't forget, will you, Sebastião?" (Jull Costa 44). The sharper-eyed Bazilio would never forget that his cousin was *very much a woman*, although taking this in a very different sense than her husband.

Cultural dependence, meanwhile, is satirized in Bazilio's being dazzled by Paris and Viscount Reinaldo by London. The novel ends with them heading to the only establishment worthy of their patronage: "And they went into the Taverna Inglesa to have a glass of sherry" (Jull Costa 439).

The vestiges of an ultraromantic mentality are similarly pilloried in Ernestinho's play—whose title, *Honor and Passion*, a merciless parody, ought to tease a knowing chuckle from the reader.

The novel engages in a serious discussion of social injustice through Juliana's aspirations toward decent working conditions. Her blackmail is the sign of an incipient class struggle; in the prim interpretation of the novelist's father, although the maid appears as the true "protagonist of the novel," in this case the portrait-painter may have used an excess of paint. Juliana's behavior would be out of place in Portugal, "where our mild customs treat servants as a sort of member of the family" (48). On the contrary, the keen observation of Queirós's work reveals the daily violence inherent in the experiences of maids and dependents—a topic, one might add, quite familiar to the author of *Iaiá Garcia*.

Finally, using Bazilio, the "Brazilian," Eça takes an X-ray of the very structure of the Portuguese empire. The fortune that Bazilio earns in Brazil is not invested in Portugal, but squandered abroad, as was the case with much of the wealth from the colonies. Luísa, in a conversation with Sebastião, shows that she understands her cousin's motives:

"And how is your cousin?"
"Fine. He's been here quite often. He's terribly bored in Lisbon, poor thing. Well, of course, *for someone accustomed to living abroad . . .*"
Sebastião sat, slowly rubbing his knees and repeated: "Yes, of course, for someone accustomed to living abroad . . ." (Jull Costa 143; italics mine)

The repetition is hardly chance, and reveals a worrying side to Luísa's cosmopolitan relative: who knows what people *used to living abroad* might have learned over there. In this context, the novel's subtitle makes even more sense: the "domestic episode" forges a concentrated space that serves as an echo chamber, amplifying the impasses and contradictions of Portuguese society. In this restricted space, the technique of concentration found a medium ripe for the author's project, while his criticism becomes even more biting as it exposes the realm of private life.

The array of topics that *Cousin Bazilio* tackles is potentially broader than that found in *Madame Bovary*. In this, Machado is certainly hitting the bull's-eye when he declares that, in Eça's novel, "adultery is simply a passing adventure here" (III, 910). He was correct, in a way; but in this he failed to see the main thrust of Queirós' conception, since Luísa's transgression is not simply the center of the book but rather serves as a Pandora's box, exposing the hypocrisy and decadence around it. Luísa's subjective anemia is a mirror for the alienation systematically imposed on women.

Zola may have considered Queirós's novel superior to the Flaubertian model because of this breadth of the criticism. For my part, I will bow out of this strange championship in which authors and works face off on an improvised football field. But I will take sides. *Cousin Bazilio* is a masterpiece and remains provocative to this day; however, it can hardly be compared to the impact of *Madame Bovary*, as its systematization of certain techniques, especially free indirect discourse, transformed the history of the modern novel. Nevertheless, for the purposes of my argument, the relevant part of Zola's take is the idea that the appropriation of a model may produce surprising results, perhaps even superior to the original model. This is the realm of *imitatio* and *aemulatio*.

Aemulatio

Now I ought to address two issues that will be decisive for my reflection.

On one hand, amid the firefight of critical articles, there emerges the idea of emulation, seen in a positive light.

On the other hand, we must reflect on Machado's terminological slip-up: he, like Eça's father, refers to realism and naturalism as if they were synonymous.

Let me begin by recalling Machado's evaluation of Eça's first novel—a most harsh one:

> That Sr. Eça de Queirós is a disciple of the author of *Assommoir* is known to all. *The Crime of Father Amaro* itself is an *imitation* of the novel by Zola, *La Faute de L'Abbé Mouret*. An *analogous* situation, *the same* tendencies; a *difference* in the setting; *difference* in the denouement; *identical* style; recollections of the other, such as in the chapter of the Mass, and others; finally, the same title. *Those who have read both certainly do not question Sr. Eça de Queirós's originality*, because he possessed it, still does, and manifests it quite affirmatively; I would even venture that this same *originality*

produced the greatest flaw in the conception of *The Crime of Father Amaro*.
(III, 903; italics mine)

Originality becomes an aesthetic flaw that leads to an artificial situation;
after all, when one changes the setting, the plausibility of the plot is under-
mined. Note the traditional criteria that back up Machado's critique; it is as if
no aesthetic dividends could possibly come from a mismatch between form
and setting. The shift that will transform this into a productive principle is
the watershed for *The Posthumous Memoirs of Brás Cubas*—beginning, as a
matter of fact, with the deceased author. However, let me signal the emergence of a notion that seems paradoxical at first, but constitutes the raison
d'être of my argument.

Although the novel is an *imitation*, it demonstrates—in a *positive
sense*—the *originality* of its author. Eça imitates, and this is precisely what
gives him his own diction! The terms are apparently contradictory, especially
within the aesthetic imposed by romanticism, which affirms the talent of the
individual in place of a recycling of tradition. The Romantic genius operates,
ideally, without models; a true demiurge of himself, he plumbs his systematic
self-involvement for enough material to create his universes.

Returning to the equation, extracted from Machado's text: Eça imitates,
which makes him original.

How to understand the formula?

Before offering an answer, let me return to Machado's criticisms. He ably
reconstructs Eça's dialogue with French tradition, not condemning Queirós's
appropriation but disagreeing with the emphasis lent to the principles of
naturalism. Machado actually uses another term, as the following passage
shows (and this general confusion between realism and naturalism ought to
be discussed):

Sr. Eça de Queirós is a faithful and most severe *disciple* of the realism
propagated by the author of *Assommoir*. Had he been a *mere copyist*, the
critic's duty would have been to leave him defenseless in the hands of blind
enthusiasm, which would ultimately kill him; *but he is a man of talent*,
who has just recently crossed the threshold of the *literary workshop*; and
I, who do not deny him my admiration, have taken it upon myself to tell

him frankly what I think of the work itself and its doctrines and practices, of which he is the pioneer in the land of Alexandre Herculano and the language of Gonçalves Dias. (III, 904; italics mine)

This passage is extremely rich, above all between the lines.

Once again, the paradoxical formula is set up: Eça is a *faithful and most severe disciple*; one might as well say, cutting away the diplomacy, that he imitates Zola. However, although he *imitates*, he is not a *mere copyist*, but a *man of talent*.

Again, the terms of the equation are within the text itself. I am not imposing a foreign framework on Machado's critique, and I seek to remain as close as possible to his vocabulary in an effort to identify the semantic fields that structure his work.

The formula now has a variation: Eça imitates, but is not a mere copyist, rather a man of talent. Talent revealed *through imitation*, but which *goes beyond mere copying.*

To ears well versed in the principles of the Romantic aesthetic, both the first equation and the second formula ring paradoxical; they verge on blotting out the distinction between original and copy, one's own voice and another's words. However, up until the Romantic explosion, since classical antiquity the literary system had been ruled by a different state of affairs, in which the common literary repertoire (tradition) was the mandatory point of departure for every "new" creation. Within this system, a dynamic ensured a balance between individual talent and tradition, to recall the terms of T. S. Eliot's 1919 essay, "Tradition and Individual Talent." The same may be seen in Machado's critical intuition, roughly sketched out in the articles on *Cousin Bazilio* and hence refined in the writing of *The Posthumous Memoirs of Brás Cubas.*

We have here the combined technique of *imitatio* and *aemulatio.*

At this point, a critical difference arises between *imitation* as a first step and *copy* as the final result. The Machadian equation becomes perfectly reasonable, indicating that he was beginning to understand the technique behind the qualitative leap implied in the writing of the *Posthumous Memoirs.* The two articles on *Cousin Bazilio* may thus be read in a new light.

The two passages touch on a model for analysis based on the classical concept of *imitatio,* followed by the necessary gesture of *aemulatio*; after all, once again, the *mere copyist* simply *imitates*, never risking the crucial moment of *emulation*. Machado's return to pre-Romantic literary practices amounts to a program of cultural politics, the subversive effects of which on traditional order appear in the striking phrase *in the land of Alexandre Herculano and the language of Gonçalves Dias.*

The poet of "Canção do exílio" [Song of Exile] was first enshrined by a famous critique by Alexandre Herculano. The Brazilian poet had his debut in 1846 with *Primeiros cantos* [First Songs], a book divided into three sections: "American Poems," "Various Poems," and "Hymns." The leading light of Portuguese romanticism hailed the work, albeit while lamenting that the "American poems" did not take up a larger portion of the book. His critique was certainly a poetic writ of emancipation, but it announced rules for that freedom: the Brazilian poet was obliged to keep his lyrical imagination circumscribed to the geography of the tropics.

For his part, Machadinho begins the transformation to Machado just when he takes on the role of an imaginary Alexandre Herculano for Eça de Queirós, lauding his merits but pointing out flaws and demanding corrections. The move was audacious, provoking reactions on both sides of the Atlantic. Two years later, an even more daring move would enshrine the Brazilian writer: the creation of *The Posthumous Memoirs of Brás Cubas.*

Emulation Post-1878

In the last two chapters, we will circumnavigate Machado's oeuvre, feeling out the semantic field of emulation in all the genres in which he worked. For the moment, however, it may be useful to insert a single example that dates from after his critique of *Cousin Bazilio*; after the emergence of the idea of emulation, it became a cornerstone of Machado's vision of literature.

There is Machado's striking analysis of the literary contribution of playwright Antônio José, better known as "o Judeu," the Jew. The essay "Antônio José and Molière" was originally published in *Revista Brasileira* on July 15, 1879, and reproduced in *Relíquias de Casa Velha* [Relics of the Old House] (1906). The question at the core of Machado's judgment rests on the problem of imitation: was the Judeu original, or did he simply reproduce previous models? To put it directly: did Antônio José emulate the masters he followed, or not? Machado puts the terms of the problem rather unequivocally:

Anfitrião [Amphytrion] proves that our poet *imitated* and *transplanted* something of Molière, to the extent that he must have had it before him, either on his workbench or in his memory; and, as this observation has not been made before, I believe it will be of some interest, at least as a literary curiosity. At the same time, I shall say *what I think of the writer and his oeuvre*. (II, 726; italics mine)

Is this not a return to the vocabulary used in his critique of Eça's novels? In Machado's take, although Antônio José *imitated* and *transplanted* Molière, he still introduced elements unique to *the writer and his oeuvre*—note the use of the verb *transplant* in the semantic field of emulation. Antônio José was not a mere copyist, but a man of talent—*as the reader will recall*, Machado said the same of the Portuguese novelist. In this passage he refines the idea; Judeu appears to have written *Amphytrion* with Molière's model before him, as if he were an apprentice reproducing famous paintings by the masters. The image is striking, and belongs to the classic register of *aemulatio*: he *must have had it before him, either on his workbench or in his memory*.

Machado's answer as to Antônio José's "originality" could not be more eloquent, and merits a long transcription in the form of a collage of quotes:

Comparing Antônio José's *Amphytrion* with those of his predecessors, one may see what he *imitated* of those models, and *what he introduced of his own line*....

Antônio José did not only *follow* recent models in this part, but he also overreached in the material from Plautus that he *imitated*....

Let us now move to what the Jew *imitated* directly from Molière....

While by this point the matter is not a situation or a new character but an idea woven into the dialogue, once again, even in *imitating* or *recalling*, the Jew remains faithful to his literary physiognomy; he may seek out *others' spices*, but only *to temper them with the sauce of his own production*....

This is the final conclusion that can strictly be drawn from the poet. He did not imitate, nor would he imitate Molière, even if he *repeated the transcriptions* seen in *Amphytrion*; he possessed originality, albeit *influenced* by the Italian operas. We must recognize that his ingenuity lacked discipline or good taste, but was characteristic and personal nonetheless. (II, 729 and 731; italics mine)

The richness of the semantic field speaks for itself here, allowing us to reconsider certain elements of Machado's literary techniques from a pre-Romantic perspective, in the context of a deliberately anachronistic aesthetic choice, the fruits of which come into focus in a reshaping of the bonds between author and reader. After all, in order to appreciate the result of emulation one must recognize the model being imitated; the technique of emulation thus implies the mastery of a solid literary repertoire on the part of the reading public. However, this is not to say that Machado's oeuvre henceforth becomes an imaginary museum, the relic of a life devoted to the library. The shift comes about as if Machado were partially recovering the pre-Romantic system, based on the dynamic relationship between *imitatio* and *aemulatio*, learning to exist as simultaneously pre-Romantic and post-Romantic. The political consequences of this aesthetic decision will be far-reaching. (Let me reiterate that this is not an effort to identify an essence—some mysterious fluid that would render the "peripheral being" unique and always identical to himself—but rather to refine a strategy that appears necessary, given the basic asymmetry of symbolic exchanges. Despite what many believe, this problem has not been made obsolete by contemporary conditions.)

Realism or Naturalism?

Machado deemed Eça "a faithful and most severe disciple of the realism propagated by the author of *Assommoir.*" Émile Zola would probably reject the label—after all, he would prefer to be considered the creator of, or at least the driving force behind, naturalism. The movement's principal theoretical text, *The Experimental Novel*, was published in 1880, the same year as *The Posthumous Memoirs of Brás Cubas* and *The Mandarin*: a true meeting of a variety of styles and aesthetic choices. For his part, the most severe disciple showed that he'd felt the blow and drew up a firm, albeit ill-mannered response, which he would never publish in full. A few of the less harsh passages were included in the preface to the second (book) edition of *The Crime of Father Amaro*, which was also released in 1880. The whole letter would only be revealed after Eça's death. Clearly sarcastic, the author mocks his critic:

> I believe that in Portugal and Brazil they label as realism, *a term that was already old in 1840*, the artistic movement which in France and England is known as "naturalism" or "experimental art." Let us accept *realism*, however, as the familiar and amiable name by which Brazil and Portugal have come to know a certain phase in the evolution of art. (176; italics mine)

The malicious sneer in the answer is evident, alluding to the gap between European novelty and Lusophone (and especially Brazilian) backwardness, in a fairly unsubtle move to suggest Machado's lack of qualifications. The matter is more complicated, however, and requires that we recall two or three factors in order to adequately understand Machado's use of the concept of realism.

First, back to the letter from Eça's father. His phrasing leaves no room for doubt: *From the point of view of the realist school that has you in its sway.*

Whence this terminological to-do?

The second element may help us understand the problem.

In the attempt at cultural renewal led by Eça's generation, the "Coimbra Question" took center stage. This was a polemic against the doctrine led by Romantic poet António Feliciano de Castilho. This new generation would fly the flag of the aesthetic defense of realism, and a desire to renew Portuguese culture—at the time, these were two sides of the same coin.

The controversy would explode in 1865, developing over the course of the famous "Conferences at the Lisbon Casino," held in 1871 and organized by Antero de Quental. The aim was clear: Portuguese culture would be thoroughly reformed, and the issues at the heart of the movement would be discussed. The series' organizer gave the opening talk, discoursing on the "Causes of the Decadence of Peninsular Peoples"—the topic of *Cousin Bazilio* was clearly on the minds of the generation as a whole. The third conference fell to Eça himself, and he spoke on "Realism as an Expression of Art."

Finally, Eça's response to the critique from Machado was entitled, revealingly, "Idealism and Realism." In this context, Machado's terminological confusion acquires yet another facet. The debate cannot be reduced to the simple gap between European novelty and tropical backwardness, as it references a specific moment in Luso-Brazilian intellectual history. To clarify the point once and for all, let us listen carefully to Eça's outburst:

> But no—pardon me—there is no *realist school*. A school is the systematic imitation of the techniques of a master. It presupposes a single origin and a fixed rhetoric or style. *Naturalism*, meanwhile, was not born of the particular aesthetic of any one artist; it is a general movement in art, at a certain point in its evolution. (Queirós, 177; italics mine)

In Queirós's prose, the terms *realist* and *naturalist* also appear as possible synonyms, although he gives Zola's method pride of place: "Naturalism is the scientific form that art has taken on" (177).

With the misunderstanding resolved, I turn to the particularly complex temporal relationship to which Eça alludes. One of Machado's main criticisms referred not to the Portuguese writer's lack of talent, but to Eça's having bent his gift to the vagaries of literary fashion. Queirós's naturalism appears to be determined not by the writer's natural inclinations, but the desire to remain up to date on the latest novelties: this is the bone of contention.

Let us see.

Seen as a literary school, naturalism succeeded realism and opposed itself to its predecessor. Despite Eça's resistance, I have no problem with using the term, given the existence of manifestos and cultural programs in this vein, as well as authors who allied themselves with one school or another. For example, in the preface to the first book edition of *The Crime of Father Amaro*, Eça recognizes that the text—although quite altered—"preserves considerable vestiges of certain concerns of the school." Emphasis on the superposition of different, but neighboring, moments in time; this is the crucial point.

Hence Eça's ironic comment. As if Machado were simply ignorant of the passage of time or the fleeting nature of fashions—and here we are talking about the author of the story "A igreja do diabo" [The Devil's Church], an inspired tribute to the inconstancy of the human condition. Now, I do not mean to occupy the reader's time with matters related to "period styles"; rather, I want to underline the subtle *temporal inversion* carried out by Eça.

In 1875, he published *The Crime of Father Amaro*, undeniably influenced by the naturalist aesthetic, keenly attuned to the *concerns of the school.* As any schoolmaster would say: ergo, this must be a naturalist novel.

(Counselor Acácio would agree, *sine dubio.*)

Just three years later, the same author releases *Cousin Bazilio.* This novel contains a dialogue, valuable while imprecise, in which Luísa's past is linked to the plot of *Eugénie Grandet,* a title by Honoré de Balzac from 1833, at the height of realism. However, it is quite clear—although Machado went for the red herring in this case!—that the most important intertextual dialogue is with *Madame Bovary,* a novel published in 1857.

The crucial element here is the inverted chronology in Eça's prose, decisive in Machado's terminological confusion. Queirós's work progressed against the tide, a move that has not been appropriately highlighted. *Cousin Bazilio* cannot be classified as a naturalist novel as easily as *The Crime of Father Amaro.* Machado erred in examining both novels through the same antinaturalist lens—or an antirealist one, in his terms. The matter demanded a deeper reading. However, Machado's stumble illuminates Queirós's stylistic leap, which the drunkard author of the *Posthumous Memoirs* would then take to its absolute limit. Machado reacted so viscerally to the success of *Cousin Bazilio* because he had sensed a path that he would shortly turn into his exclusive domain.

Let me explain myself.

Instead of following the latest fad, Eça took a crucially important step *back*—and would do it again in his next work, *The Mandarin,* in 1880, a work very different from *Cousin Bazilio* and completely unrecognizable next to *The Crime of Father Amaro.* Eça had written a novel that was far beyond what Machado could read in that moment; the Brazilian believed that his Portuguese colleague had simply sought to keep himself up to date with Zola's "realist" school. However, *Cousin Bazilio* marked the beginning of Eça's move away from the rigid naturalist model. In my analysis of the novel, the process of *formal concentration,* a characteristic of his rewriting of *Madame Bovary,* led to the *compression of literary periods and historical cultures*—here, Eça is dialoguing with the modern novel, but with contemporary Portuguese literature as well.

Didn't the writing of *The Posthumous Memoirs of Brás Cubas* also imply the simultaneous appropriation of multiple genres and styles, both varied and often contradictory? In the same vein, Machado revealed himself to be a reader of literary tradition in the broader sense, as well as a keen observer of contemporary Brazilian and Portuguese literature.

Here lies Machado's radical move: while we might say that Eça took a step backward, the deceased author, in his delirium, traveled all the way back "to the origin of the centuries" (I, 520), appropriating the whole of literary tradition with innovative freedom and a freeing irreverence. Despite his bitter criticism of *Cousin Bazilio*, the Brazilian writer would make good use of his Portuguese colleague's lesson—and if I am not mistaken, this came through the emergence of the technique of emulation as a criterion for critical reading and inventive writing.[22]

Coda

Eça de Queirós died on August 16, 1900, relatively young at age fifty-four. Machado's reaction was immediate. On August 24, the *Gazeta de Notícias* published a letter of his to Henrique Chaves.

> My dear H. Chaves. What can I say in response to this calamity? For novelists, it is as if we have lost the best of our family, the most graceful, the worthiest. And the family is not comprised solely of those who entered with him into the life of the spirit, but also those relics of another generation, and the flower of the new one as well. *What was begun with astonishment would end in admiration.* (III, 953; italics mine)

Machado's praise illuminates the image enshrined by the art of *aemulatio*: the continuous and vital dialogue between the generations. The same image had already been present in the essay "Instinct of Nationality."

Machado's grief was sincere.

(As the narrator of *Iaiá Garcia* might say.)

CHAPTER 3

Toward a Poetics of Emulation

Machado's texts are almost always rooted in parody. The narrator, however, perennially ambiguous, both parodies and negates the conflict of the two voices. He stands ambivalently between parody and stylization, without declaring an allegiance to one or the other.

—Dirce Côrtes Riedel, *Metáfora, o espelho de Machado de Assis*

The similarity of the new poem is seen as that of a good imitation, when it is the result of *emulation*. One emulates what one admires and loves: through other material means and mimetic forms, the poet invents a poem with a form analogous—but not identical to—the work authorized by custom, attempting to rival it in inventiveness and art. Emulation is a source of pleasure for the learned recipient. . .. Emulation is cumulative: the new poem aligns itself with previous works in the same genre as an authority to be imitated in new emulations.

—João Adolfo Hansen, "Notas sobre o gênero épico"

From translation to the creation of an original work through a grand model, this is the principle; but from the start, filiation to the text or texts from which Latin writers will create their works will remain the norm:

literature in the second degree, if we may put it this way, derived from pre-existing material. The Romans will give a name to this process—*imitatio*, a concept that will, to an extent, also embrace the idea of *aemulatio*: an attempt to match or outdo the original.

—Paulo Sérgio de Vasconcellos, *Efeitos intertextuais na "Eneida" de Virgílio*

. . . the fabrication of the Ancient. By this, we understand that notably Latin poetics and rhetorics—expressed in the trio of *interpretatio, imitatio,* and *aemulatio*—walk along a tightrope between the imitation of models and the criticism of that imitation. This tension constitutes the foundation of these techniques' pedagogy and their agonistics. There are countless ways for a work—be it a text or a painting—to endure within another, a phenomenon identified with the very reticular nature of artistic creation.

—Luiz Marques, "Apresentação," *A fabricação do antigo*

Drawing this return to the origins to a close, one must abandon the Greeks of antiquity to follow the Cariocas of the nineteenth century and see how the disciples of Isocrates, Aristotle, and Cicero apply the lessons they have received. . . . Upon walking down Rua do Ouvidor or Botafogo Beach, the reader will certainly come across a few dedicated students.

—Dilson Ferreira da Cruz, *O ethos dos romances de Machado de Assis*

Of Negatives

The writing of this chapter was particularly challenging, and I begin by recognizing the limits of the return I am suggesting to the notion of *aemulatio*.

Thus, I can hardly avoid emulating the last chapter of *The Posthumous Memoirs of Brás Cubas* and drawing up an introduction "of negatives."

This is not an attempt at a theoretical contribution to the examination of *aemulatio*, a central theme in classical studies. Such an ambition would overspill this essay's scope. My aim is to create a thick description of the *Machado de Assis literary system*, with emphasis on the centrality of *aemulatio* in its architecture—however, it should always be stressed, an anachronistic recycling of the classical technique of emulation.

This is not an innovative interpretation of the techniques of *imitatio* or *aemulatio*, nor a summary of their history. I will limit myself to identifying their defining elements, in order to understand the importance of the semantic field of emulation in Machado's oeuvre. Finally, I do not seek to draw up a review of the latest discussions around the centrality of *aemulatio* in artistic practices that predate romanticism.

In the chapter "Of Negatives," Brás Cubas invents an arithmetic of scarcity that serves for my reflection: "upon arriving on this other side of the mystery, I found myself with *a small sum*, which is the final negative in this chapter of negatives: I had no children; I did not bequeath to any creature the legacy of our misery" (I, 639; italics mine).

Seen from the other side, this series of "noes" paves the way for an uneasy yes. Similarly, while I hold myself back, this illuminates precisely what lies beyond my reach. The scope of this chapter's ambition lies in the intersection between two elements.

On one hand, the consciously anachronistic reinvention of *aemulatio* in its post-Romantic recycled form, through the *poetics of emulation*, sparks unexpected consequences on the level of cultural politics. The most important of these apparently helped Machado to overcome his artistic crisis, leading him to an innovative understanding of the relationship between a peripheral writer and the model provided by the "great thinking nations."

> (It never hurts to recall Eça's wounded turn of phrase, a symptom of the structural inequality in such symbolic exchanges.)

On the other hand, there is an extremely important elective affinity between the technique of *aemulatio*, the game of chess, and music. I refer to the powerful combinatorial matrices that, given a necessarily limited number of rules and conventions, produce virtually inexhaustible variants. Machado's passion for chess and music may have driven his understanding of the playful nature of *aemulatio*. To clarify: this is not a relationship of cause and effect, but rather a potential similarity between artistic and logical behaviors.

Finally, I work with the concept of emulation on two levels, drawing the distinction between *aemulatio*—a fundamental technique in the pre-Romantic literary and artistic system—and the *poetics of emulation*, a deliberately anachronistic effort developed specifically in nonhegemonic circumstances. For that matter, as the correspondence between Georg

Brandes and Friedrich Nietzsche reveals, the problem may be found at more distant latitudes and demands a comparative analysis. This is not an exclusively Brazilian dilemma, nor Lusophone, and not even Latin American, but a difficulty on a more general scale that involves asymmetrical relations of symbolic power.

The case of Machado de Assis is thus both quite local and strikingly universal—exactly like his work.

Back to *aemulatio*.

My interest as regards the first level of *aemulatio* is modest. I will simply signal its uses, observing the extemporaneous resurrection of certain forms at the second level, particularly in Machado's oeuvre. Recall the 1901 note that was added to the poem "Flower of Youth," as we saw in chapter 1:

> The classic French poets often used this form, which they called *triolet*. After long disuse, some poets of this century *have resuscitated the triolet, without scorning the older models.* (III, 181)

The vocabulary used here belongs to the classical realm of *imitatio* and *aemulatio*. Its agonic character lay in the tension between two drives: reverence for tradition on one hand, criticism of the very same legacy on the other. However, even while emulating tradition, one remained within its orbit, enriching the field with an increasing number of new solutions instead of relegating it to the Narcissean museum founded by a self-centered modernity, defined by the fetishism of the idea of originality.

Within an anachronistic reinvention of the pre-Romantic outlook, this portrait of Machado begins to take on sharper edges. The author of *The Posthumous Memoirs of Brás Cubas* would find, in the simultaneous appropriation of opposite temporalities, a realm all his own.

Aemulatio: Artistic Technique

In the previous chapter, we saw how emulation as a technique informed Machado's critique of *Cousin Bazilio*, as well as his analysis of Antônio José's legacy. In a crônica in *A Semana*, published on July 7, 1895, on the occasion of the hundredth anniversary of José Basílio da Gama's death, Machado returns to the same semantic field:

> My dear friend Muzzio, a companion of yesteryear and a critic of exceptional taste, thought those two famous verses from the *Uraguai* detestable:
>
> > A jostling group of savage chivalry
> > Who fight their battles all disorderly.[1]
>
> "That will never be onomatopoeia," he would say. "Those are simply two bad verses."
>
> I agreed that they were not melodious, but defended the poet's intentions, as he could very well have written them in a more conventional key. One day, I found in Filinto Elísio an *imitation* of those verses by José Basílio da Gama, a poor one incidentally, *but* the Portuguese bard *confessed to the imitation and its source.* (III, 660; italics mine)

The juxtaposition paves the way for an alternative reading: the imitation was hardly inspired, *but*, in exposing its source, the neoclassical poet fell under a category that Machado understood perfectly. In this context, *imitation* is not taken as a lack of inventiveness, but rather as a first and indispensable step. The next step demands emulation, an essential move; the absence of this would, indeed, condemn the author's carelessness. The defining trait of this category was defined in an article on Almeida Garrett, published in the *Gazeta de Notícias* on February 4, 1899. In this text, the terms used in the critique of Eça and the study on the Judeu are repeated wholesale.

Here is how Machado refers to the transplanting of romanticism into Lusophone literature:

> But he himself, who brought the plant—or the vaccine, as it was once called—to Portugal. . . .
>
> Garrett, being the pioneer of these new forms in his land, *was no copyist* of them, and everything that flowed from his hand bore *a mark all its own and was purely Portuguese.* . . .
>
> . . . In his books he unites the soul of the nation with the life of humanity. (III, 932–33; italics mine)

If, as writer and essayist Ricardo Piglia put it, all criticism is autobiographical,[2] then this would be Machado's confession. After all, that "certain intimate sentiment" (III, 804), famously referenced in his critical essay "Instinct of Nationality," might be precisely the vanishing point where *the soul of the nation meets the life of humanity*, forging the standard perspective of the ur-author who permanently oscillates between sameness and foreignness. One analogy to this movement might lead us back to the territory of *aemulatio*. The pre-Romantic literary system demanded that one use others' condiments as a starting point for concocting one's own seasoning. This very Machadian metaphor may also be found in the analysis of Antônio José's oeuvre: "he may seek out *others' spices*, but only *to temper them with the sauce of his own production*" (II, 731; italics mine). The metaphor is carried on in his weakness for the verb *ruminate*, an inveterate guest in Machadian texts, the best formulation of which may be found in a well-known passage from *Esau and Jacob*, published in 1904.

> Thus was Aires's conclusion, as one reads it in the *Memorial*. It will be the reader's conclusion, too, if he cares to make conclusions. Note that here I spared him Aires's work. I did not oblige him to find out for himself what other times he had to discover. The attentive reader, truly ruminant, has four stomachs in his brain, and through them he passes the facts and deeds back and forth, until he deduces the truth, which was or seemed to be hidden. (Lowe 124)

The act of ruminating presupposes the habit defined in a crônica from *A Semana*, from October 27, 1895: "I read, reread, and threeread" (III, 683). In the analogy between the acts of reading and rumination, we may glimpse a possible allusion to the realm of *aemulatio*; in both cases, after all, the first step is appropriating the other. As the available repertoire is the province of the lettered community, this type of rumination appears as a structural element of the literary system.

Many phenomena in Machado's oeuvre may be reevaluated through the lens of the intersection between his texts and concerns born of the art of rhetoric.

Recall the ease with which Luís Tinoco, the protagonist of "Aurora sem dia" [Dawn without Day], published in *Midnight Stories* (1873), becomes a sort of universal author, especially of works he hasn't examined: "From others' works he plucked a collection of literary allusions and names with which he *dispensed his erudition*, and did not have to have read Shakespeare, for example, in order to speak of *to be or not to be*, Juliet's balcony, and the tortures of Othello" (II, 223; italics mine). This passage undoubtedly criticizes the erudition by hearsay running rampant among the stuffed shirts of the literary world. However, it also calls attention to the subtle shift carried out in Machado's prose; it ends up underlining the techniques that were progressively abandoned after the Romantic revolution, highlighting them through their negative.

Brás Cubas would likewise resort to an identical strategy, bringing about the revealing combination of two authors from the very center of the Latin world of *aemulatio*: "He had no other philosophy. Nor did I. This is not to say that the university taught me none; but I simply memorized the formulas, the vocabulary, the skeleton of the subject. I treated it as I did Latin: I pocketed three verses from Virgil, two from Horace, and a dozen moral and political maxims *to dispense in conversation*" (I, 545; italics mine). To *dispense one's erudition* or *dispense in conversation*: the formula changes so as to remain identical. In the realm of *aemulatio*, the other is the inevitable jumping-off point in the creation of a collective body of knowledge, theoretically accessible to all those who participate in lettered culture.

Setting up this equivalence between rumination and *aemulatio* demands yet another step. After all, while rumination implies an act of interpretation, the technique of *aemulatio* necessarily goes a step farther, proposing an act of invention via the incorporation of someone else's material. A hermeneutic with sharpened teeth, this anachronistic return to *aemulatio* smacks of cultural cannibalism—as the Brazilian poet Oswald de Andrade would propose in the twentieth century.

The decisive element in this vein appears in one of Machado's first critical texts, "Ideas on the Theater," published in three issues of *O Espelho*. The second installment, from October 2, 1859, finds both the lexicon of emulation and the use of the verb "transplant" on the plate of the youth—then just twenty years old—who aspired to become a man of letters.

Let us read the article:

The theater has become a school for *intellectual acclimatization*, where concepts from foreign atmospheres and remote skies *are transplanted*. It rejected the nation's mission in its journey through civilization; it has no character, it reflects societies alien to our own, and it is driven by revolutions foreign to the society that it represents, a presbyope of art unable to make out that which stirs beneath its hands.

Is this due to a drought of intelligence? I believe not. Today's society is rich with talented individuals. A lack of enthusiasm? Perhaps; *but it is fundamentally a lack of emulation*. This is the legitimate cause behind the absence of the dramatic poet; this, and no other.

A lack of emulation? From whence? From audiences?

From audiences. But one must understand: from audiences because they are not drawn, as I have said, by any true or consequential seduction. (III, 792; italics mine)

We might recall that, in *The Aristotelian Telescope*, Emanuele Tesauro uses the same verb when dealing with emulation: *transplant*.[3] Machado repeats the term on other occasions, although with revealing modifications. Here, the young critic lends the verb a negative connotation. This passage, however, offers much more for the ruminant reader of Machadian semantic fields, given his concern with the incipient form of Brazilian theater.

How to explain it?

First, because this is a theater that *has no character; it reflects societies alien to our own*. It is thus foreign to the nationality that ought to define it; we are still quite far from the defender of "a certain intimate sentiment." Nevertheless, *society is rich with talented individuals*, which ought to favor the appearance of playwrights capable of reversing this tendency.

But here lies the apparently insuperable obstacle: *fundamentally a lack of emulation*. And on the part of audiences! Why? The answer is not immediately forthcoming.

If Machado believed that dramatic poets were hardly concerned with the technique of *aemulatio* and this was what was keeping Brazilian theater on thin ice, then the twenty-year-old would be the father of the forty-year-old writer, the inventor of Brás Cubas. The recipe remained the same: appropriating tradition as a whole via rumination on duly devoured authors. One step farther, and Machado would have served the entrée to the banquet that he could only prepare twenty years later, bringing Stendhal, Laurence Sterne, and Xavier de Maistre together in the note "To the Reader" in *The Posthumous Memoirs of Brás Cubas*—a respectable trio, to which he would add Almeida Garrett, in the preface to the third edition: the writer who *was no copyist*, although he introduced to Portugal flowers originally cultivated in the gardens of other lands.

The lack of emulation comes from audiences. The text is clear: *because they are not drawn by any true or consequential seduction*. And this is due to authors' lack of engagement with the nation's mission. The spectator is thus not seduced by theater because he only finds *conceptions from foreign atmospheres and remote skies*. The gravest part is that, in the binary rhythm between what is one's own and what is foreign, between here and there, *aemulatio* loses speed and energy; after all, it feeds off the permanent oscillation between the two poles. The very practice of the technique demands both the previous adoption of a model and a posterior criticism of the model one has adopted; only then is *imitatio* not the final product (a mere copy) but rather the starting point for a process of *invention*—the goal of every artist.

(*Invention*: key word.)

Machadinho's problem was, fundamentally, a *lack of emulation* . . . A drought of *aemulatio* in the classical sense, in place of the limited nationalist definition used in the 1859 article.

In the last two chapters, I will return to mapping the semantic field of emulation within Machado's oeuvre. What we have seen thus far is nothing more than an aperitif. This was how Machado defined Álvares de Azevedo in his article on Garrett: "He was our aperitif of Byron and Shakespeare" (III, 931). Once again, Machado suggests a striking affinity between the classical model and a physiology of reading sketched out in the dedication to *Brás Cubas*: "to the worm who first gnawed the cold flesh of my cadaver" (I, 511).

Time to travel back and observe the technique of emulation in its own context, the pre-Romantic period, in a long-term perspective.

Why Be Original?

Here I recall an author at the center of the Brás Cubas revolution: Lucian of Samosata, one of the most illustrious craftsmen of Menippean satire—an important genre on the path from Machadinho to Machadão, as Augusto Meyer has put it so eloquently. An author of implacable parodies, Lucian might well have been included in the note "To the Reader" at the start of the *Posthumous Memoirs.*

In a rhetorical exercise that serves the purposes of this discussion, "Zeuxis and Antiochus," Lucian turns to the legendary Greek painter and the king of the Seleucids. The men were lamenting the fame garnered by art and the praises won for a triumphant battle, respectively. The bone of contention had to do with the type of recognition an artist or a public man might desire. Zeuxis's admirers focused on the unconventional subjects of his paintings, as if their only value lay in their being unexpected, while neglecting the artist's palette and technical mastery. Antiochus's subjects praised their sovereign for an improbable victory against the Galatian army, which was larger and better prepared. The unexpected triumph was only possible because the enemy hordes were caught off-guard by the use of sixteen elephants, the king's secret weapon; awestruck, the Galatians beat a hasty retreat. Now, no general wants to be remembered for a triumph in which courage and strategy were practically irrelevant. Laurels are not always their own reward: correctly identifying merit is more important than simply praising a creator or celebrating a general. Otherwise, praise may sour into disregard for the traits that truly distinguish the man of talent or the master of strategy.

Lucian was intimately familiar with the ambiguity of certain paths to enshrinement (a dilemma that Machadinho also knew too well). After he had given a speech, those listening gathered around and, bursting with admiration, praised him, exclaiming that "his ideas [were] quite unequalled for originality."[4] Lucian was taken aback by the homage, which minimized the value of his work. This sentiment may be incomprehensible for those accustomed to the inflated Romantic value placed on genius and creativity, based on the image of the artist as an individual blessed with autonomous subjectivity and able to create without falling back on rhetorical convention. The irritated justification from the author of *A True Story*, meanwhile, sheds light on the reigning perspective in a literary system driven by the ties between *imitatio* and *aemulatio*:

> So the only attraction in my work is that it is unusual, and does not follow the *beaten track*; good vocabulary, *orthodox composition*, insight, subtlety, Attic grace, general constructive skill—these may for aught I know be completely wanting. (94; italics mine)

Lucian felt cheapened by the fact that they only mentioned the originality of his style. And he was right. Emphasizing that point in particular would mean that he was not following *the beaten track*—that is to say, that his ingenuity did not feature *orthodox composition*, or, once again, that he was unfamiliar with *the beaten track*—a graver crime still. Emphasizing originality *alone* was tantamount to judging the writer a novice, hardly familiar with tradition. A better appreciation of Lucian's talent would demand that the reader or listener be able to recognize the model being imitated so as to better savor the parodic diction of the emulation. If the audience is not familiar with the literary reference, the irony is lost, as it is a wellspring of potential meaning that demands the reader's (or listener's) cooperation in order to remain relevant. Only then does Lucian's satire attain its full power. In "Stuffed-Shirt Theory," a story published in the *Gazeta de Notícias* on December 18, 1881, and included the next year in *Loose Papers*, Machado hits the bull's-eye in his definition of irony: "that vague movement at the corner of the mouth, heavy with mystery, invented by some decadent Greek, which infected Lucian, who passed it on to Swift and Voltaire, the very look of the skeptical and the clear-eyed" (II, 294). The reference to Lucian, within my reasoning, means that Machado is buying a ticket to a period far older than Brazil under the Segundo Reinado. Xavier de Maistre wandered around the room; Machado was more ambitious, and, all without leaving his desk, traveled "to the origin of the centuries" (I, 520), ruminating on literary tradition as a whole.

Such ambition would lead the author-laborer to echo Lucian's model in the opening note to *Resurrection* (1872), turning away unreflective praises:

> What I ask of critics is this—benevolent intentions, but a frank and just appraisal. *Praises, when not founded in merit*, certainly caress one's spirit

and lend a veneer of celebrity; but those who seek to learn and wish to accomplish something *prefer the improving lesson to the flattering drone.* (I, 116; italics mine)

In the literary system prevalent before the Romantic revolution, the desire to be original would be considered frankly indecorous. Only an ignorant reader would wish to be identical to himself rather than turning to the massive contribution from all those who had successfully written before him. The person impressed with the novelty of her meager revelations must surely be the owner of a sparse library. The paradox here, according to Quintilian, is that the less prepared the tribune is, the more loquacious (similarly, the less educated the writer, the more "creative" he supposes himself to be):

For the same reason, the uninstructed sometimes appear to have a richer flow of language, because they say everything that can be said, while the learned exercise *discrimination* and *self-restraint*.[5]

Adequately selecting one's models demands intimate contact with a collective body of knowledge comprised of topoi, the whole of which is accessible to any aspiring man of letters. One's sense of proportion is honed by the need to employ selective criteria in an attempt to tackle the repertoire to be first *imitated* and then *emulated*. Emulation includes the imitation of models in terms of an exact ratio: a *lack of emulation* produces *mere copies*; an *excess of emulation* gives rise to *inaccessible products*. This formula may help to clarify Lucian's words: "I thought it gave a sort of adventitious charm, and contributed its part to the success" (94–95). The writer who is conscious of the craft considers the absolute search for novelty a false dilemma, as the greater challenge lies in contributing to the enrichment of the tradition in which he or she is operating. Otherwise, one runs the risk of falling victim to Horace's severe rebuke: "And why am I a poet, and praised, / if not because I see differences, / and know them, and mark them / just as they are? / *To blush at wisdom / is to lie; I'd rather learn*" (12).

Machado clearly understood the difference between an "artist" and a "man of talent." "O habilidoso" [The Skillful Man] is the title of one of his stories, published in 1895 in the *Gazeta de Notícias* and never reproduced in book form. In the story, João Maria—a promising youth with a talent as a painter—is unable to translate his gift into significant works of art. The reason is simple: "*Every art has a technique*; he abhorred technique, he was averse to apprenticeship, to learning the rudiments of things" (II, 1051; italics mine). The artist is only realized when he triumphs over the talented artisan; he must ultimately grow not through his talent, but through resisting the ease that such a vocation offers. Through this lens, etymology comes to the fore: the artist must first master the rules of the profession, as the words for technique (*techné*) and art (*ars*) are synonyms. This is not a matter of proffering immutable norms taken as "laws of art," but rather of mastering the creative process that defines a specific practice. At the end of the story in question, the skillful protagonist choose simply to *copy* the same painting over and over, shrinking his aspirations down to practically nothing: "This is the latest and the last frontier of his ambition: an alley and four little boys" (II, 1054). The dead-end street does not stem from João Maria's marginal circumstances; if this were the case, we would be looking at a predictable metaphor for cultural life in the *tristes tropiques*. Indeed, if the skillful hero were called Jean-Marie, lived in the Mecca of art of the nineteenth century, and still failed to understand that *every art has a technique*, the melancholy end would be the same.

In "O anel de Polícrates" [Polycrates's Ring], released in the *Gazeta de Notícias* on July 2, 1882, and reproduced the same year in *Loose Papers*, the same motif reappears in the figure of Xavier, a man of rare verbal talent, able to turn out spirited formulations and sparkling phrases as easily as he breathed, but who never published a single book, essay, short story, or even a newspaper article. The reason for this paradoxical sterility appears as a mirror image of Machado's singular artistic and intellectual trajectory. Here is how the character is described:

> He was a sackful of astonishments. Whoever spoke to him felt a sudden vertigo. *Imagine a waterfall of ideas and images*, the most original and most beautiful ones, sometimes extravagant, sometimes sublime. Note that he had utter faith in his own inventions. (II, 329; italics mine)

In the absence of a laborious apprenticeship in technique, how to overcome the two principal obstacles faced by Xavier? They lie at the core of the problem. "The first is that he was impatient, and couldn't bear the gestation period necessary for his work. The second is that he cast his eyes over such a vast array of things that he could hardly fix his gaze on any single one" (II, 330). Within this self-satisfied vision, the greater the talent, the greater the difficulty in producing anything! Talent not refined by discipline or study, that is.

A similar character sketch may be found in the case of the unpredictable Elisiário, from the story "Um erradio" [An Errant Man], published in *A Estação* in 1894 and reproduced in *Gathered Pages* (1899). The description of the protagonist might serve as a treatise on literary life in the world of the stuffed shirts that populate Machado's prose:

> He was educated in nothing, as he had studied engineering, medicine, and law, leaving at all these colleges *a reputation as a great talent lacking in diligence.* He could turn out decent prose if he were able to write for twenty minutes at a time; as a poet he was an improviser who never wrote down his verses, and so it was his listeners who put them to paper and gave him copies, many of which he lost. (II, 586; italics mine)

Elisiário comes to the same end as skillful João Maria and exuberant Xavier: "Soon he only improvised rarely, and, as he had no patience for composing while he wrote, his verses grew ever scarcer. Soon they emerged only limply; *the poet repeated himself*" (II, 596; italics mine). The ability that may be satisfied in the narcissistic contemplation of its own power does not invest in any daily honing of its talent, and instead is criticized and even pilloried in Machado's stories. An understanding of the relevance of this topic amounts to an x-ray of the literary project put forth by the author of "The Alienist."

The gap between the disciplined artist and the careless amateur sheds light on Machado's true poetics, laying bare his view of the task of the inventor. The motif appears often across any number of genres: short stories, novels, crônicas, to say nothing of criticism. Doesn't Bento Santiago show himself to be drawn down the path of least resistance? In the second chapter of *Dom Casmurro*, he confesses that he gave up writing a *History of the Suburbs* for prosaic reasons: "it was a modest undertaking, but it required documents and dates as preliminaries, *all of which would be boring and time-consuming*" (Gledson 6; italics mine). Anticipating the effort necessary to transform intuition into a published work brings yawns to the innumerable skillful characters that populate Machado's fiction: here lies the origin of the failure that invariably hounds them.

This situation helps to unveil the elements at the foundation of the *Machado de Assis literary system*: a keen study of tradition; mastery of technique; honing of talent; and discipline. Swimming against the tide of the generally heralded view of the spontaneous, prolific gift, Machado spent his life polishing his art. Instead of going for the easy and immediate result, the author of *Quincas Borba* took the image of the artist as laborer seriously.

The theme will reappear obsessively, becoming a decisive motif, a true worldview. Machadinho becomes Machado once he understands that, without a mastery of *ars*, *imitatio* will never be transformed into *aemulatio*.

Novelty? Perhaps . . .

The writer who is conscious of the craft must go *to the rudiments of things*, imitating with the aim of creating variations through the combination of preexisting elements. He seeks novelty, undoubtedly, but in order to discuss this point we must have a solid understanding of the meaning of the word.

Time to return to Lucian, now to his text *The Way to Write History*: the only work on the topic that has survived from classical antiquity, and which would be widely read and discussed during the Renaissance. The reader can only appreciate the essay by identifying the target of its criticisms—the authors, both older and contemporary, working within the same genre. Once again, and this is a crucial point: in the literary system developed around the relationship between *imitatio* and *aemulatio*, listeners and readers would ideally master the same repertoire, which articulated an objective body of knowledge transmitted through institutions of learning and exercised on public occasions, a true calling card of one's possessing a certain level of lettered culture. The best-known passages from Homer's poems were taught in Roman schools and learned by heart. Both writing and reading thus favored a playful exercise in allusions to that very collective repertoire, which also incorporated its eventual transformations. For example, Virgil knew that his readers would understand his references to Homer and would therefore be able to judge the success of his *aemulatio*. In the composition of the *Aeneid*, this factor was already woven into the making of the poem. The success of his *aemulatio* would make Virgil into a poet to be emulated in turn. During the Middle Ages many of his texts were set to music, as they were sung in schools—a common technique for memorization.

In terms of the writing of history, Lucian selects Herodotus and Thucydides as his models, casting them as *authorities* in the genre. Hence, in order to be considered an author in the writing of history one had to learn the techniques employed and topics discussed by both. To ignore the *auctoritas* of these models would earn the would-be historian an immediate disqualification from the literary system, an elimination that would be carried out by the readers themselves; after all, they knew the *Histories* and *The History of the Peloponnesian War*, and would thus be able to deny citizenship to an *auctor* whose work revealed scorn for the *authority* in the chosen genre. This authority sprang not from an individual assessment but a collective norm, objectively employed as a sort of lingua franca in the realm of emulation.

The reader may be wondering: in such a strictly regulated system, how to preserve the search for "novelty"? How to understand its role in Lucian's speech, if it, simply *gives a sort of adventitious charm*, and nothing more?

Sticking to thick description—to understand Lucian, nothing could be better than *The Way to Write History* itself:

> Enough of him. Another is a keen emulator of Thucydides, and by way of close approximation with his model starts with his own name—most graceful of beginnings, redolent of Attic thyme! Look at it: "Crepereius Calpurnianus of Pompeiopolis wrote the history of the war between Parthia and Rome, how they warred one upon the other, beginning with the commencement of the war." . . . It would be a sinful neglect to omit the man who begins like this:—"I devise to tell of Romans and Persians"; then a little later, "For 'twas Heaven's desire that the Persians should suffer evils"; and again, "One Osroes there was, whom Hellenes name Oxyroes"—and much more in that style. He corresponds, you see, to one of my previous examples; only he *is a second Herodotus, and the other a second Thucydides.*
>
> There is another distinguished artist in words—again rather more Thucydidean than Thucydides—, who gives, according to his own idea, the clearest, most convincing descriptions of every town, mountain, plain, or river. (117–19)

We already know the formula that precedes the Machadian equation: the imitator is original, as long as he is a man of talent, not a *mere copyist*. Lucian traces this caricature of Crepereius Calpurnianus with evident glee— as a *perfect copy* of his model, he betrays a poorly executed kowtowing to the *auctoritas* attributed to Thucydides. His master, meanwhile, was *a second Herodotus*, while never failing to emulate him. The anonymous historian, then, *rather more Thucydidean than Thucydides*, would be an *auctor* in his own right, seeking to create a unique mark within the realm of the necessary initial repetition.

Here lies the answer to the question about novelty: this is certainly a matter of seeking out the new. If it were not so, the copy would win out. However, we cannot confuse novelty with traumatic rupture; rather, it is an accumulation of alternatives in a combinatorial art where the potential for variations is practically infinite. The perception of this cultural tempo has nothing to do with the linear sense that came to dominate after the Enlightenment and implies that the overcoming of previous stages is a natural first step in the notion of progress. In the realm of emulation, the gesture of writing and the act of reading demand the simultaneous understanding of a variety of historical periods. This simultaneity feeds anachronistic appropriations that are made productive through the synchronous nature of the acts of reading and writing.

(It is as if the structure for *The Posthumous Memoirs of Brás Cubas* were first sketched out in the Machadian recovery of the technique of *aemulatio*.)

Chess, Music, and Fiction

In the "Sermão da Sexagésima" [Sermon of the Sixtieth], delivered at the Capela Real in Lisbon in March 1665, Antonio Vieira alluded to the combinatorial art of the rhetorical system. After comparing preaching to sowing, he noted the crucial difference between them:

God did not make the sky into a chessboard of stars, as preachers make of their sermons a chessboard of words. If one part must be white, the other must be black; if one part is called light, the other must be called shadow; if they say of one part that it has fallen, the other must be said to rise.[6]

Exactly: the world of *imitatio* and *aemulatio* recalls a chessboard. *If one part must be white, the other must be black.*[7] Across sixty-four squares, thirty-two pieces are reigned by predetermined movements and preestablished rules. In the case of the most heavily studied opening sequences and defenses, as is the case with the Spanish Opening or the Sicilian Defense, the first moves must be memorized; a veritable legion of previous matches has been carefully examined and duly codified, creating a common repertoire that every chess player of a certain level must call upon. A young player who leans too heavily on her talent will be hard-pressed to defeat an adversary who may be mediocre, but has studied the latest theoretical contributions to the game. This skillful player may be a child who has yet to meet the grand masters of the word, who has yet to be introduced to Vieira, Camões, or Machado. This does not matter: if she is in love with the game, and not victory alone, there will always come a moment in which all tactical calculations are interrupted and strategy is set aside. In this instant, the pure beauty of combinatorial art will come into play, and the young talent will finally understand the game at hand—be it on the alternating squares of the board, or on the blank page.

The future author of the *Posthumous Memoirs* would agree. Chess is an important reference in his works; in *Iaiá Garcia*, Jorge's courtship of Luís Garcia's daughter is mediated by pawns, knights, rooks, bishops, and, of course, kings and queens. The narrator's conclusion is a checkmate: "Of all the qualities demanded by chess, Iaiá was blessed with the two essential ones: a quick gaze and Benedictine patience, precious qualities in life, which is another sort of chess, with its challenges and its matches, one won, some lost, others drawn" (I, 464). The analogy is tempting, but it has its limits. The reason for this is simple: life is not quite like a chess match because in the day-to-day, rules are not always obeyed (although none can escape the final checkmate that defeats us all).

Counselor Ayres might disagree. He used to prepare himself for social life as if he were anticipating his adversary's moves in a complex game of advances and retreats: "I heard this and other minutiae with interest. I have always been given to appreciating the way in which characters express themselves and are composed, and I am often not displeased by the arrangement of events themselves. *I enjoy seeing and foreseeing, and concluding as well*" (I, 1162; italics mine). No matter; after all, the contradiction is inherent to the dispute: *if one part is called light, the other must be called shadow.*

Machado also composed chess problems, generally of the simplest sort: *The whites play and mate in two moves.* However, a problem comprising few elements may be extremely sophisticated, given the economy of resources characteristic of Machado's prose. Doesn't a novel like *Dom Casmurro* bear some resemblance to an unsolvable jigsaw puzzle, or perhaps a game of chess whose checkmate is precisely the impossibility of finishing it, as in the famous phrase from *Esau and Jacob*, "things of the future"?

(That is: the act of reading. And writing after reading. And reading to better write.)

◆ ◆ ◆

A summary-digression on the possible link between the technique of *aemulatio* and the combinatorial art of chess.

Machado: the chess-player of fiction?

(Dealing with the reader: risky moves in an imaginary game of chess.)

Or: the systematic return to *aemulatio* as a move inspired by a tight spot?

(Playing with the black pieces, Eça threatened to give checkmate in two moves: *The Crime of Father Amaro* and *Cousin Bazilio*.)

Or perhaps: *The Posthumous Memoirs of Brás Cubas*: the most successful gambit in all of Brazilian literature?

(Wilhelm Steinitz, the creator of modern chess, liked to say, "Chess is not for timid souls." To put it in the vocabulary of this essay, "Chess is not for Machadinhos.")

And that's not all: the first chess tournament held in Brazil took place in Rio de Janeiro and had six participants, among them Machado de Assis, who took an honorable third place. The championship was held in 1880, the year of the publication of *The Posthumous Memoirs of Brás Cubas*.

From Machadinho to Machadão, as Augusto Meyer put it.

I might add: a decisive shift, as though he were playing an unpredictable chess match against himself.

A chess match of words. And of clichés, and topoi, and codified techniques, and multiple variants, and textual traps, and calculating *things of the future.*

◆　◆　◆

The technique of *aemulatio* bears critical structural similarities with the game of chess.

And with music as well, which was another of Machado's passions. The topic might give rise to another book entirely, given the absolute omnipresence of references to music across Machado's work.[8] To a certain extent, Machado defines his poetics in texts where the main character is music itself, or musicians, perennially confronted with the problematic intersection between erudite music and popular compositions. In this sense, I recall the stories "The Machete" (1878), "Cantiga de esponsais" [Wedding Song] (1883), "Cantiga velha" [Old Tune] (1883), "Trio em lá menor" [Trio in A Minor] (1886), and "Um homem célebre" [A Celebrated Man] (1888).

Indeed, we may stumble upon a confession from the author in the words of Counselor Ayres: "Music was always one of my inclinations, and, if I were not afraid to venture into the poetic and perhaps the pathetic, I might say that it is now one of my regrets. If I had learned, I might now play or compose, who can say?" (I, 1142) The same counselor sketches out Flora's character in *Esau and Jacob* (1904): "Music had for her the advantage of not being present, past, or future. It was something outside of time and of space, a pure ideal" (Lowe 154). This description is a true snapshot of the character, whose ethereal nature permeates the whole narrative, disorienting everyone from the counselor to, above all, the irreconcilable twins, Pedro and Paulo. Music plays a crucial role in the plot, helping to define Flora's character. In *Counselor Ayres' Memorial* (1908), meanwhile, the names of the central couple (Tristão and Fidélia) pay homage to operas by Wagner and Beethoven, respectively. As a matter of fact, Machado was an active member of the Beethoven Club. In his youth, he waded into the battles in favor of this or that soprano, being a fervent supporter of Augusta Candiani.

Impertinent facts aside, let me concentrate on the structural aspect.

The musical scale, with its ordered sequence of tones limited by a predetermined number of notes, recalls a chessboard—although, one might say, with a reduced quantity of squares and pieces. Even so, the possible variations on the musical scale are practically infinite. A fictional take on this idea could go a long way.

Recall Hamlet's cutting words to Guildenstern, advising him that he not obey the king's orders:

> Why, look you now, how unworthy a thing you make of me! You would play upon me; you would seem to know my stops; you would pluck out the heart of my mystery; *you would sound me from my lowest note to the top of my compass*: and there is much music, excellent voice, in this little organ; yet cannot you make it speak. 'Sblood, do you think I am easier to be played on than a pipe? Call me what instrument you will, though you can fret me, yet you cannot play upon me. (3.2.329–36, 180; italics mine)

Now, imagining that "all the stories have been told already" or "all the narrative forms have already been explored" is a cliché that the literature of an author, musician, and chess player like Machado may help to overcome. In the realm of combinatorial art, there are always yet-unexplored variations to be found. After all, one can never run the full length of the compass. The Machadian texts of the second phase, composed like true scores, demand readers able to unlock their potential.

All is clarified: *aemulatio*, chess, and music are forms of combinatorial art, thought experiments that we have learned to call Machadian.

(Machado discovered an imaginary link between music, chess, and the technique of *aemulatio*, making this possibility one of the motive forces of his fiction.)

Auctoritas

An equivalence between rhetorical organization and a mental mechanism built into music and the game of chess may be gleaned from the following proviso, from Quintilian:

> If the whole of rhetoric could be thus embodied in one compact code, it would be an easy task of little compass: but *most rules are liable to be altered by the nature of the case, circumstances of time and place, and by hard necessity itself.* Consequently the all-important gift for an orator is a wise adaptability since he is called upon to meet the most varied emergencies. (291; italics mine)

The orator—and the same reasoning stands for the writer—makes use of predetermined models that ought to be obeyed. These codes, however, structured by a grammar of uses and legitimized by lettered conventions, which hold sway during a certain period of history, cannot be seen as a straitjacket meant to ensure the infinite repetition of infinitely tedious, identical discourses. If this were the case, every chess match would be a draw, all musical notes would line up in the same melody, and all mathematical calculations would produce a predictable zero sum. Once certain rules are adopted as a necessary starting point, there follows a virtually unlimited ability to adapt to specific circumstances.

As every well-trained actor knows, the spontaneity of improvisation is born of the exhaustion of interminable rehearsals.

One example comes into play here. Or perhaps two or three of them.

Within the genre of the epic, Homer was the inevitable *auctoritas*. In Latin culture, submitting oneself to the precepts of the genre meant, at a bare minimum, beginning with an imitation of the *Iliad* and the *Odyssey*; whoever failed to do this would be considered inept, not meriting the title of poet. In Horace's frank appraisal: "Homer made metres for war / and kings and the deeds of great men. . . . Comic themes need comic verse; / Thyestes' gory supper can't stand / a vulgar tone, a comic tint. Everything in its place, / I say" (13). Virgil's path was thus to follow the technical side of imitation step by step, understanding that *imitatio* is an *ars*, a specific way of fulfilling a task. This is precisely what does not apply to Elisiário or Xavier in Machado's stories.

The issue of *auctoritas* was necessarily central in Latin literature, whose first major contribution is the work of a translator—Livius Andronicus—known precisely for his translation of the *Odyssey*. Here, it is as if we were returning, *although chronologically in reverse*, to the "translation imperative." We have turned up vestiges of a structural affinity between the cultural circumstances of the Latin world, and the historical condition of Latin America—generally nonhegemonic, we might say. Or should I say the *Latin American world*?

The Romans' relationship to the Greek world was marked by singular characteristics that ought to be considered. The culture of the Latin world was never quite nonhegemonic; for the Romans, imitating and emulating the Greeks was a part of their natural right to take the spoils from the defeated. In Virgil's time, Romans were already poetic rivals of the Greeks, on par with their neighbors.

Thus, I am not looking to draw up a historical narrative based on an idealized, long-term continuum—an extremely long-term one, at that! One difference is enough to cut this off at the root: Latin cultural circumstances have become not only hegemonic, but also imperialist, while the Latin American condition is defined by secondarity in relation to the "great thinking nations." From the point of view of cultural politics, the gap between these two experiences is a glaring one.

However, I will stand by the idea of a structural affinity understood at the level of artistic and intellectual procedures.

The history of emulation in Virgil's work is vastly well known, and its volumes take a place of pride in the imaginary library stocked by Jorge Luis Borges; the Mantuan was a central figure in his conception of literature. I could add nothing to the myriad of passages scrutinized by specialists in search of the Holy Grail of Virgilian *aemulatio*.

(Whereof one cannot add to, thereof one must be silent—as Wittgenstein would say if he were a literary critic.)

I will allow myself to simply point to a structural element that Machado seems to allude to in *Esau and Jacob*.

The first six cantos of the *Aeneid* cover Eneias's flight after the fall of Troy and his journeys on the way to the Italian peninsula. The last six tell of the wars and triumphs that molded the Roman Empire. One might note that in a single poem, Virgil simultaneously appropriated both the *Odyssey* and the *Iliad*, of Odysseus's travails and the narrative of the Trojan War, in that order. If one's ability to concentrate forms and subjects were the ultimate test of the success of one's *aemulatio*, then Virgil would be the undisputed champion. For that matter, as we have seen, the *form of concentration* was Eça's method in his rewriting of Flaubert.

Returning to Machado, I will stand by the proposal of a structural affinity between the Latin relationship with Greece and the nineteenth-century Latin American relationship with Europe: in both cases, the inevitable starting point was a sense of cultural inferiority.

The success of Virgil's *aemulatio* produces the effect that we are examining in Machado's work: in adopting Homer as a model, the Latin poet transformed himself into an *auctoritas* within the genre of the epic. During the Renaissance, Virgil enjoyed great prestige and would often garner more praises than his master. The *Aeneid* would become an invaluable authority. It comes as no surprise, then, that the opening verses of *The Lusiads* do not seek to emulate the *Iliad* or the *Odyssey*, but rather the *Aeneid*. Even the title of Camões's poem suggests it: the word *lusíada* does not appear once in the text. The title both pays tribute to Virgil and emulates him. Just as the *Aeneid* celebrates the deeds of Aeneas, *The Lusiads* sings the conquests of the Portuguese people, and not merely the heroics of Vasco da Gama; there is a broadening of the historical scope here that, in poetic translation, drives Camões's enterprise. The success of this *aemulatio* would lead Camões to the status of *auctoritas* in turn. Bento Teixeira, for example, when drawing up his *Prosopopeia* in 1601, seeks to emulate not Homer, nor Virgil, but Camões himself.

An author who begins with *imitatio* and succeeds in the later stage of *aemulatio* can easily become an *auctoritas*. The deliberately anachronistic updating of this procedure is the equivalent of a declaration of independence, coming from authors in nonhegemonic areas, as their inherent secondarity is now no longer an insuperable obstacle but rather the first, necessary step of the artistic process. In this sense, we may return to the letter from Eça to Machado that mentions the first part of the critique of *Cousin Bazilio*. The reader now beholds a new missive entirely: "the article, by virtue of its distinction and the talent with which it was composed, *honors my book, almost increasing its authority*" (227; italics mine). The vocabulary chosen here is perfect, as Queirós's *aemulatio* of the Flaubertian model would transform the Portuguese novelist into an unquestioned *auctoritas* in the Lusophone world.

Machado understood perfectly.

Hence his bitter reaction.

The Lusophone world, I said. The borders of this world are clear and ought to be indicated. The poetics of emulation is a subjective answer of great aesthetic intelligence, but it cannot change the objective situation that is a structural imbalance in symbolic exchanges. This is a crucial point; if it were not, one would inevitably fall into embarrassingly naive praises of the peripheral condition as the ultimate cause of the inventiveness implicit in the procedure of the poetics of emulation.

Everything in life comes with compensations—some will say.

I am not among them.

Beyond this, I will return to the Achilles' heel of my hypothesis. Deep down I am responding to the questions that have probably occurred to the reader: as an "answer," are the poetics of emulation the "exclusive" product of nonhegemonic circumstances? Is the hierarchy of *auctoritas* based solely on political and cultural asymmetry, or does it also involve a purely "technical" side? What is the difference between *aemulatio* employed within a single political and cultural context, and the *poetics of emulation* that take place between a nineteenth-century Brazilian author and an eighteenth-century Irish writer?

Machado, as he himself recognizes in the "Note to the Reader" that opens the *Posthumous Memoirs*, is emulating Laurence Sterne. Here, my hypothesis seems perfectly precise; after all, at least in principle, there is no questioning the asymmetry between them in the universe of the hierarchical Republic of Letters.

For his part, and in a spirit not unlike Lucian's, Sterne embarked on a parodic emulation of the budding tradition of the British novel, which was then being forged by the works of Samuel Richardson and Henry Fielding, among others. Thus, *The Life and Opinions of Tristram Shandy, Gentleman*, with its first two volumes originally released in 1759, parodies earlier titles such as Richardson's *Pamela, or Virtue Rewarded* (1739) and above all, Henry Fielding's *The History of Tom Jones, a Foundling*, published in 1749. Fielding had already paved the way in 1742 with the release of *Joseph Andrews*, a rol-licking take on *Pamela*.

At the end of chapter 4, I will return to the differences between Sterne's and Fielding's vision of the novel in order to show how Machado discusses them in the same "Note to the Reader," albeit rather cryptically. To start with, I point out that the rise of the British novel was bolstered by the presence of an internal system of emulation whose dynamics fostered the genre's vitality.

An *internal* system of emulation: this is an example of practices of emu-lation between authors on the same hierarchical level, coming from the same hegemonic context. To put it directly: the poetics of emulation may exist even in the absence of *external* asymmetry in power relations. *Aemulatio*, understood as a dominant artistic practice in the pre-Romantic period, did not represent "inferiority" but rather an invitation to invention.

Internal asymmetry, however, is inevitable, as *aemulatio* assumes the presence of authors whose *auctoritas* must be recognized by contemporaries as well as those who follow, even if that recognition comes in the form of parody.

Here stands the greatest hurdle for the hypothesis I am putting forth: the poetics of emulation must not be confused with any sort of "essence" of peripheral cultures. On the contrary, it comprises a body of techniques that favor a certain aesthetic, independent of latitude. At the end of chapter 5, and in the conclusion, I offer a way around this impasse.

Machado-Virgil?

A poet like Virgil was faced with a complex, challenging situation. He needed to emulate the Latin tradition that immediately preceded him, but also the Hellenistic legacy, plus—as if that weren't enough—the classical Greek tra-dition. As an authentic representative of the basic dilemma of Latin culture, he needed to make this relationship with the legacy of Greek civilization productive, somehow.

A writer like Machado de Assis was faced with a challenging, complex situation. And for reasons that were structurally similar to those troubling Virgil. A Brazilian writer, a *Latin* American writer, needed to productively define his relationship with Western culture, especially in relation to the "great thinking nations." Moreover, *after February 1878*, Machado could hardly leave one Portuguese-language contemporary out of the equation.

Seen from this angle, this mission was even less likely to succeed than Virgil's.

Machado's case had an additional complicating factor. As the language of the empire, Latin occupied a hegemonic position that would last through the seventeenth century and even into the eighteenth, although French was beginning to take on the role that English has assumed today, as the universal linguistic currency. Portuguese, meanwhile, never moved beyond its condition as a secondary language, even during the height of the Portuguese Empire: "minor literature" written in Portuguese is, one might say, doubly minor. This perverse arithmetic did not pass Machado by. In a letter to Joaquim Nabuco on August 1, 1908, he congratulates his friend on his talks at American universities but laments the secondarity of their language:

> Thank you for all of them, especially the one regarding Camões's place in literature. It is both good and indispensable to claim a rightful place for our language, *and in this, international political services will not be less important than purely literary ones.* It is truly sad to see us considered, as you note, in a subaltern position in relation to Spanish. (III, 1092)

Machado doesn't even mention French, to say nothing of English, because in those cases the subaltern position would be unquestionable: in any serious fight, Portuguese isn't even a contender. This is the gist of a crônica from October 11, 1896, from the *A Semana* series. Here, Machado draws up an imaginary letter to the Russian czarina. In the middle of this fictional exercise, a concrete fact takes center stage:

> Czarina, if these lines should come to your hand, do not follow the example of Vítor Hugo, who, upon receiving a leaflet from Lisbon, wrote back to the author, "I do not know Portuguese, but with the aid of Latin and Spanish, I am reading your book" . . . No, I don't even ask that you reply. Have the lines translated into the language of Gogol, which they say is so rich and sonorous, then read them straightaway. (III, 737)

The small act of revenge—Lusophonizing Victor Hugo's name—is some consolation, but does not change Portuguese's *subaltern position in relation to Spanish*. Once again, the "translation imperative," which concerned Machado as well, rears its head.

The association between the Latin author and the *Latin* American writer may seem arbitrary, as if we were imposing the specters of our squabbles onto Machado and then using hermeneutical tweezers to pluck passages from his texts that confirm our obsessions.

Be that as it may, I will remain faithful to the method of thick description by continuing to consult the author's texts.

In a letter to José de Alencar on February 29, 1868, in response to the latter's introducing him to Castro Alves, one finds an interesting parallel: "Choosing myself as Virgil to the young Dante, that is to say, as the soothsayer who comes to us from the land of Moema" (III, 896). Machado would thus be *Il Duca* to Castro Alves, the young poet of *Espumas flutuantes*. The parallel has a darker side: Virgil, Dante's guide through Hell and Purgatory, must abandon him just as he enters Paradise . . . And who would Castro Alves's Beatrice be?

In the story "O esqueleto" [The Skeleton], published in the *Jornal das Famílias* in October and November 1875, the narrator turns to the Latin poet to describe Dr. Belém, the owner of an expansive personality: "We lunched happily; the doctor was as he seemed to be generally, speaking of serious or frivolous things, alternating a philosophical reflection with a jibe, a story of his youth with a quote from Virgil" (II, 817). An echo of this wandering disposition appears in "An Errant Man." As we have seen, this story pokes fun at Elisiário, the creator of visionary projects, none of which are ever brought to fruition—but this is just nitpicking, for the legion of skillful characters in Machado's prose. One friend makes a casual comment about life in the backlands of Ceará, and Elisiário immediately begins imagining his conquest of the territory: "He would harvest everything, plants, legends, songs, dialects. He told the story of the common country man's life, he spoke of Aeneas and quoted Virgil and Camões, to the great surprise of the servants, who stopped in their tracks with slackened jaws" (II, 589–90).

I do not attribute much more to these passages than the typically Machadian oscillation between the popular and the erudite, contemporary and classical, an oscillation that produces its own destabilization. Insofar as possible, criticism ought to rise to the level of complexity produced by the ur-author, instead of lowering it to the monotonous game of conjecturing and confirming one's own hypotheses.

In terms of the association that I am putting forth, it is important to find more definitive references in Machado's texts to the author of the *Aeneid*. And, even if they do exist, I do not intend on presenting them as "evidence." That would be falling into the entertaining ingenuity of those critics who believe that they are turning up hidden codes, secret messages, allusions to this or that, and dedicate veritably Benedictine efforts to deciphering them. As if one could find the *key to the writing* for the whole of Machado's works! My aim is another altogether: with no pretense of exhausting the complexity of the writer's profile, I wish to sketch a new portrait using the colors from his own palette.

In this spirit, I turn to chapter 26 of the *Posthumous Memoirs*. Here, young Cubas is informed of his father's plans for him: he is to marry and dedicate himself to politics. Indifferent to these aspirations, the dead-author-to-be puts pen to paper, writing precisely the verses of the *Aeneid* emulated by Camões in the first verses of *The Lusiads*: "*Arma virumque cano*"—"*As armas e os barões assinalados*" [Armes, and the Men above the vulgar File],[9] as Camões put it. In a spate of free association that recalls Sterne, Cubas plays with a number of combinations, as if he were an *avant la lettre* adept of concrete poetry:

> I was going to write *virumque*—and it came out *Virgil*, and so I went on:
>
> | | | |
> |---|---|---|
> | Vir | | Virgil |
> | | Virgil Virgil | |
> | | Virgil | |
> | | | Virgil |
>
> My father, a bit put out by such indifference, rose, came to my side, cast a glance at the paper. . . .
>
> "*Virgil!*" *he cried out.* "*That's you, my boy,* precisely; your bride is called Virgília." (I, 549; italics mine)

Brás Cubas is Virgil—and, although this is only the case because of a pun, the alignment between their roles is striking. In *Esau and Jacob*, after all, the very structure of the *Aeneid* seems to provide the model for characterizing the rivalry between Pedro and Paulo. In chapter 45 (fittingly titled, "Muse, Sing . . ."), Counselor Ayres seeks to ennoble the perennial dispute between the brothers by turning to classical literature:

> When lunch was finished, Aires gave them a quote from Homer, in fact two, one for each one, telling them that the old poet had sung about them separately, Paulo at the beginning of the *Iliad*:
> "Muse, sing the wrath of Achilles, Peleus's son, ill-boding wrath for the Greeks, that sent to Pluto's house many strong souls of heroes and gave their bodies to be a prey to birds and dogs."
> Pedro was at the beginning of the *Odyssey*:
> "Muse, sing that astute hero who wandered so many years after the destruction of sacred Ilium."
> It was one way to define each one's character and neither took the illustration badly. On the contrary, the poetic quotation served as a private diploma. The fact is that both smiled with faith, acceptance, thanks, without finding one word or syllable with which to contradict the aptness of the verses. (Lowe 97)

The counselor does not mention the *Aeneid*; the model, however, is that of Virgil's composition, with an unexpected juxtaposition of the two Homeric poems in the image of the growing hostility between the two brothers.

One crônica from *A Semana*, published on January 7, 1894, bears even more suggestive terms, shot through with a diction that we would later learn to call Borgesian:

> At times I gaze on a yard in Rome, where some old rooster wakes up the illustrious Virgil, and I wonder if it is not the same rooster that wakes me up, and *if I am not the very same Virgil*. This is the period of tame madness that comes over me in sleep. Then I walk up the Via Appia, turn on Rua do Ouvidor, and run into Maecenas, who invites me to dine with Augustus and a veteran of the Companhia Geral. (III, 597; italics mine)

Machado may be *the very same Virgil* because he has discovered, in emulation, the possibility of resuscitating a worn-out technique in the wake of romanticism. The same technique employed by Virgil in his confrontations with the legacy of classical Greece. The deliberately anachronistic return to *aemulatio* allows one to formulate an alternative to the situation of nonhegemonic cultures, only exacerbated by the use of a language considered secondary in the hierarchy of the republic of letters. Now, if *aemulatio* demands the previous step of *imitatio*, secondarity is no longer experienced as anguish and may rather be seen as a field of possibilities, driven by an internal logic that implies crucial consequences in terms of cultural politics.

But let's hold our horses! My reflection may lead to a fallacy: secondarity brings its own advantages, since peripheral circumstances stimulate innovation. The literary system and the capitalist system would thus move in opposite directions ... This posture leads to an inevitable praise of backwardness, as if it ensured a mysterious epistemological advantage inaccessible to artists from central countries. In the case of nonhegemonic contexts, I am thinking of strategic moves, not essential characteristics: while the artistic techniques that comprise the poetics of emulation may be found, *separately*, at any latitude, then *the simultaneous occurrence of all of them* might generally characterize the *potential* of a nonhegemonic situation.

The development of the poetics of emulation springs from the horizon perfectly characterized in the unrestraint of Oswald de Andrade: "Filiação" [Filiation], the *felix culpa* of the peripheral inventor. What follows is the joyful enumeration of his debts:

> *Filiation.* Contact with the Brazil of the Caraíba. *Où Villegaignon print terre.* Montaigne. The natural man. Rousseau. From the French Revolution to Romanticism, to the Bolshevik Revolution, to the Surrealist Revolution and Keyserling's technicized barbarian. *We walk.*[10]

In the case of Machado's literature, one must move forward—but above all, backward—through the unending flow of time periods, a primary characteristic of the delirium inaugurated by the *Posthumous Memoirs*. This is a deliberately anachronistic poetics, *thus imitating in a modern form* the classical technique of *aemulatio.* This is a crucial point: I am referring to a *reverse anachronism*, productive in its inversion of the normal chronology of literary history. This is not a matter of projecting current values onto tradition, but rather the contrary, rethinking these values with a basis in that tradition.

In the crônica in *A Semana* from January 7, 1894, the idea is summed up in an eloquent formula: *"All is sea, and without a shore,* as Ovid said in the words of Bocage" (III, 598). When spoken in Portuguese the poet seems to be another, just as Ovid's Latin lends a new tinge to Bocage's diction. An upside-down anachronism, a two-way anachronism, an interminable back-and-forth between sameness and foreignness.

The poetics of emulation, too, were intuited by any number of authors. This is what I will show now, with a focus on the Hispanic American world.

Emulation: Anachronistic Poetics

Since the techniques of the classic form of *aemulatio* have been defined, I will focus on a description of the elements that characterize the *poetics of emulation*, understood as a deliberately anachronistic update of that technique. I will linger on the phenomena of the distinction between *inventio* and *creatio*; the compression of historical periods; deliberate anachronisms; the primacy of reading over writing; and the centrality of translation. The interrelationship between these elements comprises the dynamism behind the practices common to writers and artists in nonhegemonic circumstances—among them Georg Brandes, Machado de Assis, Czeslaw Milosz, Eça de Queirós, and Domingo Faustino Sarmiento, besides so many others.

> (Once again, this is not a matter of speculation preceding the examination of a given *corpus.* The itinerary in this essay is the opposite: the comparative study of texts stimulated the formulation of a hypothesis.)

It is as if the Latin American authors share a fundamental affinity with Lucian: he himself a Syrian, embracing and dedicating himself to a culture that, at least in principle, was not his. The Lucianic gaze is irreverent and establishes a certain distance, just like his eminently parodic literature. A foreign style, we might say.

On April 24, 1950, a young Colombian journalist published a defiant article in *El Heraldo*, the Barranquilla newspaper. His text mulled over the "problems of the novel," and opened on a provocative note:

There has not yet been written in Colombia a novel evidently and *fortunately influenced* by Joyce, Faulkner, or Virginia Woolf. And I say "fortunately" because I don't think we Colombians can be an exception at this point to the *play of influences.* . . . If we Colombians are to take the right path, we must position ourselves inevitably within this current. The lamentable truth is that it has not happened yet and there is not the slightest sign of it ever happening.[11]

The journalist was twenty-two years old and sought to make his mark through incisive statements, ultimately arguing that the Colombian novel suffered from the same weakness as nineteenth-century Brazilian theater: *fundamentally a lack of emulation.* We are already familiar with the swift antidote. The Brazilian author would take it upon himself to dispatch the poultice: the systematic, selective appropriation of material not one's own.

In 1931, a slightly more experienced Cuban intellectual, at age twenty-seven and with a stay in Europe under his belt, had outlined the same principle. This similarity should come as no surprise, as it is evidence of the clear presence of common strategies employed in nonhegemonic contexts faced with the "great thinking nations."

Let us consult this second article:

All art needs *a tradition of craftsmanship.* In art, the *crafting* is just as important as the raw material of the work. . . .

That is why it is indispensable for youths in America to have a profound knowledge of the representative values of art and modern literature in Europe . . . *in order to master their techniques through analysis* and thus hit upon constructive methods that may be suited to translate our Latin American thoughts and sensibilities with the greatest effect. . . . When Diego Rivera, a man in whom pulses the soul of the continent, tells us, "My master, Picasso," this declaration shows that his line of thinking is not alien to the ideas I have just laid out.[12]

Latin American artists needed to *master the techniques* inaugurated by European vanguards in the first decades of the twentieth century: the opposite path from the one followed by "skillful" João Maria. The laborious process of learning these artistic techniques implies the desire to be *fortunately influenced* by models, accepted as *authorities*, given the superior craftsmanship put into their creations.

This is the semantic field of *imitatio* and *aemulatio*, with all its innumerable variants: *filiations*, from Oswald de Andrade, *play of influences*, from Gabriel García Márquez, the eagerness to *master techniques*, from Alejo Carpentier.

After his programmatic article, García Márquez would wait seventeen long years while nobody met his expectations. Since none stepped forward, he released *Cien años de soledad* . . . Carpentier also took seventeen years to publish *El reino de este mundo*, a fundamental text in the formation of modern Latin American literature. The novel was published in 1949—but the famous prologue, in which he presents the concept of *lo real maravilloso* (the marvelous real), came out on April 8, 1948 in *El Nacional*, a Caracas newspaper.

The coincidence is striking: two aspiring men of letters, in different decades and different countries, arguing for similar principles and producing works that would change the field of Latin American literature in the twentieth century.

But the encounter may be more striking still.

In another context, in another century entirely, with concerns of his own, Machado supports a related move, with the breadth of view that characterized his second phase. In 1882, in the preface to *Contos seletos da Mil e uma noites* [Selected Stories from the *One Thousand and One Nights*], a book organized by Carlos Jansen, he reasons:

> The *Thousand and One Nights* has met the fate of many other *inventions*: they were *exploited* and *looted* for their content. It was inevitable, just as it was inevitable that composers would take poets' most personal and sublime creations to mold them to their inspiration, which is certainly rich, elevated, and sublime, *but parasitic nonetheless*. (III, 918; italics mine)

This passage is very rich. Here Machado broadens the field available to *aemulatio*, including a dialogue with the arts. Theater has taken over literature, which comes together with music or is appropriated by it. For that matter, musician and chess partner Artur Napoleão would do the same with

Machado: both of them put their names to the song "Lua da estiva noite" [Moon of a Summer's Night].

In commerce between the arts, the specificity of this or that object is less important than the trait that underlies them all. The artistic process *is parasitic nonetheless*, inevitably taking a preexisting work as its starting point: this is the most powerful sense of the word *inventio*.

The vocabulary here is certainly varied, and the periods distant, but the basic intuition is unmistakable: Machado de Assis, Oswald de Andrade, Alejo Carpentier, and Gabriel García Márquez are working with the same semantic field, sharing similar discursive strategies.

How to understand this resonance, within the framework I have been sketching?

By way of a response, one might recall the philosophy of Pedro Henríquez Ureña. In *La utopia de América*, an important collection of essays, one of the dominant themes is precisely the relationship between the Latin American intellectual, European culture in general, and North American culture in particular. This is the constitutive presence of the other, that is, taken as the model for the definition of cultural identity. Underlying the distance "between imitation and inheritance,"[13] proposed as the correct methodology for considering the problem, we find the central axis for the poetics of emulation:

> We have the right—*inheritance is not theft*—to move freely within the Spanish tradition, and, whenever possible, *outdo it*. Moreover, *we have the right to all the benefits of Western culture*.
>
> Where does the ailment of imitation begin, then?
>
> Any literature will feed off foreign inflows, imitations, or even thefts: this will not make it less original. . . . However, the case turns serious in the absence of transformation, when the imitation remains an imitation.
>
> Our sin, in America, is not *systematic imitation*—which did no harm to Catullus or Virgil, neither Corneille nor Molière—but rather *diffuse imitation*. (53; italics mine)

The explicit nature of this passage makes it reinforce the possibility of identifying a common strategy in dealing with the inevitable presence of foreign elements in the definition of one's own intellectual and artistic identity. Machado speaks of *looting*, Henríquez Ureña of *thefts*, Oswald de Andrade prefers *filiations*, Carpentier argues for the need to *master European techniques*: these function as synonyms, alluding to similar aesthetic procedures. Hence the gap between "systematic imitation" and "diffuse imitation": the latter only demands that one unquestioningly reproduce the norm being adopted, while the former implies the desire to outdo the model at hand while still engaging in a productive dialogue with it. I have translated the terms used in the keen reflection proposed by the Dominican critic: on one hand, diffuse imitation, an act which closes in on itself, evokes *imitatio*, limited to the role of mere copy; on the other hand, systematic imitation, which opens itself up to critical developments, points to *aemulatio*, raised to the ability to produce novelties within tradition.

The project of developing a literature based on "systematic imitation" implies the return to the technique discarded by romanticism but inherent in the mastery of *aemulatio*. Such a model would be based on the steps described by Henríquez Ureña: assimilation, appropriation, and transformation of the model. The poetics of emulation thus allows us to bring together Machado de Assis, Gabriel García Márquez, Alejo Carpentier, Jorge Luis Borges, and Pedro Henríquez Ureña, among so many other thinkers and inventors. (Note that I refrain from calling them creators—and I have good reasons for doing so.)

Emulation and Cultural Politics

The most economic form of clarifying the political consequences of the anachronistic return to emulation would be to recall the dilemma faced by Domingo Faustino Sarmiento during his exile in Chile, in the 1840s. How to bring readers to *El Progreso*, the newspaper he had founded, if the European and North American papers were also available and even got to Santiago de Chile *first*? To understand his predicament: Sarmiento filled a good part of *El Progreso* by compiling articles from foreign periodicals. Now, how to compete with publications whose news are always "fresher" and whose perspectives tend to shape readers' opinions? Why wait for the selection of news and feature articles if the reading public already had access to the texts in the original language and could do without translation entirely? Sarmiento's response to this is exemplary, and reveals the structural element underlying the defining procedures of the poetics of emulation:

> Our daily outdoes the best-known in Europe and America, for the quite obvious reason that, being one of the last newspapers in the world, we have at our disposition, *to select from in the best possible way*, all that the other newspapers have published.[14]

Upon reading Sarmiento's spirited reply, the reader will probably think of the works of Oswald de Andrade. And he is quite right, as this is a strategy related to cultural cannibalism—that is, Oswaldian anthropophagy.

Similarly, in search of these structural affinities, one might mention another article from young García Márquez, "The Possibilities of Cannibalism." Published in 1950—the same year that Oswald de Andrade completed *A crise da filosofia messiânica* [The Crisis of Messianic Philosophy], the essay in which he built on the consequences of cultural cannibalism—García Márquez's text moves in a similar direction. "Cannibalism would give rise to a new concept of life. It would be the beginning of a new philosophy, a new and fecund path for the arts" (400).

Faithful to the monomania that drives this essay, I shall return to the author of "The Alienist." The crônica in *A Semana* from September 1, 1895, is dedicated to alleged cases of cannibalism from Guinea and a rural part of Minas Gerais. Machado's ironic conclusion might just as easily have been penned by Oswald or García Márquez:

> Refrains are crutches that the strong should cast away. When the custom of cannibalism returns, there will be nothing to do but trade "Love one another," from the gospels, for this doctrine: "Eat one another." After all, these are the two refrains of civilization. (III, 673)

The reappearance of this subject sheds light on the meaning of the poetics of emulation: developing strategies to deal with the constitutive presence of the other, adopted as both model and authority.

Sarmiento's attitude suggests that being perennially at the forefront may be an insurmountable limit: those in such a position have nothing before their eyes. This is why vanguards soon cease to be iconoclasts and become zealous guardians of their own memory, in a proliferation of institutional oxymora: *museums* of *modern* and *contemporary* art. The lagging position staked out by the editor of *El Progreso* ensures him an unexpected advantage: everything is available to him, spread out like items on an endless menu, in a perspective that defines a new way of understanding art and thought in nonhegemonic circumstances. In the crônica on a hypothetical return to cannibalism, Machado confesses: "We do nothing more than spin round and round, as the other used to say" (III, 672). Certainly, and, above all, *as the other used to say*, in the oscillation that defines the power of reverse anachronism.

A deceased author *avant la lettre*, Sarmiento did not need to wait for the tomb to live through Brás Cubas's delirium. Pressured by objective conditions that he could not alter, linked to the concrete fact of unequal political and economic relations, he *invented* a subjective way of facing down this impasse, returning to the *origin of the centuries* in his own style.

In Sarmiento's words, within the realm of aesthetics and thought, the last may at times be the first, simply because they choose *from the whole of tradition* those specific elements that most directly interest them.

Once again, to return to the most important element: this is a *potential*, but one that demands a deliberate move to be fully realized.

◆　◆　◆

A question appears: mightn't this link between Machado and these various Hispanic-American authors be artificial? The dialogue between Brazilian culture and the Hispanic-American world remains practically nonexistent even today. Nevertheless, the association with Sarmiento is propped up by an article published in the *Gazeta de Notícias* on July 9, 1888. Here, Machado recalls his (almost) encounter with the Argentine.

His impressions of the occasion merit a transcription:

> When I contemplate the swift progress of the Argentine nation today, *I invariably recall the first and only time I saw Dr. Sarmiento*, the president who succeeded General Mitre in governing the Republic.
>
> It was in 1868. A few friends and I were at the Club Fluminense at Praça da Constituição, where the Imperial Secretariat is today. It was nine o'clock at night. We saw a man who had stayed there the night before enter

the tearoom. He was not young; he had *large and intelligent eyes*, was clean-shaven, somewhat plump. He did not linger long; *now and then he gazed at us, while we examined him in turn, without knowing who he was.* This was precisely Dr. Sarmiento, come from the United States where he represented the Argentine Confederation, having left there because he had just been elected president of the Republic. He had met with the emperor and came from a scientific demonstration. Two or three days later, he continued on to Buenos Aires.

The impression that man left on us was truly profound. In that fleeting vision of the president-elect, one might say that we glimpsed the future of the Argentine nation. (III, 1013; italics mine)

The scene is pure fiction. Machado and his friends look curiously at Sarmiento.

The Argentine returns their gaze, equally intrigued.

But for all this, they do not exchange so much as a word.

Or perhaps this is not the case. Machado and Sarmiento dialogued many times, unawares; both used their works to invent an alternative way out, turning the political circumstances they could not change into a productive aesthetic and intellectual factor.

◆　◆　◆

In the next century, another Argentine would reformulate Sarmiento's question. In the terms proposed by Ricardo Piglia in his study of the novels of Witold Gombrowicz, the question tackled by Machado and Eça returns once again:

What happens when one belongs to a secondary culture? What happens when one writes in a marginal language? . . . Here, Borges and Gombrowicz become more similar. We have only to recall one of the fundamental texts of Borges's poetics: "*The Argentine Writer and Tradition.*" What to say of tradition? . . . *How to become universal, in this suburb of the world?*[25]

These questions—and it would not be difficult to string together a host of quotations with similar inquiries—help to define the political repercussions of the poetics of emulation. Once again, they *have nothing to do with any outdated ontology of the periphery*, and simply refer to a concrete situation of inequality in cultural exchanges. The poetics of emulation brings together an array of techniques employed by intellectuals, writers, and artists involved in asymmetrical relations, and occupying the less-favored side of such exchanges—be they cultural, political, or economic in nature. Practices of emulation, however, are not the exclusive province of one context or another.

A striking manifestation of this phenomenon is that an incredible variety of authors appeal to the same semantic field when addressing the issue. In Milton Hatoum's story "Encontros na península" [Encounters on the Peninsula], a young, hard-up Brazilian writer is lucky enough to meet a Catalan woman looking to learn Portuguese quickly. The motive is somewhat peculiar: "'I don't want to speak it,' she said firmly. 'I want to read Machado de Assis.'"[16] This was a case of a tardy, but nonetheless delicious bit of revenge. Victoria Soller, a disciplined student, has ended her relationship with the Lisbon native Soares, a man obsessed with proving the superiority of the literature of Eça de Queirós. Predictably enough, the Catalan comes to disagree with her ex-lover. Her dialogue with her Portuguese teacher echoes Ricardo Piglia's question:

> It's clear that Machado's narrators are horrid, ironic, and all geniuses. And the man was cultured, as a matter of fact. Extremely cultured, *verdad*? The nineteenth century in France produced any number of great writers of prose. *But how could Machado de Assis have appeared in the suburbs of the world?*
>
> Mysteries of the suburbs, I said. Or perhaps of the *literature of the suburbs*. (105; italics mine)

From this perspective, Carpentier's reference to Rivera is crucial, and sheds light on the intersection between Piglia and Hatoum: *When Diego Rivera, a man in whom pulses the soul of the continent, tells us, "My master, Picasso."* Long after the advent of the Romantic revolution, the process of passing on the craft within painting schools preserved the model of *imitatio* and *aemulatio*, as aspiring painters would have to submit to intense training based on the diligent reproduction of canvases by the masters.

Picasso's trajectory is exemplary, and allows us to add depth to our reflection. He began his career by patiently learning the technique of his craft by copying masterpieces. Even in his most iconoclastic period, he continued to emulate tradition as well as contemporary colleagues, Matisse in particular.

Exactly like Virgil and Camões.

Precisely like Machado and Eça.

Shouldn't we recall Picasso's origins? A native of Málaga, a true center of the periphery, he traveled to Madrid—central in Spain, but a peripheral space in the artistic system—and then finally came to Paris, the center of the artistic world. In any case, he needed to adapt to this new environment before he could conquer it. A remarkable exhibition sought to do justice to this dimension of the Spanish painter's art. I am referring to the 2008 show "Picasso et les maîtres," which revolved around the idea of a new interpretation of the painter's oeuvre and, above all, his artistic strategies.

In a provocative essay, "Picaso cannibale: Deconstruction-reconstruction des maîtres," the curator suggests: "This painting of painting practiced by Picasso is, as I have said, a form of cannibalism."[17] In her vision, Picasso could only become an icon of twentieth-century art when he began to consciously appropriate tradition, in a double-edged process intrinsically tied into *imitatio* and *aemulatio*, comprising what I have called the poetics of emulation. This is how I have interpreted her observation that "one of the characteristics of this period is the use of repetition as a form of creation."[18] Now, *repeating in order to innovate* was the essence of classical technique. The most provocative inventors in nonhegemonic cultures, whether consciously or not, developed a strategy of updating aesthetic procedures that predated the Romantic idealization of the ideas of "genius," "subjectivity," and "creation."

In such a situation, a typical indulgence for creators of hegemonic cultures is the idle dispute to determine who is the most "original," in the effort to defend an impossible aesthetic primogeniture. In nonhegemonic cultures, for those who work with marginal languages, such a statement will take on an unintended comic tone. The originality bias may thus be swapped out for the development of textual complexity. Reading appears as the source of all invention, able to shatter hierarchies, conjure unexpected temporalities, and sometimes turn them on their head entirely.

After all, as Machado saw all too clearly, Virgil might well be seen as a Brazilian at Pedro II's court, or an Englishman in Victorian London. Everything rests on the radicality of one's reading. I recall the crônica from *A Semana*, published on November 11, 1894:

Antiquity surrounds me on all sides. And I am not put off by it. There is an aroma to it that, *even when applied to modern things, seems to touch on their essence. . . .*

Gladstone *is an old man and obstinately refuses to age.* An octogenarian, he might well content himself with the sweet career of Macrobius and only come to be published once he went to the cemetery. He does not want this; not he, and not Verdi. One writes operas, the other left Parliament with a cataract, had an operation on the cataract and published the *Aeneid* in English to show the English how Virgil would write in English, had he been English. *And is Virgil not English?* (III, 629; italics mine)

The *old man who obstinately refuses to age* is the image of the reverse anachronism that allows for the poetics of emulation to be formed. However, this is a two-way anachronism in a flow between a number of temporalities. In the same crônica, Machado adds a proviso: "I shook out the newspapers and came up to the window. Antiquity is excellent, *but one must rest a bit and breathe modern airs*" (III, 630; italics mine). It is as if nonhegemonic writers were always more *original* the more they *imitated* tradition and, at the same time, addressed the issues of their time. The paradox, as the reader already knows, is scarcely apparent.

One, Two, Three

As we have seen, the most prominent elements of the poetics of emulation are three in number: the distinction between *inventio* and *creatio*; the compression of historical periods; and deliberate anachronism. Other elements that stand out are the primacy of reading over writing and the centrality of translation.

Emphasis on the distinction between two verbs, which today are commonly used as synonyms. *Create*, from the Latin *creare*, implies producing something new at the very instant of creation: the utopian *creatio ex nihilo*, creating from nothingness (or, in the Romantic sense, creating exclusively from oneself). *Invent*, on the contrary, from the Latin *invenire*, implies a much more modest act, as it means to *find* or *discover*, often doing so by chance. To *invent* thus suggests the relevance of preexisting elements, which must be combined in new arrangements and relationships. It appears as if *inventio* is a matter of always setting up a new game, taking advantage of the pieces already set out on the board—to return to the chess match of words characteristic of *aemulatio*. The subtle semantic difference between the two verbs may give rise to equally different portraits of the two.

On one hand, when she imagines originality as *creatio*, the author is following in a Romantic model, imagining herself to be a true demiurge. On the other hand, when envisioning originality as *inventio*, the author is transformed into a keen reader of tradition through the recycling and rumination that lead to the celebration of "filiations," in the Oswaldian spirit, ensuring one's entry into the circle of tradition.

This understanding of invention casts it as a fundamental procedure in the poetics of emulation, given that its corollary allows for a valorization of reading's priority in relation to writing—and, in the case of nonhegemonic cultures, the centrality of translation in the development of one's own tradition.

To invent is to form a complex system that juxtaposes historical periods, literary genres, and conflicting interests. The experience of this simultaneity drives a view that sets literary craftsmanship apart, favoring the phenomenon of the "compression of historical times," a defining feature of nonhegemonic contexts.

Once one has accepted the necessary precondition of the juxtaposition of historical periods and literary genres, literature conceived in nonhegemonic conditions will inevitably include a number of different traditions simultaneously. In Piglia's words: "Secondary and marginal literatures, set apart from the great currents of Europe, have the opportunity to create a unique, 'irreverent' take on the great traditions" (73).

Such irreverence is stimulated by the compression of historical times, as the simultaneous presence of multiple historical periods leads to a welcome expansion of one's repertoire, characteristic of inventors in peripheral cultures. This broadening demands an effort toward synthesis that may *potentially* produce a particularly critical gaze. The keenness of this gaze is more than an individual trait—it is a structural fact.

The seemingly chaotic combination of centuries of tradition and different literary genres—to say nothing of the return to reading and writing practices characteristic of the pre-Romantic period—helps to reshape the critical

and theoretical aspects of the "deliberate anachronism" as outlined in Jorge
Luis Borges's famous short story, "Pierre Menard, Author of the *Quixote*."

As invention favors the compression of historical periods, this very
compression drives the effort to bring together periods that may be very different or far-flung, as well as the move to mix a variety of at times contradictory genres. This strategy gives rise to an effect discussed in the fiction of
the author of *El hacedor*. In the search for Pierre Menard's invisible oeuvre,
Borges intuited a new way to read:

> The technique of deliberate anachronism and fallacious attribution. That
> technique, requiring infinite patience and concentration, encourages us to
> read the *Odyssey* as though it came after the *Aeneid*, to read Mme. Henri
> Bachelier's *Le jardin du Centaure* as though it were written by Mme. Henri
> Bachelier. This technique fills the calmest books with adventure. Attribut-
> ing the *Imitatio Christi* to Louis Ferdinand Céline or James Joyce—is that
> not sufficient renovation of those faint spiritual admonitions?[19]

Deliberate anachronism is a form of reading that consists of the invention of new relationships within literary history. Such a method tends to
relativize the traditional hierarchy of the acts of writing and reading, suggesting an inversion with a clear elective affinity with Machado's innovations. In
this sense, his constant dialogue with the reader takes on another hue.

The time has come to show, *theoretically*, that while we are peripheral
and nonhegemonic, in the end this is precisely why we may undertake a radical rereading of the whole of tradition: and here lies the task of the poetics
of emulation.

And here we see the leap to *The Posthumous Memoirs of Brás Cubas*.

The same move may be found in the verses of Roberto Fernández Retamar. I recall his poem "¿Y Fernández?," in which he remembers his father:

> Como un raro, un viejo, un conmovedor Romeo de provincia
> (Pero también Romeo fue un provinciano).

> Like an odd, old, touching Romeo from the provinces
> (But Romeo, too, was a provincial).[20]

I would like to conclude this chapter here.

However, I will repeat that I do not seek to turn the poetics of emulation into a naive paean to the peripheral condition. Deep down, this outdated jingoism hobbles a more urgent consideration: if the poetics of emulation are so promising, why do the objective conditions of cultural hegemony remain indifferent to them?

A question pregnant with questions that would take us far along . . .

(Quite far indeed: I will return to this hurdle in the conclusion.)

CHAPTER 4

The Decisive Years

Machado de Assis also had his "break" around '79 (the year in which the first *Westerners* appeared in the *Revista Brasileira*). If the Master had died after the publication of *Iaiá Garcia*, in '78, he would have left an oeuvre in which poetry and prose were balanced at the same level of mediocrity. But at age forty came the "break." The *Westerners* were followed by *The Posthumous Memoirs of Brás Cubas* (81), *Loose Papers* (82) . . .

—Manuel Bandeira, "O poeta"

We may thus declare that Machado developed an original combination of Menippean satire with the autobiographical perspective of Sterne and Maistre, all the while highlighting certain philosophical elements. *Brás Cubas* is the novelistic philosophical tale in a comical tone, a moralist's manual set to a reveler's rhythm. In this book virtually no sentiment, belief, or behavior escapes corrosive derision or the spirit of satire and parody.

—José Guilherme Merquior, "Gênero e estilo das
Memórias póstumas de Brás Cubas"

What first claims the attention of the critic in the fiction of Machado de Assis is his heedlessness of the dominant styles and the apparent archaism of his technique. . . . Curiously, the archaism seemed brusquely modern, in the style of the vanguard in our century, which also tried to suggest the whole by the fragment, the structure by the ellipsis, emotion by irony, and grandeur by banality.

—Antonio Candido, "An Outline of Machado de Assis"

I would like to conclude by returning to the image of the glass and the wine, which Machado de Assis used to identify both that what his book had in common with its models and that which differentiated it from them: "The glass may be the work of the same school, but it bears another wine." As for the glass, the similar work makes it clear that all were produced by the same workshop. The mark is engraved into the crystal: this glass is of Shandean origin.

—Sérgio Paulo Rouanet, *Riso e melancholia*

There is great ambition in a writer who, over the course of his first books, tries out practically every genre made available to him by the literature of his time, including an opera libretto that has apparently not survived.

—José Luiz Passos, *Machado de Assis: O romance com pessoas*

1878: A Year Like No Other

The year 1878 was difficult for the writer Machado de Assis.

Difficult, but very prolific. Or perhaps difficult because it was so prolific.

In the indispensable *Bibliografia de Machado de Assis* compiled by José Galante de Sousa, the reader will find thirty-five entries dating from the year that *Cousin Bazilio* was published—not counting the novel *Iaiá Garcia*, apparently completed in September 1877 but published at the start of the following year. Galante de Sousa does not include it in the list of texts composed in 1878.

There is a bit of everything in this flurry of production from Machado.

From January 1 to March 2, he publishes *Iaiá Garcia* in *O Cruzeiro*. The model was more than familiar for Machadinho's loyal followers: a Benedictine work ethic and aesthetically Franciscan results. Even if we accept Galante de Sousa's dating, can we imagine that Machado published the novel without at least one last revision, simply casting his eyes over the final version of the manuscript? In this case, 1878 appears even more productive.

Meanwhile, a variety of other texts were constantly appearing in a number of vehicles.

For example, fantasies—signed with the pen name Eleazar—such as "O bote de rapé" [The Snuff Boat] and "A sonâmbula" [The Sleepwalker], which the author did not include in subsequent collections.

A few stories—highlights being "The Machete" and "Na arca" [On the Ark], the latter republished in *Loose Papers* (1882).

A waterfall of crônicas—signed with the pen names Manassés and, more commonly, Eleazar.

Not to neglect the sonnet "Círculo vicioso" [Vicious Circle], a fixture in anthologies, dated 1878 and published in the *Revista Brasileira* the following year. These verses may be read as an indirect meditation from the author on his personal impasses:

> The firefly danced in the air impatiently:
> "Oh how I wish that I could be that yellow,
> That burns in the eternal blue, a candle far!"
> And yet the star gazed on the moon with jealousy:
>
> "If only I could copy such transparency,
> Which, from the Grecian column to the Gothic sill,
> Has contemplated lovers' faces sighingly!"
> And yet the moon gazed on the sun with bitter will:
>
> "Oh misery! If I could be that giant ball,
> Immortal clarity, the sum of all that's light!"
> The sun, though, leans his brilliant chaplet o'er the wall:
>
> "I'm burdened by this numen's aureole bright . . .
> I'm wearied by this blue, unbounded parasol . . .
> Why could I not be born a firefly at night?"[1]

The vicious circle refers to the eagerness to copy the other so perfectly as to be confused with it, an impulse that inevitably puts rivalry at center stage. Perennially dissatisfied with what we are, we project onto the other—seen as an insuperable model—the image of the fullness that we lack. The French thinker René Girard called this desire to be the other "metaphysical," a paroxysm of mimetic desire. The circle closes in an eternal recurrence of the same: the distinction between the firefly and the sun is one of scale, not nature.

Similarly, in the realm of *aemulatio* one cannot avoid the obligation to imitate the *auctoritas* of the genre at hand. The circle only becomes vicious if it remains limited to a simple copy, or if it is reduced to pure envy. But not in psychological terms; recall Quevedo's comments on Aristotle's *Rhetoric*:

> Emulation is a certain pain provoked by the excellence that we see in another like us, and of which we judge ourselves capable; it does not cause pain because the other possesses it, but because we do not possess it as well. This is a noble pain, just as envy is vile and infamous.[2]

One does not yearn to be exactly what the other is, but to hone one's own abilities. Quevedo's synthesis may be better appreciated if we compare it to the original text. Aristotle analyzes emulation in book 2, chapter 11 of *Rhetoric*:

> Emulation is a pain at the apparent presence, in the case of those like us by nature, of honourable goods possible for ourselves, *not* because our neighbor possesses them, but because *we* do *not* possess them. Hence, Emulation is good and a mark of a good man, as envy is mean and a mark of a mean man, since the former, through his emulation, prepares himself to win the good things, while the latter, through his envy, aims at depriving his neighbor of them.[3]

The strong sense of emulation is clarified in the reference to *those like us by nature*—that is to say that we, too, may obtain that which they possess because, at least in principle, this is not a matter of talent alone, but also laying claim to tradition. Envy focuses on the other and its creations, while emulation depends on the possibility of perfecting an artistic model; this does not boil down to psychology, but rather the aim of mastering certain rhetorical techniques. Quevedo has perfectly incorporated the lesson and his summary preserves the goal of conquering *the excellence that we see in another like us, and of which we judge ourselves capable.* The psychological aspect is displaced by concerns of technique; and all are potentially equal, as one's capacity may be developed through careful study.

Imitation and emulation are vital for the poet, the writer, and the artisan; in their absence, one remains a *mere copyist.* Recall the semantic field of *augeo*—in Latin, "to increase." *Auctor* is also derived from *augeo.* The element of *aemulatio* is thus also foreseen in the very word that names the writer; the author is, at one extreme, an "increaser," as he, in the act of emulating, contributes to tradition and presents the possibility of other emulations.

This intuition becomes steadily more systematic for Machado in his articles on *Cousin Bazilio.* His vocabulary traces the gap between the *mere copyist* and the *man of talent.* I may suggest that the reader return to chapter 2, particularly the *"Aemulatio"* section, in which I discuss the systematic emergence of the idea of emulation in Machado's harsh critique. I will recall it here through a single quotation, which illuminates the semantic field I am reconstructing:

> Sr. Eça de Queirós is a *faithful and most severe disciple* of the realism propagated by the author of *Assommoir.* Had he been a *mere copyist,* the critic's duty would have been to leave him defenseless in the hands of the blind enthusiast, who would ultimately kill him; *but he is a man of talent,* who has just recently crossed the threshold of the *literary workshop.* (III, 904; italics mine)

In this light, Eça's calm reaction to the severe analysis from his Brazilian colleague takes on another meaning entirely. In a letter sent from England on June 29, 1878, in the effort to strike up a correspondence with Machado, the author of *Cousin Bazilio* chooses his diction carefully; and in thanking his interlocutor, he slips into what seems involuntary self-praise:

> I hoped to delay no further in thanking you for your excellent article of the sixteenth. Although opposed to me, and inspired in a practically political hostility towards the realist school—the article, by virtue of its distinction and the talent with which it was composed, *honors my book, almost increasing its authority.* Once I have read your other articles I will permit myself to

discuss your opinions on this one—not in my personal defense (as I do not merit one), not in defense of the grave defects of my novels, but in defense of the school that they represent and which I consider a superior factor in the moral progress of modern society. (227; italics mine)

The publication of *Cousin Bazilio* would transform Eça into the reigning *auctoritas* in Portuguese-language novels, a position he would maintain for a considerable time. His take on Machado's first article—that it *almost increases the authority* of his book—heralds the divergence between the two writers. Here, everything depends on the emphasis one puts on the terms of the phrase.

Almost—one might say, as Brás Cubas declares, that *the work in itself is everything.*

Or: *increasing its authority*—that is to say that the criticism contributes to the novel's success, especially in terms of the controversy it sparks.

Young Machado used identical terms in 1863 when he published two plays, *O caminho da porta* [The Path to the Door] and *O protocolo* [The Protocol]. In a letter to his friend Quintino Bocaiúva, we come across the key word:

> I will publish my debut comedies; and I do not wish to do so without consulting *your competence.* . . .
>
> But can that which was baptized on the stage with applause be transferred to paper without great inconvenience? Does not the difference between the two mediums of publication alter the judgment, changing the value of the work?
>
> It is in order to resolve these questions that I appeal to your *literary authority.* (III, 1028; italics mine)

Emphasis on Machado's understanding of the importance of a given medium in the transmission of literary experience, as well as the modern relevance of the question: *Does not the difference between the two mediums of publication alter the judgment, changing the value of the work?* Machado appears as a possible precursor for the contemporary idea of transmedia storytelling!

For the time being, however, I will repeat the point that the publication of *Cousin Bazilio* transforms Eça into an *auctoritas* in the world of the Portuguese-language novel.

In 1893, Valentim Magalhães—then director of *A Semana*—kicked off a competition with the following question: "What are the best six novels written in the Portuguese language?" In addition to the *Posthumous Memoirs*, Machado had published *Quincas Borba* two years earlier; but *Dom Casmurro* would have to wait another seven years, which put him in a relatively unfavorable position on the whole. Eça had already written some of his most renowned titles: *The Crime of Father Amaro* (1875), *Cousin Bazilio* (1878), *The Mandarin* (1880), *A relíquia* [The Relic] (1887), and *Os Maias* [The Maias] (1888). The competition was open, meaning that any person could send in his or her verdict to the newsroom. On September 23, the results were announced: *The Maias* was the grand champion with ninety-four votes; *Cousin Bazilio* had eighty-one supporters; *The Posthumous Memoirs of Brás Cubas* got sixty-four recommendations; *The Relic*, fifty; *The Hand and the Glove*, forty-nine; and, finally, *O Ateneu* [The Ateneu] rallied forty-one faithful readers.

Three novels by Eça, two by Machado and one nod to Raul Pompeia. The Portuguese writer's primacy was supreme. Of course, he also enjoyed similar prestige in Portugal.

A previous competition in Coimbra, in 1884, had sought to identify the three greatest writers in the Portuguese language; and the results were surprising, clarifying changes in prevailing literary tastes. In first place was Eça with 473 votes; runner-up went to Alexandre Herculano, with 202 followers; in third, unexpectedly, came Aluísio Azevedo, with a solid 195 votes; José de Alencar had 174 admirers; Machado was granted the consolation of fifth place and 164 votes; and, finally, Camilo Castelo Branco garnered 139 supporters.[4]

Such results are not always worth their weight; it would be a trivial mistake to consider them unassailable critical verdicts. However, they do shed light on the authority that contemporaries lent to Eça. This is why he seeks to open up a debate with Machado on realism, looking to pontificate on thorny ground. The terms of the letter are clear, and come with a slight ironic taste: "Total acceptance on the part of a literature so original and progressive as is Brazil's comes as an inestimable honor—for me and for realism, in the end, it is *a splendid confirmation of influence and vitality*" (228; italics mine).

The harshness of the criticism from Machado is a negative demonstration of the force of Queirós's aesthetic choices; the vehemence of his censure
sheds light on the movement's importance. Machado does not take the bait.
Even if he had once contemplated the possibility of continuing the dialogue,
one wrong step from Eça made such a conversation unlikely.

The wrong step seems to have been taken by his editor, Ernesto Chardron.
On July 27, he sends a letter thanking the author of *Helena*, and onto this
polite gesture he tacks a business proposal that one might judge imprudent,
at the very least. Chardron, with one eye on the Brazilian publishing mar-
ket, sends the letter along with the frontispiece to the new edition of *Cousin
Bazilio*, as well as the first edition of *The Capital*. The other side of the proofs
bore the following printed affirmation, drawn up before consulting Machado:

> We declare before the law that the literary property of this work in the
> Empire of Brazil, belongs to Sr. J. M. Machado de Assis.—Eça de Queirós—
> Ernesto Chardron. (229)

Beyond swallowing Eça's undeniable success, Machadinho was being
offered the job of literary agent for his younger colleague—the same one
who had *just recently crossed the threshold of the literary workshop*. The topic
was touchy, as few aspire to the role of second violin. Even a music lover
might spurn the suggestion.

Recall how Machado sought to justify the harshness of his analysis:

> One of my rivals accuses me of finding nothing good in *Cousin Bazilio*.
> He did not realize that, in addition to declaring the author's talent (which
> would be childish to deny) and recognizing his gift for observation, I noted
> the elegance of a few pages and the perfection of one of his characters. This
> does not strike me as denying everything to a book, *and to a second book at
> that*. (III, 909; italics mine)

To translate Machado's observation: Eça ought to be seen as a beginning
novelist, still lacking an oeuvre per se, the whole of which would justify his
immediate enshrinement. Admirers should check their haste, then, as the
Portuguese author was (still) green and had simply published *a second book*.

In the novel that Machado released amid this controversy, there is one character who may help us imagine his reaction upon reading the note from Eça and Chardron—the note, once again, drawn up without the Brazilian's consent to the terms proposed by the shrewd editor. In *Iaiá Garcia*, our eyes are drawn to a prideful dependent who reacts, as vigorously as possible in a patriarchal society, to the humiliations imposed by her position. In a decisive passage, Estela tries to explain to her father why she did not allow her protector's son to take certain liberties. Her response to her limited circumstances might be seen as a life's philosophy—that is, the exercise of a pragmatic code of ethics, when faced with an adverse environment (a project dear to Machado):

> Then she told him of Jorge's passion and the whole episode in Tijuca, the root cause of the events narrated in this book; she showed to him heatedly and eloquently that, in refusing to give in to Jorge's passion, she had sacrificed certain advantages to preserve her own decorum—a sacrifice made even more respectable by how much she had loved Valéria's son. What was she asking of her father now? *Very little, and very much*: she asked that he accompany her, that *he leave the life of dependence and servility that he had followed until then*; thus might he respect her and respect himself. Her father listened, dumbfounded. (I, 508; italics mine)

Meek Sr. Antunes does not understand his daughter: why risk the family's security by denying Jorge what was, essentially, his "right"? After all, *she had loved Valéria's son*.[5] Estela's own sense of dignity sheds light on the limits imposed by a legitimate sense of amour propre: she is a dependent, but she is not the property of her protector's son.

Machadinho describes Estela's brio with revealing sympathy. The business proposal from Eça and Chardron came at the worst possible moment; Machado never responded, although that is almost unnecessary to say.

The Portuguese writer felt the blow. Although we cannot establish a simple cause-and-effect relationship, the virulence of his first reply to Machado's criticisms is telling. As we saw in chapter 2, without the slightest pretensions of subtlety, Eça aggressively suggested that Machado has not read Zola's novel *Faute de l'Abbé Mouret*, writing that he "stumbled upon an advertisement for *Faute de l'Abbé Mouret in a French newspaper* or spotted it in a bookseller's window" (171; italics mine).

The sardonic reply would only be published in full after Eça's death. This, however, made little difference. In 1880, on the occasion of a new edition of *The Crime of Father Amaro*, Eça held nothing back. Here he is still visibly bothered by the accusation of plagiarism:

> The intelligent critics who accused *The Crime of Father Amaro* of being simply an *imitation* of the *Faute de l'Abbé Mouret had, unfortunately, not read the marvelous novel* by Mr. Zola, possibly the origin of all his glory. The chance similarity between the titles led them to err.
>
> Knowing the two books, *only corneal obtuseness or cynical bad faith* would allow one to liken this lovely, idyllic allegory, combined with the moving drama of a mystical soul, to *The Crime of Father Amaro*—which, as you may see in this new work, is, in the end, simply an intrigue between clerics and devout women woven and whispered in the shadow of an old cathedral in the Portuguese countryside.
>
> I would like to take this moment to thank the Criticism of Brazil and Portugal for all the attention it has devoted to my works. (I, 8; italics mine)

Corneal obtuseness or cynical bad faith: the torpedo had a specific target. The severe reader of *Cousin Bazilio* would need to blaze a new path.

Next, winter would descend in full blast.

At the end of the year—on December 27, to be precise—Machado, the model civil servant, takes a medical leave. An intestinal ailment and problems with his eyes demanded serious treatment. He and Carolina went to Nova Friburgo, only to return in March.

He returns recovered, and even plump. In a letter sent to José Veríssimo on December 1, 1897, he recalls this period, perhaps nostalgic for his old self: "I was pleased to hear what you had to say of the good effects of Nova Friburgo. I went to the place thin as a cadaver, some seventeen years ago, leaving quite fat, *ce qu' on appelle* fat, and will always recall the place fondly" (III, 1042). The topic returns in a letter from February 1, 1901, to the same friend: "Nova Friburgo is a blessed land. It was there that, after a long illness, I recovered my lost flesh and battered spirits" (III, 1055).

He had never traveled so far. Machado would return from Nova Friburgo in good spirits, and plump to boot. And, above all, as the author of the first version of *The Posthumous Memoirs of Brás Cubas*, partly dictated to Carolina during the periods when his eye problems prevented him from writing.

The year might have been difficult.

But its conclusion could not have been more favorable.

1879: Eve

The year 1879 was an even more crucial year for the development of my hypothesis.

First of all, a stark difference: in this period, Machado publishes just five pieces. Just like the future readers of the deceased author: *perhaps five*. He likely devoted most of his time to revising and producing the final version of the manuscript brought from Nova Friburgo.

But that is not all.

Within this slim production, the highlights are texts that work precisely with the semantic field of emulation, with its corresponding vocabulary: plagiarism, originality, imitation, and copy.

We have seen the study of the works of Antônio José, a text that serves as a true bridge between the critique of *Cousin Bazilio* and the Brás Cubas revolution. Thus, I would ask once again that the reader return quickly to chapter 2 and take another look at the eloquence of the terms employed in the long article dedicated to Judeu.

Even so, I will repeat a few passages in which Machado invokes the perspective of *aemulatio*:

> Comparing Antônio José's *Amphytrion* with those of his predecessors, one may see what he *imitated* of those models, and *what he introduced of his own line.* . . .
>
> While by this point the matter is not a situation or a new character but an idea woven into the dialogue, once again, even in *imitating* or *recalling*, the Jew remains faithful to his literary physiognomy; he may seek out *others' spices*, but only *to temper them with the sauce of his own production*. (II, 729 and 731; italics mine)

On the eve of the completion of the *Posthumous Memoirs*, Machado refines this method, leaning on the framework used to analyze Eça's work. This strategy would be fully developed in the note ("To the Reader") that opens the *Posthumous Memoirs*, as well as in the preface to the third edition of the novel, released in 1896.

There's still more.

Later in 1879—specifically, on October 15, in the *Revista Brasileira*—Machado published fragments of a text that is difficult to discuss: not because of its quality or lack thereof, but due to the surprising nature of his aesthetic choices. This is an atypical object that stands out from all the rest of his production over the course of a long career, starting with its inspiration. "The matter of this poem is strictly historical. . . . Such is the episode that I set myself out to commemorate, and which readers may find in volume 3 of the *Annals of Rio de Janeiro*, by Baltasar da Silva Lisboa" (III, 227).

This is the mock-heroic poem "O Almada" [Almada], a narrative poem recalling a truly laughable episode dating from 1659, in Rio de Janeiro. One comes to see that the anecdote must be this way for the heroic-comic genre to make sense, as it feeds off of the clash between epic diction and trivial subject matter.

The episode had already served as fodder for José de Alencar's *Alfar-rábios* [Old Books], published in 1873 and comprising three narratives, "O Garatuja" [The Scribbler] "O Ermitão da Glória" [The Hermit of Glória], and "Alma de Lázaro" [Soul of Lazarus]. In the first story, Alencar re-creates the story in the form of a novella written in satirical, almost picaresque prose.

Machado was the first author in the history of Brazilian literature to reflect systematically on the oeuvre of his contemporaries as well as embracing the whole of tradition, keeping himself reasonably up to date as to the foreign fiction of the time. Hence, his reworking of the old anecdote seems to be making a subtle statement. Machado appears to amend Alencar's literary gesture, insinuating that, given its truly cartoonish dimensions, the incident demanded the use of a genre already established by tradition—the mock-heroic poem—rather than a historical chronicle of the colonial period.

Machado's intervention remains an ironic one. In 1856, Alencar had his literary debut in the Segundo Reinado (1840–89) with a merciless attack on the epic poem "Confederação dos Tamoios," by Gonçalves de Magalhães. One of Alencar's main arguments had to do with the inadequacy of the epic as a genre in dealing with the material at hand. The next year, he published *O Guarani*. In Alencar's logic, prose had taken the place of poetry. In the case of "Almada," the mock-heroic poem takes the place of the historical chronicle.

The episode that served to inspire "Almada" may be summed up in two or three sentences.

These were the years of priest and administrative prelate Dr. Manoel de Sousa Almada. On one occasion, with apparently no motive, his servants attacked a notary public, who then appealed to general magistrate Pedro de Mustre. Over the priest's emphatic protests, an investigation was opened; and when the general magistrate refused to stop the proceedings, he was summarily excommunicated! General indignation was aroused by Dr. Almada's arbitrary revenge, the excommunication was suspended and the case sent to Lisbon.

(The curtain falls.)

The poem was never republished in book form by the author, or even published in full.

(Just as well.)

The poem doesn't even seem to justify the effort that went into composing it—not to mention the diligence demanded by the task of reading it. By way of demonstration, the opening verses ought to suffice:

Celebrate, muse, the wrath of Almada
Who Rio's church filled with awe.
And if for learned Boileau, for grave Elpino
You inspired songs, and for them you wove
With docile hands such immortal garlands,
Then pardon me if I dare to undertake
A task of such scale. (III, 230; italics mine)

The reader may identify the spirit of *aemulatio* in the highlighted verses, as the model to be followed is respectfully announced; this does not raise the lines above their clear mediocrity. And what to say of the conclusion?

Thus proclaiming, vanishes the figure
(Who was no more nor less than Sloth).
Then the startled curates
To the ground throw themselves, and beating
Nine times their chests, nine times
The hard ground kissing in tears,
Plead to the sky that from the eternal books
The barbarous decree be scratched. (III, 282)

This would be the tone expected from a mock-heroic poem, where the deliberately cartoonish effect stems from the mismatch between noble diction and common subject matter. Even so, how to understand the appearance of "Almada" on the eve of the *Posthumous Memoirs*? Can we imagine the deceased author alongside the verses: "Plead to the sky that from the eternal books / The barbarous decree be scratched"?

The "Note" allows us to clear up the enigma:

I observed insofar as possible the rules of the genre, being to *parody the tone, style, and proportions of epic poetry*. In Canto IV I dared to *imitate* one of the most beautiful pages in antiquity, the episode of Hector and Andromache, from the *Iliad*. . . .

Dinis did not stop at the single *imitation* quoted. He made many of the *Iliad*, which I have not seen remarked on by anyone to this day, *perhaps because they were overlooked*. I will summarily point them out. . . .

Now I will say that it is not some timidity that I publish this book. In its genre there are primarily two celebrated compositions that served me as *models*, but which *are truly inimitable, Lutrin* and *O Hissope*. A bit of ambition, however, led me to set myself to the task and persevere at it. This was not to *compete* with Dinis and Boileau; I am not so presumptuous. . . .

Given this explanation—necessary for some, idle for others—I will deposit my books in the hands of the critics, asking that they frankly point out that which merits *correction*. (III, 228–29; italics mine)

In the last passage, we see an echo of the preface to *Resurrection*:

The critics will decide whether the work corresponds to the aim, and, principally, if the laborer is suited for it.

This is what I ask, with heart in hand. (I, 116)

But we are privy to a change in the author's tone. Offering something *with heart in hand* is one thing; asking for a frank and possibly merited *correction* is another. This correction, moreover, may only be made by the reader—and this leap will structure the essence of Machado's prose in the second phase.

Machado rewrites himself countless times until hitting upon the diction that will enshrine his work.

The mention to critical authorities defines the framework within which "O Almada" must be understood: *two celebrated compositions that served me as models, but which are truly inimitable,* Lutrin *and* O Hissope.

Boileau's poem in six cantos, *Le Lutrin*, composed from 1674 to 1683, is an unavoidable authority in the genre. In it, two priests delve into an infinite discussion as to the best position to place a lectern—an entertaining pretext to clarify where the author falls in the dispute between ancient and modern thinkers. Boileau's poem served as a model for António Dinis de Cruz e Sousa in composing *O Hissope*, published posthumously in 1802. The Portuguese poet's work, just like that of his Brazilian follower, would make use of a historical episode presented in a mock-heroic mold.

Machado's note reveals a full understanding of the history of the genre. Moreover, it displays a deliberate use of pre-Romantic discursive practices. His knowledge in this field manifests itself in the vocabulary associated with the semantic field of emulation: *parody the tone, style, and proportions of epic poetry.*

Naturally, I am not proposing that definitive conclusions be drawn from passages such as those extracted from the note to "Almada." Nevertheless, Machado's vocabulary here does feed into my hypothesis. His reference to the *imitations* executed by António Dinis that were only not identified *perhaps because they were overlooked* implies the key element in the technique of emulation: a circuit in which production and reception share an identical repertory. The classical technique of *aemulatio* functions on fixed models, albeit multiple ones; the modern and deliberately anachronistic practice of emulation enjoys greater liberty, even aided by the progressive collective forgetting of that very repertoire. However, in both cases, the direct quotation from or allusion to classical sources is the defining move in literary art, revealing one's link to tradition—a *copious* source of imitable models, texts hence ripe to be emulated. Ironic intentions should not be neglected here: how many contemporary readers must have noticed the link between Alencar's prose and Machado's poem?[6]

A *copious* tradition, I said.

The word "copy" bears an etymology that is practically forgotten nowadays. In Latin, *copy* evokes a plurality of meanings: "abundance, power, wealth, faculty, license, permission." The full meaning of "copious" may only be found in the pre-Romantic literary system. *Abundance*, in and of itself, authorizes *license, permission* to reproduce the *wealth* contained in the model. This *faculty*, however, may only come to fruition once *imitation* adds new elements to the source. To reduce the term *copy* to the mere reproduction of the same would mean reducing it to a vulgar sense only dominant in post-Romantic vocabulary. From the perspective of *aemulatio* this semantic reduction would be reprehensible; this would mean losing the chance to enrich the original that lies at the heart of emulation.

In the prologue to the third edition of *Quincas Borba*, Machado justifies his decision to not dedicate an entire novel to Sofia Palha, the immediate cause of Rubião's ruin: "Sofia is entirely contained here. To continue with her would be to repeat her, and *repeating the same may well be a sin*" (I, 642; italics mine). Repetition *and* difference: this is the leitmotif of the technique of *aemulatio*. As has already been clarified, *imitatio* is not an end in and of itself, but it is the first step in a technique that comes to fruition in the indispensable *aemulatio* of the chosen *auctoritas*-model.

Machado turns to the classical sense of the noun on a few occasions. In the short story "On the Ark," published in *O Cruzeiro* on May 14, 1878, and reproduced in *Loose Papers* (1882): "And only with great effort could Noah, Ham, and the wives of Shem and Japeth contain the two combatants, whose blood began gushing *copiously* [em grande *cópia*]" (II, 307; italics mine).

In "O segredo de Bonzo" [Bonzo's Secret], a story published in the *Gazeta de Notícias* on April 30, 1882, and also included in *Loose Papers*, the word returns twice more: "And I say the news of the week because these pages are drawn up every eight days, *in great copiousness* [em grande *cópia*]" (II, 307; italics mine). Shortly thereafter: "The assembly acclaimed Diogo Meireles; and the afflicted began seeking him out *in such copious numbers* [em tanta *cópia*] that he had no hands free to measure them" (II, 328; italics mine).

The equivalence between *copy* and *abundance* is revealing, above all in the two stories at hand. Machado follows Lucian's lesson closely and parodies both biblical language and the sixteenth-century style of Fernão Mendes Pinto.

Back to literary chess.

Every player of a certain level must copy long-standing strategies—the Caro-Kann Defense, for example, one of the most solid defensive systems for the player using black. The first sequence of moves will necessarily repeat countless other matches. However, *and precisely because of this*, as the middle game approaches, the conceivable variants become truly incalculable. The dynamics of a system of combinatorial art oscillate between these two poles: on one side, predictability, and on the other, improvisation.

In a commemorative note meant to pay tribute to the bookseller Garnier, published in October 1893 and reproduced in *Gathered Pages* (1899), Machado defines the famous establishment: it was "a place for conversation and encounters" (II, 654). In characterizing the space, Machado's use of the noun once again evokes Latin etymology:

> It would be unnecessary to recall what this bookstore was, *so copious and so varied*, in which there was everything from theology to novellas, the classical book, the recent composition, science, imagination, morality, and technique. (II, 655; italics mine)

Picking out this vocabulary reveals how Machado's literary project began progressively mixing a variety of time periods, both in the juxtaposition of styles and periods and in the careful recycling of terms, whose spectrum of meanings had been reduced by the Romantic revolution. This method, one might add, was defined by Machado.

In chapter 1, I mentioned the idea of resuscitating the triolet, *"without scorning the older models"* (III, 181; italics mine).

Let us examine the recurrence of the principle in the critical essay "A nova geração" [The New Generation], published in the *Revista Brasileira* on December 1, 1879, literally on the threshold of the Brás Cubas revolution. This is how he references the use of Alexandrine verse in Brazilian poetry:

> French influence is still visible. . . . This is not new in our tongue, or even new to us; since Bocage a few attempts have been made to *acclimate* it;

Castilho worked it in with great perfection. The objections that one may raise as to the Alexandrine verse's foreign origins are feeble and without value. Literary theories become worn, but *literary forms must be renewed as well.* What else did the Romantics do from 1830 to 1840, if not *seek out and rejuvenate a number of archaic forms?* (III, 814; italics mine)

Machado ably turns the spell against its caster. Despite their defense of the aesthetics of creation and their praises of the genius as the demiurge of himself, the Romantics themselves (in Machado's view) resorted to the very techniques at the foundation of the poetics of emulation, a factor that becomes especially relevant in the case of Brazilian Romantic poetry. And so, if *literary forms must be renewed*, why not accomplish this through a move already quite familiar to the reader: *seek out and rejuvenate a number of archaic forms?* In a typically Machadian twist, romanticism is seen as an unexpected counterfeit of the literary system that Romantic values themselves relegated to perennial ostracism.

The constant use of the verbs "transplant" and "acclimate" should be understood in the same tenor. This is why *the objections that one may raise as to the Alexandrine verse's foreign origins are feeble and without value.*

Of course! Nationalistic prejudice, elevated to the status of literary criterion, became normalized under romanticism. Only then did literary history move to define itself in terms of national determination. In the pre-Romantic context, *acclimate* and *transplant* were verbs that denoted a precise action as essential as it was codified, as one inevitably started out by working with another's repertory in the process of developing one's own work.

We must note, however, that Machado also used the verb in a different sense, one still shackled to the Romantic spirit—and thus contrary to my argument. Here I am referring to his first critical texts.

In "The Past, Present, and Future of Literature," a long article published in two installments in *A Marmota* on April 9 and 23, 1858, the young critic is a perfect model for the style of the period. He even deplores authors' use of French literature, following a line of reasoning that the 1879 essay turns upside down:

Few, a very few, have set themselves to studying such an important form as the novel; even despite *our pernicious contact with French novels*, which examines, applauds, and enshrines our youthfulness, with so few scruples about *wounding national susceptibilities*. (III, 788; italics mine)

This is just as we saw in the previous chapter, in the essay "Ideas on the Theater" from the same period, where the verb *transplant* took on a pejorative sense in that it suggested little attachment to the traits of the nation. Here the same reserve takes on a moralistic hue, as *national sensibilities* also include the rejection of realism and naturalism.

An identical sense of the word had been employed in the 1858 article, in a discussion around the virtual absence of a thriving Brazilian theater:

Transplanting a French dramatic concept into our language is a task that any biped versed in cursive may attempt. And what comes of this? Exactly what we have before us. Art has become an industry; and with the exception of half a dozen successful attempts, our theater is a fable, *a utopia*. (III, 789; italics mine)

The act of *transplanting* a foreign idea results in the fanciful nature of *our theater*. The young critic's specificity ought to be noted here: as *to acclimate* necessarily implies starting out with a foreign object, through the grafting on of plants from a variety of climates, this makes it such that the *place itself* may not be constituted; hence, given the predominance of the French style, Brazilian theater becomes an involuntary metonym for *utopia*.

Two decades after this predictable judgment, the *same* author will defend the use of the French Alexandrine in local poetry: after all, *the objections that one may raise as to the Alexandrine verse's foreign origins are feeble and without value*. Indeed, my efforts here seek to shed light on the gap between these two authors.

Two authors, I said; that was no typo.

To insist on the rigorous unity of an author who moves through clearly different, and at times completely opposite, stages—isn't this ultimately a hermeneutical magic trick?

The critic ought to accompany the metamorphoses of an author instead of imposing easy labels, tautologically justified in the comforting shadow of a single proper name.

I will offer a symptomatic example of the use of this semantic field from the well-intentioned author of the *Chrysalids*. Let me present a long collage of quotations from "The Feuilletonist," published in *O Espelho* on October 30, 1859.

> One *European plant* that has rarely acclimated among us is the feuilletonist.
>
> Whether this is a defect of its organic properties or an *incompatibility with the climate*, I cannot say. I am simply stating the truth.
>
> Nevertheless, I said—*rarely*—which supposes *at least one case of serious acclimation*. As for that which falls outside this exception, the reader has already seen that it is born stunted, with stingy proportions.
>
> The feuilletonist is native to France, where it was born, and where it lives at its leisure, as if in bed during the wintertime. From there it spread across the world, or at least where the great vehicle of the modern spirit took on greater proportions; and here I speak of the newspaper. . . .
>
> In the feuilletonist's appreciation for the local element, I fear that I may fall out of favor by denying the affirmative. I shall simply confess certain exceptions. In general, the feuilletonist here is utterly Parisian; he bends to a strange style, and tends to forget, in his ruminations on the *boulevard and the Café Tortoni*, that he is standing on a muddy macadam street, with a thick lyrical tent pitched in the middle of the desert.
>
> Some go to Paris to study the physiological aspects of their colleagues over there; needless to say, they have degenerated physically as well as morally.
>
> It must be said: national color, in extraordinarily rare exceptions, has overtaken the feuilletonist among us. *To write feuilletons and remain Brazilian is truly difficult.*
>
> However, as all difficulties level out, he might well take on more local color, more of an American likeness. Then he might do less harm to the independence of the nation's spirit, so shackled to these *imitations*, these mimicries, this *suicide of originality and initiative*. (III, 958–60; italics mine)

This is a provocative text, to be ruminated step by step.

The first part of the passage leans on an organicist vocabulary, based on the opposition between native soil and plants that are not merely intruders, but also resist adaptation. The effort itself seems useless, as the results generally boast *stingy proportions*, something like a garden irremediably past its bloom. In Machado's understanding, the feuilleton—come from France—may be seen as one of the first cases of the systematic exportation of an artistic fashion, made international with the help of a powerful means of communication: *the great vehicle of the modern spirit; and here I speak of the newspaper.*

Despite the conventional and even conservative nature of young Machado's observations, his association between a particular form of communication (the newspaper) and the internationalization of an aesthetic form (the feuilleton) merits attention, as his intuition remains fresh. This is the thrust of another article, also from 1859—"The Newspaper and the Book"—released in the *Correio Mercantil* in two parts on January 10 and 12, dedicated "to the Sr. Dr. Manuel Antônio de Almeida." The author of the *Memórias de um sargento de milícias* [Memoirs of a Militia Sergeant] had been Machado's protector when he became a typographer's apprentice at the Imprensa Nacional. Why not pay him a simple homage? Such a gesture of gratitude would surely earn the approval of Sr. Antunes . . .

Bursting with enthusiasm, young Machado does not hesitate to defend the emergence of a medium of communication able to eclipse all predecessors: "The newspaper is more than a book, closer to the nature of the human spirit. Does it nullify the book as the book will nullify the page of stone? I am not loath to admit it" (III, 946).

In this passage, Machado is alluding to a famous work by Victor Hugo. Indeed, a character from *The Hunchback of Notre Dame* summed up the revolution sparked by the Gutenberg Galaxy in a famous turn of phrase. Archdeacon Dom Claude compares the printed book with the cathedral, concluding pessimistically: "'Alas!' he said, 'this will kill that.'"[7] The book would destroy the building.

The definitive edition of Victor Hugo's novel dates from 1832. The narrative, however, takes place in 1482—just a few decades after the advent of movable type. The narrator himself justifies the archdeacon's suspicion: "It was the pulpit and the manuscript, the spoken and the written word, taking fright at the printed word" (192).

The priest's melancholy may help us understand that pointing out the obvious error in his prediction is less important than observing Machado's opening up to the vision of the book as not a definitive medium closed in on itself, but rather one subject to the modifications of contemporary history.

This sense remains current and relevant, although it was not developed within the traditional framework of commentaries on the adaptation of the feuilleton.

The second part of the passage reiterates his condemnation of *these imitations, these mimicries, this suicide of originality and initiative.* The rejection of the French style is a reverse affirmation of a nationalist project, supported during the same period for Brazilian theater. Thus, *to write feuilletons and remain Brazilian is truly difficult.*

However, amid a thicket of predictable turns of phrase, the young critic threatens to surprise us. While the feuilletonist at Dom Pedro II's court seems to have successfully adopted the foreign form, he still *tends to forget, in his ruminations on the boulevard and the Café Tortoni, that he is standing on a muddy macadam street.* As he waxes rhapsodic on the beauties of the City of Light, his shoes are sunk in dirt; the elegant prose of one who lets his pen run across the page is met unexpectedly with the misaligned jolt of *a thick lyrical tent pitched in the middle of the desert.* Something seems not to fit this new framework of the acclimated feuilleton, although the young critic can only perceive this misalignment in a minor, almost caricatured key. He identifies the break only to condemn it, falling back on the centuries-spanning cliché that casts the tropics as a desert for men and ideas alike.

(The deceased author's greatest conquest, meanwhile, lies precisely in converting this misalignment into a compositional principle. If one composes feuilletons in the shadow of *a thick lyrical tent pitched in the middle of a desert* and is only met by the "airs of Paris," in Brás Cubas's words, then an entire corrosive worldview hangs on the development of this contrast.)

Unearthing this side of young Machado is important, because it reveals that the study of the semantic fields of his literature does not always bolster my hypothesis.

The literature of an ur-author tends to rise above critical formulations, as the potential plurality of its meanings hobbles any attempt to cramp an oeuvre into a one-note interpretation.

Still, critical efforts may be equally creative. For this to be the case, criticism must reconstruct the internal processes behind fictional creation, feeding into an investigation of literature itself, something not necessarily found on the surface of the work at hand.

Time to finish our examination of "O Almada."

A consultation of the notes included alongside the poem allows us to read it with fresh eyes, now with a new understanding of what seemed an extemporaneous exercise.

Machado displays his *filiations*, as Oswald would put it, in exemplary fashion. In Canto I, the third stanza recalls the swallows' perennial flight from one continent to the other:

> Just as the Christian soothsayer who the martyr heroes
> Sang piously, passing one day
> Through the ancient Greek land, rallying in a band
> The very birds, he contemplated they who once,
> Tearing as then through the blue space,
> Went from the Ilisos to African shores. (III, 231)

The note identifies the model for the last two verses: "Chateaubriand alludes twice to the migration of swallows from Greece to Africa. Once in the *Itinerary*, part I . . . [and] in the *Martyrs*, Canto XV" (III, 317). Falling back on the authority of the French poet legitimizes the Brazilian's use of the reference, in a repetition that emulates the model being adopted. This model, meanwhile, will be turned upside down by the irreverence of Brás Cubas and his deliberately inappropriate comparisons—not the least of which being the very prose of the deceased author, an absolutely singular update on the interminable *Mémoires d'outre-tombe*, to say nothing of Lucian's *Dialogues of the Dead*.

Machado notes a similar usage in the case of José de Alencar, reviewing Alencar's novel *Iracema* in the heat of the moment, in an article published in the *Diário do Rio de Janeiro* on June 23, 1866 (the year after the book's release). Machadinho compares Alencar's tale to a famous title by Chateaubriand; after all, extremely similar episodes feature in both stories. This is the moment in which Celuta, the indigenous wife of René, reveals her pregnancy. In *Iracema*, Martim also discovers that he is to be a father. Here is the young critic's analysis:

Iracema will reveal this good news to Martim; there is an identical scene in the *Natchez*, and we may permit ourselves to compare it to that of the Brazilian poet.

When René, as the poet of the *Natchez* tells us, was certain that Celuta bore a child in her breast, he drew close with sacred respect and embraced her delicately, so as to do her no harm. "'Wife,' said he, 'heaven blessed your entrails.'"

The scene is certainly lovely; it is Chateaubriand who speaks to us; *but the scene in* Iracema *is, to our eyes, more felicitous.* The wild Ceará native appears before Martim's eyes, adorned with maniva flowers, clasps his hand, and says to him:

"Your blood already lives in Iracema's breast. She will be mother to your child."

"A child, you say?" exclaimed the Christian joyfully.

He knelt there, and, encircling her with his arms, kissed his spouse's fecund womb. (III, 851; italics mine)

It would be foolish to imagine that Machado lets himself be carried away by a limited critical nationalism in his evaluation of Alencar's scene as superior. Indeed, the dialogue between man and wife is more suggestive than the omniscient narration in the *Natchez*. To say nothing of Alencar's linguistic work; he introduced a Tupi-Guarani diction into the Portuguese language, comprising an extremely lively literary language, as we may glean from the contrast between Iracema's lyrical simplicity and the direct tone of Martim's question. Furthermore, the author of *O Guarani* always recognized Chateaubriand as the ultimate authority in developing an "American poetry." Young Machado considers the possibility that the imitation of a model may be artistically superior, but has still not understood the technical dimensions of *aemulatio*. He would need another few years before fully incorporating this intuition as a founding literary principle.

This is precisely what happens in "Almada."

Let us turn to another note.

In Canto II, stanza 8, the verse "For the arm of great Almada to stretch" (III, 235) merits the following justification: "*Espraiar o braço* [the arm to stretch] is a translation of *épanouir la rate*—not mine, but by Filinto Elísio" (III, 319). Like a poetic sampler or a precursor of "uncreative writing,"

Machado incorporates another's translation, without any distinctive features, into his own poem. This is the crucial point. Moving beyond the traditional form of allusion or citation, the author of "Almada" takes radical control over the other's words. The reader who skips over the note or happens not to know the works of Filinto Elísio will consider Machado the *creator* of the verse "For the arm of great Almada to stretch." To the benefit of his poetic *invention*, Machado adopts the criterion he once used to examine the theater of Antônio José: the foreign as a condiment for the homespun.

The simple move to compose a mock-heroic poem sheds light on the path that Machado would radicalize with *The Posthumous Memoirs of Brás Cubas*. This seems to be the most fruitful way to understand poetic composition within a forgotten form.

On one hand, the genre calls for the use of sublime language and a literary structure similar to that of the epic, the use of rich metaphors and the development of sharp-witted conceits; but the topic of the poem must be banal or even farcical. The obvious mismatch between epic form and trivial content is the source of the comic imbalance, the genre's dominant tone. Doesn't the strength of the *Posthumous Memoirs* also stem from similar disproportions? Remember the truly laughable comparison between the deceased author's narrative and the Pentateuch! The method is woven into the fabric of the book and remains a hallmark of the novels from the second phase, short stories, and crônicas. "Almada" thus regains a place in the pantheon of Machado's production—albeit as a warm-up exercise, where the author stretches his muscles before undertaking a more serious challenge.

Aemulatio and the Reading Public

On the other hand, this exercise highlights the true bridge from *imitatio* to *aemulatio*, based on the constant recycling of tradition—an irreverent recycling, which spurs a sense of desacralization typical of Machado's finest style. Here lies the most productive aspect of the return to the mock-heroic.

Let me explain.

A heroic effort from a representative of literature produced in one of the suburbs of the world (to recall the terms used by Ricardo Piglia and Milton Hatoum), as part of an attempt to tackle the whole of tradition: this must inevitably have a comic edge to it, as if there were a structural asymmetry between one's circumstances and one's aesthetic project. This subject will reappear in countless of Machado's stories, crônicas, and even in his poetry.

Indeed, Machado may be seen to sample with the freedom of some of today's hip-hop stars, especially in his poetry. This attitude will be heralded from the start of his production.

In the poem "Minha mãe" [My Mother], published in *Marmota Fluminense* on September 2, 1856, and never reproduced in book form, the reader is informed straight out that this is an "Imitation of Cowper." The young author may well have been alluding to the well-known poem "On the Receipt of My Mother's Picture" by William Cowper, a staple in anthologies of the period. In an echo of the classical form, painting and poetry come together in the formula of an "imitation of . . ."

In the decades that follow, the technique will be perfected.

In *Phalaenae*, Machado's second book of poetry, released in 1870, we find "Uma ode de Anacreonte" [An Ode by Anacreon], a theatrical text in Alexandrine verse (and we have already been privy to his verdict on the French origin of the form). At one point, a poem by Anacreon is read. At the end, the reader is invited to consult this revealing clarification:

> Sr. Antônio Feliciano de Castilho is the author of the translation of this little ode, which led to the composition of my tableau. It was immediately after reading the *Lírica de Anacreonte*, from the immortal author of *Ciúmes do Bardo*, that I had the idea to put into action the ode from the poet of Teos, sprung so Portuguesely from the hands of Sr. Castilho that *it seems more original than translation*. (III, 181; italics mine)

The importance of translation in Machado's oeuvre is widely known, reinforcing the centrality of the translator's task in the construction of canon in nonhegemonic cultures. In a sense, to translate and to acclimate are related actions. Many of Machado's verses came from the appropriation of translations. His first book—"this little worklet," as *A Marmota* announced in June 1861—was the translation of a "satire in prose," *Queda que as mulheres têm para os tolos* [The Liking that Women Take to Fools]. Take the case of "Lira chinesa" [Chinese Lyre], also from *Phalaenae*, comprising eight short poems. Machado's explanation is as follows:

The poets imitated in this collection are all contemporaries. I found them in
the book published in 1868 by Mrs. Judith Walter, a distinguished traveler
said to possess a profound knowledge of the Chinese language, and who
has *translated them in simple and common prose*. (III, 181; italics mine)

Later in the same book, Machado offers up his version of Friedrich
Schiller's "The Gods of Greece." His lack of contact with the original is not
an insuperable obstacle. "I do not know German; I translated these verses
through *the translation in French prose* by one of the most well-regarded
interpreters of the language of Schiller" (III, 316; italics mine). Machado
takes a variety of paths: from original to translation, *which seems more original*, and from prose to poetry. Origin does not matter; what takes preference
is the lyrical inspiration that the poet gathers indiscriminately.

In *Americanas* [Americans], a book released in 1875, the reader will find
"Potira," a narrative poem that reiterates the move to sample others' poetry.
The verses

Deep hollow
Of the earth, that common mother, open in her breast,
Embraces and protects them (III, 102; italics mine)

demonstrate his ability in the art of casting old clothes as a new outfit. In a
discreet note, Machado reveals his source:

See G. Dias, Últimos cantos, 159:
. . . When my body
To *the earth, that common mother* . . . (III, 182; italics mine)

Nothing more is said; the reader is simply shown the authority being
honored in the recycling of his work. The same book includes "Cantiga do
rosto branco" [Song of the White Face], where Machado clarifies:

This composition is not original; the original itself is indigenous. It belongs
to the tribe of the Mulcogulges, and was translated from their tongue by
Chateaubriand (*Voyage dans l'Amérique*). Those savages were renowned as
poets and musicians, as were our Tamoios. . . . The celebrated ode is the

composition that I have transported to our language. The title in the *prose translation* by Chateaubriand is—*Chanson de la chair blanche*. (III, 316; italics mine)

Machado eagerly takes advantage of the *prose translation* of a poem, looking to retranslate it poetically even in the absence of any knowledge of the original tongue. Given the frequency of this practice, we might call it a method. Emphasis on the fluid processing that Machado uses on his models. Today's young people consider themselves *creators* in a new sense, mixing rhythms, lyrics, and any number of art forms in new arrangements. Machado already had a truly *inventive*, inexhaustible mechanism at his disposal: the realm of *aemulatio*.

Here is the most complete translation of the circuit:

Homer and Virgil have *served mock-heroic poets on more than one occasion.* Let us not speak of Ariosto or Tassoni here. In *Le Lutrin*, Boileau *parodied* the episode of Dido and Aeneas; Dinis *followed in his footsteps* in the dialogue between Gonçalves the scrivener and his wife, and both did so in a situation analogous to the episode *in which I imitated the immortal scene by Homer.* (III, 228; italics mine)

We have come back to the circle between the firefly and the sun; but it is no longer vicious.

Homer is the ultimate authority in the epic. Virgil imitated him, and did so with such skill that he also became an *auctoritas.* Hence, both have necessarily *served mock-heroic poets on more than one occasion.* It could not be otherwise; they provide the inevitable starting-point for those seeking to parody the epic. Why would Machado not imitate Boileau, if Dinis himself *followed in his footsteps?* Even his vocabulary is a sort of resurrection of pre-Romantic forms and terms. Recall Lucian's words from the previous chapter: "So the only attraction in my work is that it is unusual, and does not follow the *beaten track*" (94; italics mine)

One must follow the path blazed by the masters in order to refine one's technique. This is because the reading public will ideally be familiar with the authoritative works at hand, and will demand that the apprentice poet display the fruits of his studies through allusions or even direct citations.

In this sense, the definition of an "instinct of nationality" takes on a new hue. Machado may have been thinking of the indissociable bond between effective readers and potential authors—and in that order. This is why he gives writers a particular task:

> Whoever examines current Brazilian literature will recognize in it imme-diately, as its principal characteristic, a certain instinct of nationality. Poetry, novels, all the literary forms of thought seek to dress themselves in the colors of the nation, and there can be no denying that such a concern is a symptom of the vitality and abundance of the future. The traditions of Gonçalves Dias, Porto Alegre and Magalhães *are thus continued* by the generation already formed and the next which is still stirring, *just as those past continued* the traditions of José Basílio da Gama and Santa Rita Durão. (III, 801; italics mine)

At first glance, the passage seems to align itself automatically with the nationalistic drive that defined the main thrust of nineteenth-century litera-ture. After all, not only do *all the literary forms of thought seek to dress them-selves in the colors of the nation*, but this trait is also *a symptom of the vitality and abundance of the future.* However, the next sentence allows for a different interpretation, or at least introduces some nuances. To an extent, the *colors of the nation* are defined by the hues of the spines of countless books, and not by a faithful portrait of the landscape.

The "instinct of nationality" remains the conscious drive towards the development of a textual corpus via the confection of an imaginary library. This is a remarkable chain of readers, carrying on a common tradition that comes into focus just as the circle starts to fail. Machado glimpses the promise of a virtual universe of authors to be formed around a repertoire of shared readings. This perspective would authorize a new take on that famous definition: "What one ought to demand from the writer above all is *a certain intimate sentiment*, which makes him a man of his time and his nation, even when dealing with matters distant in time and space" (III, 804; italics mine). That *certain intimate sentiment*, if I am not forcing my hand, also echoes in the collective memory constructed—at least partially—around the library. Machado justifies his stance by calling upon the authority he respects above all: "And I shall ask if *Hamlet, Othello, Julius Caesar,* or *Romeo and Juliet* have anything to do with English history or the British territory, and if, nevertheless, Shakespeare is not both a universal genius but also an essentially English poet as well" (III, 804).

The last page of the essay is remarkable, offering a masterful synthesis of my project:

> With due exceptions, the classics are not widely read in Brazil. Among those exceptions, I might name a few writers whose opinions diverge from mine on this point, but who know the classics perfectly. In general, however, they are not read, which is a literary ill. *To write like Azurara or Fernão Mendes would be an unbearable anachronism today.* Each time has its style. But studying the most refined forms of language, *extracting a thousand riches from them, which by virtue of their age are made new*—I cannot find a reason to scorn this. The ancients did not have everything, nor do the modern; with the riches of one and the other, we *enrich the common purse.* (III, 809; italics mine)

This text was written in 1873. The year before, Machado had published *Resurrection*, and he would release *The Hand and the Glove* in the next year. Read in isolation, the passages I have underlined here do not seem conclusive, as the two novels in question were far from shaping an innovative understanding of the technique of *aemulatio*. However, within the context I have been building, the idea of studying the classics takes on a special power—this is a way of *extracting a thousand riches, which by virtue of their age are made new*, the very technique that leads to the leap of the *Posthumous Memoirs*.

The literal reproduction of forms from the past produces an *unbearable anachronism*—this, nobody is questioning. However, the return to pre-Romantic literary practices in post-Romantic times may give rise to a rich sense of strangeness, whose aesthetic consequences draw the line between the first and second Machados. Although the terms of the equation were already set down in 1873, he was not yet prepared to formally incorporate them into his literature. The impact from the success of *Cousin Bazilio* may have been what was lacking for the perennially prim author of *Iaiá Garcia* to tackle the risk of reinventing himself.

That is why the systematic appearance of the semantic field associated with emulation may be traced to his response to Eça's success.

Even more surprising is that, many years before the Brás Cubas revolution, the young critic found himself already on the path that would lead to his enshrinement. In a long essay reviewing the theater of José de Alencar, published in three parts in the *Diário do Rio de Janeiro*—on March 6, 13, and 27, 1866, he reflects:

> *Verso e Reverso* [Verse and Reverse] earned its warm reception, not only for
> its merits, but also for its *novelty of form*. Until then, Brazilian comedies
> *had not sought out the most esteemed models*; the works of the late Pena, rich
> with talent and a solid comic vein, were intimately linked to the traditions
> of the Portuguese farce, which is not to discredit them, but to define them;
> if the author of *O Noviço* [The Novice] had lived, his talent—which was of
> the most auspicious—would have moved along with the time, *uniting the
> progress of modern art to the lessons of classical art*. (III, 871; italics mine)

The *novelty of form* was the result of a broadening of repertoire: beyond working with a single nucleus (be it Portuguese farce or the French naturalist novel), an author of talent must seek out more sources, taking on a wider perspective. The more an author owes to tradition, the more influence she will receive, the more *filiations* she will recognize, and she will find herself ever freer and more inventive. Machado offers a mirror image of the aesthetic choice that allows him to imagine the *Posthumous Memoirs*. A similar method appears in his short stories dedicated to music. Martins Pena, although undoubtedly talented, could not develop his craft because he did not seek out *the most esteemed models*, to be found in the *lessons of classical art*.

And where else?

Such passages clarify that Romantic praises of genius have an element that is considerably less noble than defenders of the aesthetic of creation might argue. I refer to the emergence of a mass urban audience unable to identify allusions, citations, and appropriations simply because of an unfamiliarity with classical repertoire.

The problem is not exclusive to Brazil, but rather a symptom of the emergence of the cultural industry at any latitude. Carlos Monsiváis, one of the most important Hispanic-American essayists of the past century, summed up the dilemma in *Las alusiones perdidas*, a remarkable manifesto.[8] These lost allusions allude in turn to the novel by Honoré de Balzac, *Les Illusions perdues*, concluded in 1843. Those who read the Mexican author and do not immediately make the association between the two books become unwitting evidence for his argument.

Hence Machado's veiled critique of the readers who were unable to make out Dinis's imitations, *perhaps because they were overlooked.* To repeat the question: and what to say of these readers who did not link "Almada" and *O Garatuja*? Here, the deceased author's pessimism takes on a pragmatic tone:

> The fact that Stendhal admitted to having written a book for a hundred readers is a source of surprise and consternation. What comes as no surprise, nor will likely provoke any consternation, is if this book does not garner even Stendhal's hundred readers, nor fifty, nor twenty, or even ten, if that. Ten? *Perhaps five.* (I, 513; italics mine)

The dwindling numbers of the reading public drive the irreverence with which Brás Cubas addresses them: when one is steering close to something so tiny, why not risk everything on a promising hand? Who says that bluffs have no aesthetic potential? In the ever-cited passage, scantiness becomes an unexpected source of freedom:

> The work in itself is everything; if it pleases you, fine reader, my work is paid for; if it does not please you, I will pay you with a flick of the finger, and farewell. (I, 513)

We must tread carefully, however, when drawing automatic links between this condition and the shaky quality of Brazilian circumstances. They were truly unenviable, especially during the nineteenth century; nevertheless, the steady appearance of an urban mass audience ignorant of the classical tradition is a generalized phenomenon, a defining element of cultural modernity in countries like France and England.[9] Sliding unmediated from jingoism to self-flagellation may not be the best way of dealing with the local elements of a cosmopolitan predicament.

Machado's Camões

Time to discuss a little-studied facet of Machado's oeuvre: his theater works. The play *Tu só, tu, puro amor* [Thou, Only Thou, Pure Love], whose title comes from a line in *The Lusiads*,[10] was written amid the celebrations on the three-hundredth anniversary of the poet's death and performed at the Teatro D. Pedro II on June 10, 1880. The text would be published in the *Revista Brasileira* the next month, in the July 1 edition. The play was written for the occasion and has since failed to draw attention.

We would do well, however, to heed the author when he speaks about his aims:

> The conclusion of the noble loves of Camões and D. Catarina de Ataíde is the subject of the comedy, a conclusion that would lead to the subsequent adventure in Africa, and later to a departure to India, from whence the poet would one day return with immortality in hand. I have not sought to portray the court of D. João III, nor do I know if the minimal proportions of the text and the urgency of the occasion would permit it. But I did seek to make the poet contemporary with his loves, *not lending them epic*, and hence *posthumous*, tones. (II, 1139; italics mine)

Machado's Camões is not, therefore, the author of *The Lusiads*, but the young poet famous for his songs and, above all, for his loves and adventures. Nothing more: no *epic* tones, nor *posthumous* ones, without the comfortable retrospective vision that reduces the complexity of an existential and artistic trajectory to the empirical declaration that Camões wrote *The Lusiads* and became the greatest poet in the Portuguese language, an unrivaled authority in the epic—that in any language, one might note. Now, he might not have survived the shipwreck. He might not have put himself to the task of completing his masterpiece: a *boring and time-consuming* task, as the casmurrian narrator might put it, with an uncertain payoff. How many skillful men abandoned their tasks midway through, relegating themselves to the myriad of secondary names and irrelevant dates that populate literary histories?

The Camões of *Thou, Only Thou, Pure Love* resembles the author I imagined in the second chapter: Machadinho, a severe and somewhat prim reader of *Cousin Bazilio*, still a long way from Machado, the singular author of *The*

Posthumous Memoirs of Brás Cubas. Now, he might not have written that novel and simply continued on his pallid way as the author of novels in the *touch-me-not* style. Machadinho might not have survived the shipwreck of his illusions or his illness in late 1878.

Or the winter that finally arrived, in February 1878.

All my efforts thus far are synthesized in the way Machado hopes to understand Camões: *not lending them epic*, and hence *posthumous*, tones.

Back to the play.

The young poet, entangled in amorous adventures and shows of courage, rarely exercises his talent. His adversary in the plot, Pêro de Andrade Caminha, does not pardon this lack of seriousness. In romantic histories of Portuguese literature, Caminha has been repeatedly cast as Camões's rival—a story that Machado seems to have accepted unquestioningly. Onstage, Caminha sets himself against the future author of *The Lusiads*, going so far as to declare:

CAMINHA (displeased): The poet! The poet! He contrives a few witless verses and becomes a poet on the spot! You squander your enthusiasm, Sr. D. Manuel. A true poet is Sá, the great Sá! But this sluggard, this spare-time brawler . . .

DOM MANUEL: Do you believe, then? . . .

CAMINHA: That the youth has some talent, much less than his presumption and the blindness of his friends would suggest; *some talent I will not deny him*. He writes sufferable sonnets. And his songs . . . I will say that I have read one or two, and they were not too poorly scrawled. Well, then? With good will, *more effort and less pride*, spending his nights not lazing around the taverns of Lisbon *but meditating on the Italian poets*, I tell you that he may come to be . . .

DOM MANUEL: Finish.

CAMINHA: He is finished: a sufferable poet. (II, 1140; italics mine)

The reference to Francisco Sá de Miranda is a well-aimed blow. A poet who approached his craft with gravity and discipline, he studied law at the University of Lisbon and traveled to Italy from 1521 to 1526, living alongside notable names of the Renaissance such as Ariosto and Pietro Bembo. His works would bear the mark of this period abroad. Once back, he became a voice for this new aesthetic, bringing forms like the sonnet, song, and deca-syllables, among others, into Portuguese. The emphatic mention—*A true poet is Sá, the great Sá!*—offers up a model of authority for the young talent, still more taken by taverns than libraries.

In a harsh exchange, Caminha offers severe words of advice: "Go to Italy, Sr. Camões, go to Italy" (II, 1148). In this case, "going to Italy" is more than a change of scenery; it suggests a journey through time, shedding light on the formal novelty of Machado's techniques.

Curiously enough, the same symbol appears in *The Mandarin*, Eça de Queirós' novel released in 1880, which represented a significant departure from *The Crime of Father Amaro* and *Cousin Bazilio*. After one character errs and imagines a Goethe inspired by Portuguese lands, Meriskoff, "a doctor in German from the University of Bonn," like any academic worth his salt, can't resist the temptation to correct him:

> "Madam, the sweet land of Mignon is Italy: *Do you know that fortunate land where the orange tree flowers?* The divine Goethe was referring to Italy, *Italia mater* . . . which will always be the true beloved of all sensitive souls!"[11]

Machado practically repeats the words of *The Mandarin* in a letter to a close friend on April 20, 1903. The author of *O abolicionismo* was in Italy at the time; Machado imagined him "treading on the beaten earth of so many centuries of the history of the world. I, my dear Nabuco, still bear that mark of youth, which the Romantic poets taught to love Italy" (III, 1063).

> (The paths of literature always cross: those same verses by Goethe, cited in the original German, are the epigraph to Gonçalves Dias' "Song of Exile.")

In both cases, for Machado as well as Eça, "going to Italy" meant adopt-ing pre-Romantic literary models and laying claim to another literary regis-ter. This is why the future author of *The Lusiads* is given a harsh reprimand: without this journey through time, he will never move beyond his state as an author "with neither art nor learning" (II, 1150). Machado's Camões runs the risk of winding up as João Maria, the "skillful man" from the story "O habilidoso"! Only exile and abandoning the easy life of the court will allow the poet to change his destiny. At the end of the play the emergence of the epic poem is heralded, in the anticipation of those ever-repeated verses:

> Canst thou see there, in the far immensity of these *seas which never ship has sailed before,* a resplendent figure leaning over the balconies of the dawn and crowned with Indian palms? It is our glory. (II, 1155; italics mine)

Even in a piece written for the occasion, Machado finds himself chewing over the model of *aemulatio,* understood in a broad sense as a technique for the assimilation and transformation of models enshrined as authorities in their respective genres.

Moreover, the dilemma of this Machadian Camões recalls the impasse faced by Machado himself.

Turned inside out, of course.

It is difficult to imagine the author of *Helena* involved in bohemian brawls or playing at the braggart. He could always behave with care and prudence.

An ideal son-in-law—the kind that is more appealing to fathers than to brides.

Deep down, the issue is the pitfall that any author of talent must steer around if she does not wish to condemn herself to the fate of the skillful youth. After all, talent must be a means to further development, and not an end in and of itself.

In the case of Machado's Camões, this was a matter of maintaining his hormones under control long enough to acquire the discipline and knowledge necessary in order to produce his masterpiece.

On the very day that the play *Thou, Only Thou, Pure Love* was performed at the Teatro D. Pedro II, Machado published a sonnet in a special edition of the *Jornal do Comércio.* It is entirely composed under the sign of a successful emulation—successful both historically, relating the Portuguese explorations to antiquity, and literarily, holding the writing of *The Lusiads* up against enshrined models:

> When, turning the mysterious key
> That shut the gate to the Orient,
> Gama unfurled the new blazing land

Before the eyes of the valorous crew,

A resplendent vision may have shown
Him in the future the sonorous
Horn, which would sing the famous deed
To the ears of kin and strange alike.

And said: "If in another, ancient age,
Troy sufficed for man, now I wish
To show that humanity has grown more human.

As you shall not be the hero of a fierce song,
But you shall defeat time and boundlessness
In the voice of another modern, gentle Homer." (III, 165)

This new Camões not only goes to Italy: he also visits Hellas. In the speech imagined by the Brazilian writer, the Portuguese poet considers the feats of Vasco da Gama superior to those chronicled in the classical world. If the limit imposed by the Columns of Hercules—once considered impassable—was what condemned the Mediterranean to the role of mare nostrum, then it was the Portuguese who opened the door to wide oceans and new lands. Likewise, the poet offers up his epic as a decisive difference: while, in the ancient age, Troy sufficed for man, the new conquests now call for another modern, gentle Homer who will unite, no longer divide.

The Camões of the play and the Camões of the sonnet illuminate the journey from Machadinho to Machadão. The paths are different, but the final stops come together in their mastery of the technique of *aemulatio*.

Machadinho had to abandon the literary models tailored around the young *senhoritas* and respectable ladies of the court of Emperor Pedro II. In "The Instinct of Nationality," for example, one comes across the following appraisal (reproduced in full in chapter 2):

The moral tendencies of the Brazilian novel are good, on the whole. *Not all are irreproachable from beginning to end*; there will always be something *for a severe critique to point out and correct*. But the general tone is acceptable. (III, 805; italics mine)

Indeed.

The path was not a short one.

Here, then, is one way of understanding Machado's leap: while most of his contemporaries were pricking their ears to catch the latest fad, the author of "A Visit from Alcibiades" was traveling to Italy—but, like the Camões from his sonnet, he did not merely travel to the physical peninsula. He frequented all periods as if they occupied the same historical instant, defined not by the linearity of the calendar, but by the simultaneity of the moments of reading and writing. Emulation offers up another kind of temporality, denying linearity and negating irreversible conquests; this is not to promote traumatic breaks, but rather to contribute to enriching the common repertoire, promising a synchrony between any number of periods and traditions. One notable example is Dante in Canto IV of the *Inferno*, when he sees "four great shades" come towards him. Virgil, his guide, clarifies the situation:

> "Note well,"
> My master began, "the one who carries a sword
> And strides before the others, as fits his role
>
> Among these giants: he is Homer, their lord
> The sovereign poet; the satirist follows him—
> Horace, with Lucan last, and Ovid third:
>
> That lone voice just now hailed me by a name
> Each of them shares with me; in such accord
> They honor me well."[12]

Virgil is the fifth poet in the Pantheon, and Dante presents himself as the youngest star in the constellation. Only by recognizing the authority of his precursors is he able to rub shoulders with them. Over the long reign of the literary practices that preceded the Romantic period, allusion, citation, and appropriation were pillars of a larger whole defined by the pair comprised by the gestures of *imitatio* and *aemulatio*. It was the aim of every author to transform him- or herself into an *auctoritas* in a given genre, finding "great shades" around the library with whom to face off.

In the context of the Brazilian nineteenth century, the aesthetic consequences of this anachronistic about-face would carry far along.

Emulation and Authorship

The next step demands the development of this possibility, as we saw in Machado's texts from 1878 and 1879: the eve of the debut of the deceased author's prose.

Or, as we have just seen in the play *Thou, Only Thou, Pure Love* and in the sonnet "Camões": another way of unveiling it.

Time to consult *The Posthumous Memoirs of Brás Cubas*, first released in the *Revista Brasileira* in 1880 and the following year as a book.

I shall start by recalling the terms of the note "To the Reader":

> The fact that Stendhal admitted to having written a book for a hundred readers is a source of surprise and consternation. What comes as no surprise, nor will likely provoke any consternation, is if this book does not garner Stendhal's hundred readers, nor fifty, nor twenty, or even ten, if that. Ten? *Perhaps five.* This is, in fact, *a diffuse work* in which I, Brás Cubas, while adopting the *free form* of a Sterne or a Xavier de Maistre, cannot say whether I have added a few *grumbles of pessimism.* That may be. The work of a late man. I wrote it with *the pen of mirth and the ink of melancholy*, and it is not difficult to predict what may come of this mixture. (I, 513; italics mine)

This is the key passage, indeed, the rite of passage for Machado de Assis. The narrator of the *Posthumous Memoirs* places writing and reading on the same level. It is as if the "Note to the Reader" were acquiring an autobiographical tang: literally memorialistic, as the writing reveals the recalling of texts previously read. Machado not only interprets the writers with whom he is dialoguing, he also proposes a concept with which to frame their techniques: *free form*. Moreover, Machado distorts this *free form* in his own sense.

He does not embark on interminable digressions or travel around his room, driven solely or principally by a spirited sense of humor. As he himself suggests, his chosen route calls for a copilot: the *pen of mirth* must be joined to the *ink of melancholy*, and from this unexpected meeting of opposites springs the peculiarity of the works from his second phase. Machado brings the eighteenth and nineteenth centuries together in the figures of Sterne, Xavier de Maistre, and Stendhal, staining humor with the somber tones of melancholy. Remember that the possibility of juxtaposing a variety of historical periods and mixing literary genres anticipates the Borgesian technique of deliberate anachronism.

The narrator of the *Posthumous Memoirs* inserts himself into a field ruled by the technique of *aemulatio*, transforming it through a modern appropriation. In addition to naming the models for his writing, he clearly lays out the aim of emulating them. Take the prologue to the third edition, released in 1896, and *reread it from the perspective proposed here*—it becomes revelatory, essential:

> What makes my Brás Cubas *an author all his own* is what he calls "grumbles of pessimism." The soul of this book, as lighthearted as it may seem, carries a bitter and harsh edge, *which is far from coming from its models*. The glass may be the work of the same school, *but it bears another wine*. I shall say no more so as not to begin criticizing a dead man, as he painted himself and others as he saw fit and best. (III, 513; italics mine)

His vocabulary could not be more direct, and belongs entirely to the semantic field of emulation. The description is so precise that it dispenses further comments. The reader already understands the *deliberate* nature of the deceased author's allusions to the practice of emulation. Emphasis on the conceptual craftsmanship: *the work of the same school*, as the mold is the same for everyone, as it is set by the common repertoire and enshrined by the tradition of rhetorical use. However, the same glass always *bears another wine*, as *aemulatio* only occurs in affirming its difference.

(Starting in the mid-1870s, growing awareness of the technique of *aemulatio* begins to define the style that we will learn to call Machadian.)

In the *free form* imitated in the *Posthumous Memoirs*, there emerge *grumbles of pessimism*—an element *that is far from coming from its models*. While the starting points include Sterne, Xavier de Maistre, Garrett, and Stendhal, the final destination is the metamorphosis from Machadinho to Machadão (it can never hurt to fall back on the acuity of Augusto Meyer.) Hence, if the glass is of the same artisan, the wine reveals a *terroir* all its own—which, like any good harvest, demands long and patient cultivation.

◆   ◆   ◆

Machado's metaphor invokes the fate of the carmenère grape, vanished from European vineyards around 1860 after the great phylloxera plague, an invasion of insects led by the vineyard-phylloxera. For decades, it was believed that the legacy of a long tradition had been lost.

Much later, an uncommon sort of wine started to come out of Chile, apparently prepared from the merlot grapes in the region. Specialists were intrigued and set about studying the variety.

The oenologists would come to a surprising conclusion: this unknown merlot strain was the fruit of the only carmenère crops that had survived the phylloxera plague. The discovery came in 1994, from French ampelographer Jean-Michel Boursiquot. The carmenère grape was saved because, once *transplanted* to Chile, and unwittingly bred together with merlot varieties, it *acclimated* perfectly, leading to the development of a *terroir* of its own for its production.

A sort of vineyard archaeology, the short history of the carmenère grape might well inspire a mock-heroic poem.

Or perhaps Sarmiento, the editor of *El Progreso* (the newspaper published in Chile in the nineteenth century) may have been right after all. To return to the passage cited in the third chapter:

> Our daily outdoes the best known in Europe and America, for the quite obvious reason that, being one of the last newspapers in the world, we have at our disposition, *to choose from in the best possible way*, all that the other newspapers have published. (II, 3)

The story does not end here. In Europe, the method of choice to prevent future phylloxera attacks was the importation of resistant American varieties into European vineyards. It remains the dominant technique to this day; and so we might say that each glass of European wine does, indeed, *bear another wine.*

A South American wine.

◆   ◆   ◆

The long path that Machado took on the way to understanding *aemulatio* may be evidenced in a contrast. I return to the opening note of the first edition of *Resurrection* (1872); here, Machadinho recognizes the need to consult previous models, but still lacks a broader vision of the complex technique of *imitatio*—which, as I have said countless times, always includes the later gesture of *aemulatio*:

> What follows is the opposite of what came before. *The more we examine the models*, we penetrate into *the laws of taste and art* and understand the extent of our responsibility, *the more our hands and spirit shrink from the task*, although this itself arouses our ambition, no longer presumptuous, but rather thoughtful. This may not be *the law of geniuses*, to whom nature has given the almost unconscious power of supreme audacity; but it is, I believe, the law of middling aptitudes, the general rule of intelligence. (I, 116; italics mine)

The first part of the passage follows the preliminary steps in the technique of *aemulatio*, but the conclusion remains shackled to the affirmation of the creator as demiurge. While the two first sentences might well belong to the handbook of the Brás Cubas revolution, the final sentence implies an embarrassing retreat: one step back, and two to the side. The author of *The Hand and the Glove* seems to believe in the *law of geniuses*, whose motto is *creatio ex nihilo* and whose norm is ever-autotelic, indifferent to the imitation of any model. In this post-Romantic perspective, emulation can only be the result of a lack of talent, derived from the *law of middling aptitudes*: the rule of thumb for intelligences sans *terroir*. Thus, systematic acquaintance with tradition does not drive the reader to emulate it: *the more our hands and spirit shrink from the task*, spurring a sort of formulaic modesty, doubtless meriting medals of honor for exemplary literary good behavior.

(And yet the opening paragraph from the *Posthumous Memoirs* is worth more than a collection of medals.)

The note "To the Reader," expanded in the prologue to the third edition, resuscitates another idea of originality—no longer limited to creation, but focused on literary memory. The writing of new texts, then, is linked to the laws of *invention*. If Machado consciously assimilated the Sternian technique of digression, he did it in the style of Montaigne, as his digressions always play with literary references.

Oblique ones, at times.

Here lies the secret of the cryptic passage in the note "To the Reader." Given the importance of this text for my argument, I will repeat part of the previously quoted section:

> The work of a late man. I wrote it with the pen of mirth and the ink of melancholy, and it is not difficult to predict what may come of this mixture. Add to which the fact that serious people will find in the book with some *appearance of a pure romance*, while frivolous people will not find *their usual novel* here; and thus it will be deprived of the esteem of the serious and the love of the frivolous, which are the two main pillars of opinion. (I, 513; italics mine)

We maintain a striking relationship with the titles of the novels of the eighteenth century: the long titles that helped to define the tradition of the modern novel. The best way to understand this is to emphasize our subtle discarding of the apparently useless level of detail favored by writers of the 1700s.

For example, *The History of Tom Jones, a Foundling*, released in 1749, has become plain old *Tom Jones*. Likewise, *The Life and Opinions of Tristram Shandy, Gentleman*, published a decade later, becomes *Tristram Shandy*. Now, the parallelism in these titles suggests a debate that shook the eighteenth century in England; and returning to that debate may clarify the subtleties of Machado's vocabulary.

Fielding, fully aware that he was looking to create a new model for narrative, noted that he had "properly enough entitled this our work, a history, and not a life; nor an apology for a life."[13] This choice is striking and reveals his desire to discipline the story through an organizing structure: the travels of a character through the world, concentrating the focus of the narrative on his trials and tribulations. In the author's words:

When any extraordinary scene presents itself . . . we shall spare no pains
nor paper to open it at large to our reader; but if whole years should pass
without producing anything worthy his notice, we shall not be afraid of a
chasm in our history; but shall hasten on to matters of consequence and
leave such periods of time totally unobserved. (68)

A decade later, Sterne unveiled that which Fielding's choice had dis-
guised. Sterne's vocabulary, striking a parodic pose before *Tom Jones*, sheds
light on the strength of the internal system of emulation that takes place
between two authors in the same hegemonic context. As I have stated again
and again, the techniques at the core of the poetics of emulation operate
independently of latitude.

Let us listen to Sterne's Lucianic diction:

If my hypercritick is intractable, alledging, that two minutes and thirteen
seconds are no more than two minutes and thirteen seconds . . . and that
this plea, though it might save me dramatically, will damn me biographi-
cally, rendering my book . . . a professed Romance, which, before, was a
book apocryphal . . .[14]

Apocryphal because the digressions that destabilize the narrative teleol-
ogy threaten the aim to unite *novel* and *history*, as the constant interruptions
in the flow of action by any number of comments hobble any linear, organizing project. The two conceptual pairs implied a special moment in the
definition of the European historical experience, made corporeal in a simple
analogy: *history* was to *novel* as *life* was to *romance*.

In the eighteenth century in England, *history* invoked the discipline
and regular meter of the idea of *novel*, while *romance* operated alongside the
unpredictability tied to the word *life*. Contemporary reception of the two
words may shed light on the difference. *Romance* evoked the use of fantastical, disorganized, implausible narratives—Romanesque in the negative sense
of the word. However, such censure implied a definitive choice on the part
of the reading public; the relative disfavor suffered by *romance* suggested the
privilege of the *novel*, a story told according to certain parameters that would
supposedly produce a true panorama of the most significant events in the
trajectory of a given protagonist.

The deceased author overcomes this dichotomy by uniting the two models: in Machadian terms, Sterne's *romance* is translated as a *pure romance*, while Fielding's *novel* becomes a *usual novel*. Machado fuses mirth and melancholy, brings the eighteenth and nineteenth centuries together, and mixes *novel* and *romance* in an eloquent demonstration of the phenomenon of the compression of historical periods.

There is another passage very similar to the note "To the Reader"; I am thinking of chapter 112 of *Quincas Borba*. It merits a full transcription:

> This is where I would have liked to use in this book the method of so many others—old, all of them—in which the matter of the chapter is summarized: "How this happened thusly, and more to that effect." There's Bernardim Ribeiro; there are other glorious books. In foreign tongues, without rising to Cervantes or Rabelais, I could be content with Fielding and Smollett, many of whose chapters can already be read just by the summary. Pick up *Tom Jones*, Book IV, chapter 1, and read the title: *Containing five pages of paper*. It's clear, it's simple, it doesn't fool anyone; there are five pages, nothing more, whoever doesn't wish to read them won't, whoever does will, and it is for the latter that the author obligingly concludes: "And now, without any further preface, I proceed to our next chapter." (I, 738)[15]

Indeed, the juxtaposition of distant historical periods and conflicting visions of literature will come to define the tone of his prose. Machado puts Cervantes and Rabelais together with Fielding and Smollett, without forgetting Bernardim Ribeiro, a Portuguese writer and poet from the Renaissance. In this pantheon we can find precursors and representatives of the clash between *romance* and *novel*, suggesting a subtle take on literary history. Machado's appropriation is meditated, lending strength to the category of *pure romance* in opposition to the notion of *usual novel*.

But there's more.

Machado ties the form of the novel to a specific sort of reception. Structurally, writing and reading are thought of at the time; they are twin models. *Novel* commands the *esteem of the serious*, while *romance* supposes the *love of the frivolous*.

There's still more.

This reflection, after all, would be hardly Machadian at all if I were to content myself with a binary opposition: this reader versus that reader. In this case, one would simply need to decide which kind of reader one wanted and then write the same book eternally, doubling down on previously established solutions. The deceased author takes a step beyond this, recognizing the possibility of losing the support of both those *main pillars of opinion*, as his *Stilmischung* (mixture of styles) runs the risk of displeasing everyone at once.

Whether serious or frivolous, the reader can no longer count on the clarity of a monochromatic universe. A new fiction of reading is coming into view. Machado not only casts himself as an irreverent reader of tradition, but he also calls upon his audience to take part in the fictional construction through the development of a technique of reading, with collage as its defining procedure. This I propose to call collage-reading, a fundamental element in appreciating the truly Machadian literary form.

CHAPTER 5

Forms of Emulation

With the publication of *The Posthumous Memoirs of Brás Cubas* and the first *Cantos ocidentais* [Western Cantos], the name he first gave to his *Westerners*, Machado de Assis came to the acme of his career. From then on he would remain at the same level, but would rise no farther—a difficult feat, certainly. The artist had found his perfect form, fulfilling his inspiration completely.

—Lúcia Miguel Pereira, *Machado de Assis*

Machado's critique of the new novel by Eça is solid, reflexive, thorough, and uncompromising. When he attacks Eça's naturalist principles, he defies the prestige of the most-read author in the Portuguese language at the time. Machado in 1878 was nothing more than a writer who was famous among his compatriots, but lost on the margins of the metropolitan world.

—Valquiria Wey, "Reflexiones sobre una crisis: 1878 en la obra de Machado de Assis"

The fate of this essay ["News of the Present Brazilian Literature—Instinct of Nationality"], meanwhile, becomes increasingly doubtful under our counterfactual hypothesis: at the very least, since Machado did not in fact

die in 1878, we will always have to decide if this essay redeems itself on its
own merits in the midst of his reputed mediocrity, or if it stands out at the
expense of Machado's novels as a whole.

—Abel Barros Baptista, *Em nome do apelo do nome*

The "meeting" of these "similarities" then sets off a controversy on a more
superficial level, such as the concern over whether the supposed "originality" of an "artist" might be compatible with the certainty that he also
"suffered influences" from abroad. "Influence," in his case, taken as a euphe-
mism to soften the more apt words, *emulation* and *copy*.

—Guiomar de Grammont, *Aleijadinho e o aeroplano*

These references help to understand how Machado read and made use of
known texts in the act of reading his own. . . . The ruminant reader with
four stomachs in his brain which the narrator references in *Esau and Jacob*
was Machado himself, an extraordinarily active machine for digesting
other's discourses and reworking the byproducts into discursive elabora-
tions that ran inverse or contrary to the intentions of the source text.

—Ivo Barbieri, "O lapso ou uma psicoterapia de humor"

M. de A.

After our initial journey around *aemulatio* in Machado's works, the time has
come to discuss his concept of authorship; after all, the dominant motif in
his critique of *Cousin Bazilio* revolves around notions of copying, plagiarism,
and imitation. The return to a classical perspective represents a questioning
of authority conceived purely in terms of autonomous subjectivity. Tracing
this issue across the other five novels in the second phase allows us to deepen
the study of *aemulatio* in Machado's oeuvre.

In *Quincas Borba*, published in 1891, we find a broadened consideration
of the idea of authorship by means of a questioning of the acts of reading
and writing. Chapter 113 presents the reader with the following situation:
Rubião, the faithful but dim follower of the philosopher Quincas Borba,
inherits his master's fortune and starts spending it rashly.

✦ ✦ ✦

A brief detour.

Rubião will never understand that the motto "to the victor, the potatoes," does not represent an end but rather a means to obtain future stability, *things of the future*, the meaning of which he never quite grasps. In Quincas Borba's fable, as laid out in chapter 6, the moral is clear:

> Imagine a field of potatoes and two starving tribes. There are only enough potatoes to feed one of the tribes, *who can thus gain enough strength to cross the mountain and go to the other slope, where there are potatoes in abundance*; but, if the two tribes peacefully divide the potatoes in the field, neither will be able to nourish itself sufficiently, and both will die of malnutrition. Peace, in this case, is destruction; war is preservation. One of the tribes exterminates the other and collects the spoils. . . . To the vanquished, hate or mercy; *to the victor, the potatoes*. (I, 648–49; italics mine)

Rubião accepts the prize (the potatoes, in this case his inheritance) but forgets about the responsibility that it brings with it: taking care of Quincas Borba the dog, first of all, but above all crossing the mountain—to wit, wisely investing the sum at hand, or at the very least making prudent use of it. In the bellicose code of ethics of the creator of Humanitism, the first potatoes only serve to *gain enough strength to cross the mountain*. The *potatoes in abundance* only lie on the far slope.

Of course, on the contrary, Rubião spends all his energies in the process of frittering away his unexpected riches.

Rubião was indeed an ignoramus.

✦ ✦ ✦

Back to chapter 113.

Rubião decides to sponsor a political newspaper, whose owner is looking to take advantage of the country bumpkin's naïveté. One day he visits the newspaper's offices and happens to read an article by Camacho, a lawyer and journalist unburdened by scruples. Rubião simply suggests a minor change in the text—adding an adjective. Naturally, Camacho adopts his patron's corrections; and this provokes an unexpected reaction:

Rubião applauded the article; he thought it excellent. Perhaps lacking in vigor. *Vendors*, for example, was well said; but it would be even better as *vile vendors*. . . .

"Vile vendors, vile vendors," Camacho repeated quietly. "It already sounds better. Vile vendors. I accept," he concluded, *making the emendation*. . . .

"Very good!" said Rubião, *feeling himself in no small way author of the article*. (I, 738; italics mine)

Through a good-humored association of ideas, Rubião arrives at the conclusion that he is the author of the little article. In Machado's words, the character's attitude provides the motif for a new chapter: "If that were the method of this book, here you have a title that would explain everything: Of how Rubião, satisfied with the *emendation* to the article, composed and ruminated on so many sentences *that he wound up writing all the books he had ever read*" (I, 738; italics mine). This line of reasoning brings up a problem of logic—namely, the exceptionally rapid transition from Rubião, reader of books, to Rubião, author of those very books. The narrator, nevertheless, offers the key to this apparent impasse:

There is an abyss between the first phrase, of which Rubião was a coauthor, to the authorship of all the works read by him; it is true that the hardest step was going from the phrase to the first book;—from then on the path was swift. No matter; even so, an analysis would be long and tedious. Better to leave it at this: for a few minutes, *Rubião felt himself the author of many works by other people*. (I, 739; italics mine)

This passage recalls the spirit of a number of Jorge Luis Borges's most famous short stories, especially among those who study the concepts of reading and authorship. Machado and Borges blur the borders between the two acts: reading is to write with one's eyes; writing updates the posthumous memory of previous readings. The innovative *arrangement* of preexisting elements emerges as more productive than the drive to *create* new elements, clarifying the centrality of *inventio* in the poetics of emulation.

This unique notion of parasitism as a method of composition shows itself again in a crônica from *A Semana*, published on November 22, 1896. The text is inspired by a news item: "A landholder from Rio Grande do Sul shot himself in the head and vanished from the number of the living." The suicide was surprising; though the owner of vast estates, the cause of his death "was the conviction that the man must be poor" (III, 742). Machado does not miss the opportunity to illuminate an odd comparison with Brazilian daily life and classical memory, this juxtaposition being one of the hallmarks of his second-phase style: "The reverse of this case was well known, being that citizen of Athens who neither had nor owned a drachma, a poor devil convinced that all the ships coming into Piraeus belonged to him; he needed nothing more to be happy" (III, 742–43). The corollary of this realm of the "as if" might well illustrate Rubião's writing method.

As the *cronista* puts it:

On the contrary, if your steward believes that he wrote *The Lusiads*, he will proudly read the poet's stanzas (if he can read); he will repeat them by heart, will interrogate your face, your gestures, your mutterings, and will spend hours before the display cases looking on the copies of the poems shown there. (III, 743)

In the next novel—*Dom Casmurro*, published in 1900—the issue of authorship takes a similar swerve. At the start of the narrative, Bento Santiago explains that the title of the book sprang from a specific incident. One day as he returned home, he met a young poet who resolved to recite his complete works. Santiago naturally wound up dozing off, which infuriated this unpublished genius; his revenge was to dub his neighbor uncourteous. The narrator, for his part, clarifies the cognomen: "Don't look it up in dictionaries. In this case, *Casmurro* doesn't have the meaning they give, but the one the common people give it, of a quiet person who keeps himself to himself. The *Dom* was ironic, to accuse me of aristocratic pretensions. All because I nodded off!" (Gledson 4). This sense of the word had already appeared in the story "So-and-So," from 1884: "*Until then he had been a perfect casmurro*, who did not attend company meetings, did not vote in political elections, did not go to the theater, did nothing, absolutely nothing" (II, 437). Then, as we saw, he is transformed by the reading of a newspaper article about himself—an anonymous text, lauding him. "So-and-So"'s dour cast is cured by the reading. Bento Santiago did not have the same luck: writing did not help him kick the habit, much less mend his foibles.

In the narrative, *casmurro* also means not being polished enough to put up with the train-car poet for many long minutes. "Dom" was tacked on for comic effect, since Bento Santiago, far from being an aristocrat, was in fact was on a downward slide (albeit diligently preserving the shadow of his past elegance). The narrator is not put out, however. In fact, he turns the mean-spirited nickname into the title of his memoirs, conceding a revealing homage to the young poet:

> Still, I couldn't find a better title for my narrative; if I can't find another before I finish the book, I'll keep this one. My poet on the train will find out that I bear him no ill will. And with a little effort, *since the title is his, he can think the whole work is.* There are books that only owe that to their authors: some not even that much. (Gledson 4; italics mine)

The method takes a radical turn.

In *The Posthumous Memoirs of Brás Cubas*, the deceased author converts his readers (or scarcity thereof) into the foundations of his writing.

In *Dom Casmurro*, the narrator proposes an impossible simultaneity between the act of writing—*if I can't find another before I finish the book, I'll keep this one*—and reading, a corollary being the partial transference of the attribution of meaning over to the reader. Here I am not referring to a metaphorical sense, but to the creation of textual frameworks specially developed to achieve this end.

In his last two novels, Machado continues his exploration of this method via a surprising checkmate. Let us set up the board.

In theory, both *Esau and Jacob* (1904) and *Counselor Ayres' Memorial*, released in 1908, the year of Machado's death, are texts pulled from the diaries of Counselor Ayres: this is the framing fiction of the reading, as proposed by Machado de Assis.

Or by M. de A., as the note to the reader in *Counselor Ayres' Memorial* is signed.

And that is the question.

Is the reader accessing pages taken from *Counselor Ayres' Memorial*? Or is this a wink to the reader from *Machado de Assis*?

The notes that open both volumes clarify the (false) riddle.

In *Esau and Jacob*, everything seems more or less clear. One has only to consult the note to the reader—the unsigned note, one might point out.

> When Counselor Aires died, seven notebooks in manuscript were found in his desk, firmly bound in cardboard. Each one of the first six was numbered in order, with roman numerals I, II, III, IV, V, VI penned in red ink. The seventh bore this title: "Last."
>
> The reason for this special designation was not known then, nor is it known now. Indeed, this was the last of the seven notebooks, with the distinction that it was the thickest, but it was not part of the *Memorial*, the diary of remembrances that the counselor had been writing for many years and which constituted the subject of the previous six. It did not bear the same order of dates, indicating both the hour and the minute, as the previous ones. It was a single narrative; and although the very figure of Aires played a prominent role in it, with his name and title of counselor, and by allusion, some of his adventures, it did not thus belong to the previous six. Why, indeed, "Last"? (Lowe 1)

This is another wink to the reader—or another flick of the finger, should the reader fail to smile at the allusion to the typical recourse to the intervention by the "editor," who "finds" a manuscript and brings it to light after purging it of all possible shortcomings in terms of decorum or verisimilitude. Recall, for example, *The Fortunes and Misfortunes of the Famous Moll Flanders*, by Daniel Defoe, from 1721.[1]

In Machado's context, the most suggestive model in this respect is *Manon Lescaut* by Prévost, published in 1731 as the seventh volume of the *Memoirs and Adventures of a Man of Quality*, attributed to the fictional marquis de Renoncour. *Manon Lescaut* proposes a fictional pact that has since become famous: the marquis comes across the failed knight Des Grieux and listens to the tale of his turbulent relationship with the heroine, Manon Lescaut. The book is thus the transcription of the narrative of the Chevalier des Grieux.[2]

The *seventh volume*, I said.

And which was *still set apart from the content of the six notebooks* previously composed by the Marquis de Renoncour.

Indeed.

Let us return to Machado's novel.

At first there is no doubt: the (anonymous) writer of the note to the reader is the *reader* of the Counselor's manuscripts, responsible for the posthumous publication of not his diary, per se, but rather a narrative in which the Counselor is also a character. The publication of *Esau and Jacob* is effected by an anonymous reader who, on a fictional level, does not necessarily align with Machado de Assis. This reader is literally the organizer of the publication, responsible for selecting certain of the Counselor's texts.

This is a false riddle! The critic may not always rely on the art of the *cronista*, as defined by Machado in *A Semana* on October 11, 1897: "I like to hunt out the minimal and the hidden. Where no one sticks his nose, there goes mine, with the narrow and keen curiosity that uncovers that which is veiled" (III, 772).

"Not always," however, doesn't mean "never."

The riddle may be false, but the game with the initials is real and may become even more interesting.

Consult chapter 12, "That Man Aires," in *Esau and Jacob.*

Let us begin at the end of the previous chapter, "A Unique Case!," when the Counselor breaks into the narrative. Plácido, a zealous advocate for spiritism, spares no efforts in the attempt to convert the diplomat to this new creed. And, quite unlike Bento Santiago on the train, Ayres remains attentive (albeit indifferent to his interlocutor's enthusiasm):

> "Come, come," he said, "come help me convert *our good friend Aires.* For the last half hour I have tried to inculcate in him the eternal truths, but he resists."
>
> "No, no, no, I am not resisting," *chimed in a man of about forty,* extending his hand to the new arrival. (Lowe 31)

At the start of the next chapter, the narrator—that is, the narrator taken from the manuscript notebooks of Counselor Ayres—paints a full portrait of the character who has just arrived: Counselor Ayres himself.

Confused?

Switching angles: here, the reader finds a complete description of the author of the manuscript, who is also, at the same time, the character being described.

The man Aires who just appeared still retains some of the virtues of the times, and almost none of the vices. Do not attribute such qualities to any motive. Nor should you believe that homage is intended to that person's modesty. No sir, it is the pure truth and a natural attribute. In spite of his forty years, or forty-two, and perhaps because of this, *he was a fine specimen of a man.* A career diplomat, he had arrived just a few days before from the Pacific, on a six-month leave.

    I will not take too long to describe him. Just imagine that he wore the marks of his profession, the approving smile, the soft, cautious speech, the well-timed gesture, the appropriate turn of phrase, all so well distributed that it was a pleasure to hear and see him. Perhaps the skin of his clean-shaven face was just about to betray the first signs of age. Even so, his mustache, which was youthful in color and in the energy with which it twirled into fine, stiff points, would give an air of freshness to his face, when the half century of his life arrived. His hair would do the same thing, just vaguely graying, parted in the middle. On the top of his head was the beginning of a bald spot. In his buttonhole an eternal flower. (Lowe 32; italics mine)

This portrait continues for another four paragraphs. The narrator is liberal in his definitions, having assured us: *I shall not take too long to describe him.* The reader may be left with a bee in her bonnet, especially if she adheres to the Machadian tactic outlined in a crônica from *A Semana* on October 27, 1895. In a delicious discussion provoked by the news of a suit against several spiritists—careful there, Plácido!—the narrator confesses his disorientation: "The learned will have an easy answer; I, a simple layman, can find none. I let myself rest between the Code and the Constitution, taking one article here, another there, *I read, reread, and threeread*" (III, 683; italics mine).

    In his memoirs, Ayres draws up a narrative in third person where he includes himself as a character, a supporting actor in the plot, but one who merits a painstaking analysis of his person and character. Technically, this scenario does not present insurmountable difficulties. However, given the Counselor's reserved nature—being a man given to blending into the background so as to focus on others—the move is surprising.

    The short-circuit grows more intense, as the author of the note to the reader takes it upon himself to underline the apparent discrepancy—*Why*

Last?—but offers no answer. The matter seems to be unsolvable: *it was not understood then, nor is it now.* The silence from the reader, who also happens to be the editor, is yet another of the *questions without an answer* in the Machadian oeuvre.

In this context, the note to the reader in *Counselor Ayres' Memorial* deserves to be read in full:

> Those who have read my *Esau and Jacob* may perhaps recognize these words from the *preface*: "In the leisure of his office he was writing the *Memorial*, which, if the dead or dull pages were cut, would barely suffice (and might yet) to kill time on the boat over from Petrópolis."
>
> I was referring to Counselor Ayres. The time having come to print the *Memorial*, it was found that the part concerning a period of two years (1888–1889), *if trimmed of some circumstances, anecdotes, descriptions, and reflections—might serve for a continuous narrative*, which may be of some interest, despite being in the form of a diary. There was no unwillingness on my part to draw it up like the other volume—neither unwillingness nor ability. Here it is as it was, but hewn and sparing, preserving only that which concerns the same matter. The rest will appear someday, if some day comes.
>
> *M. de A.* (I, 1096; italics mine)

First of all, those who have read *Esau and Jacob* may observe a change in tense: in the first novel we read that Ayres "had been writing the *Memorial*," not that he "was writing the *Memorial*." Moreover, what had been a note to the reader is now a "preface."

Nitpicking details, typical of the search for the philosopher's stone. This is not my case. I have said, resaid, and threesaid: I do not seek to shrink the complexity of the path that led from Machadinho to Machado down to the limits dictated by my hypothesis.

That said, however, one crucial point emerges from these details.

The previous short-circuit—as for the Counselor, the author of the *diary of recollections*, and "that man Aires," the character in *Esau and Jacob*—touches Machado himself.

M.A., that is.

If the note read, "Those who have read *Esau and Jacob*," we would have evidence for the hypothesis of a deliberate indistinction between *Machado de Assis* and *Memorial de Aires*; the riddle would go on for some time. However, the inclusion of a possessive adjective makes the scale lean toward the more trivial hypothesis: "Those who have read *my Esau and Jacob*," that is to say, those who read the novel by Machado de Assis.

I reiterate: the hermeneutic riddle is a false one, and that is precisely why the literary game is authentic. The question, *Why Last?*, returns in the image of a double-edged, contradictory agreement.

In both novels, the reader of the texts that are published is denied direct access to the Counselor's memoirs; he can only read excerpts that have been previously selected by the authors of the notes. In *Esau and Jacob*, it is an anonymous censor; in *Counselor Ayres' Memorial*, M. de A.—for that matter, does he simply put his name to the opening note or does he also undertake the task of producing a *pruned and sparing* narrative? The text is ambiguous: "The time having come to print the Memorial, *it was found that . . .*"

Found by whom?

Moreover, the textual operation carried out by M.A., the reader, consists in removing all the hallmarks of the diary as a genre from the *Memorial*. The process as described—*if trimmed of some circumstances, anecdotes, descriptions, and reflections*—transforms the Counselor's annotations into something else entirely, "a continuous narrative, which may be of some interest, *despite being in the form of a diary*." The reader of *Counselor Ayres' Memorial* truly never has access to the diplomat's diaries, only to the mediated form established by a previous act of reading.

Machado's final two novels therefore situate the act of reading in an authorial position. By making a selection of the Counselor's writings, the anonymous reader constitutes the possible meanings of the text. Hence, the frustrated enigma of the Notes to the Reader is important not as some literary game of hide-and-seek, but as a provocation that activates the reading's potential.

In the terms that Machado proposes, the questioning (or broadening) of the concept of authorship implies the reshaping (or broadening) of the role attributed to the reader. The symmetry of the formula necessarily follows the rigorous parallelism between the acts of reading and writing.

It would be silly to link that questioning and this reshaping to the technique of *aemulatio* alone. This is not a simple, monocausal process. However,

I am confident in the new hues that emulation and its techniques bring to this new portrait of the author of *Resurrection*.

(Portrait or photography: let the reader decide for herself. After all, collage emerges as a structural principle of the Machadian assimilation of *aemulatio*.)

Just Before

I need to clarify the path from the questioning of the notion of authorship to the structural relevance of collage, via a rethinking of the scope of the reader's role.

Let me begin with a contrast. The text at hand is "Brother Simão," published in the *Jornal das Famílias* in June 1864, and reproduced in *Tales from Rio* (1870).

The story includes elements that will become hallmarks of Machado's second phase, although here they are crammed into a traditional framework. To borrow a metaphor from the visual arts, one might call this a study for future works. The heart of the sketch is a less-than-invigorating story: Simão, a young and romantic idealist, falls in love with his cousin, an orphan adopted by his family. Helena is the name of the beautiful orphan, just like the heroine of Machado's third novel, released twelve years later. The two characters share identical social circumstances: they are dependents, only able to dream of social ascension through marriage. Guiomar from *The Hand and the Glove* was more cunning; she ingeniously managed to escape a marriage to the nephew of her protector, thus avoiding a lifetime spent in the eternal circle of dependency. Estela from *Iaiá Garcia* proved prouder; she gave up a love that might have been true, her hand forced by the precarious nature of her situation. A reflection on the limits of the social framework defined by hierarchies, privileges, and a culture of favors, a fixture in Machado's novels, was apparent from his first short stories.

Simão is predictably tricked by his parents, who wish to impede his relationship with Helena. In this story, virtue finds no reward. Disillusioned by the false news of his cousin's death, the young man—a Jansenist lost in the tropics—abandons the company of men and takes religious orders. His eccentric, misanthropic behavior draws the attention of friars and novices alike: is he a saint completely devoted to serving the Lord, or is he simply hiding his madness under a religious habit?

Here the story takes a more interesting—and Machadian—turn.

First of all, two levels of narration emerge. And one of them, the "source" of the tale, can only be imagined by the reader. After Brother Simão's funeral, it is discovered that he wrote "some fragments of his memoirs" (II, 152). Eager to understand their brother's withdrawn ways, the friars decide to read the papers, involuntarily making him an author deceased—and we know the explosive result of the inversion of this naive procedure, in the form of the deceased author. The brothers' decidedly impious curiosity drives the narrative, evoking the oblique voyeurism behind one's reading of novels. For its part, the tale offered to the reader is the result of the examination of "the author of this narrative [who] despises that part of Memoirs which is completely devoid of importance" (II, 153). As with *Counselor Ayres' Memorial*, the reader of the story does not have access to the text by Brother Simão, but rather a reconstruction mediated by the narrator's reading. The reader of the story must content herself with the narrator's recollections of the *"Memoirs to Be Written by Brother Simão Águeda, Benedictine Monk"* (II, 153). Since the monk never finished his text, why not give a posthumous form to the writing, filtering it through the gaze of one who came after him? The figure of the author who knows himself to be primarily a reader is already present in the structure of this story.

Let us examine the nature of Brother Simão's memoirs.

In the words of the narrator, who happens to be the text's first reader: "They were, for the most part, incomplete fragments, truncated jottings and insufficient notes; but from the whole one may gather that Brother Simão was truly insane during a certain period" (II, 153). While the incompleteness and lacunae on display here may recall the prose of the *Posthumous Memoirs*, another question arises around a new comment on the manuscript.

The first time that Simão returns home, his cousin's name is strategically ignored. However, in the process of fulfilling his evangelizing mission, the monk visits a town far into the countryside of the state. To his surprise— although the reader might have easily seen this twist coming—at the end of his sermon, "a couple entered the church, husband and wife: he an honorable laborer, . . . she, a lady esteemed for her virtues, but of an insuperable melancholy" (II, 157). The woman is—who else?—Helena. Upon recognizing her cousin, she faints in the middle of Mass. The sermon is briefly interrupted, the friar identifies the new arrival and understands the fraud he has been living, as well as the stratagem his parents employed to separate him from his cousin. The narrator goes on: "In the friar's manuscript there follows *a series of ellipses laid out in eight lines*. He himself does not know what happened" (II, 157; italics mine).

Note the use of typographical resources, a method that would be enshrined in the *Posthumous Memoirs*, in a text from 1864—although here they are simply suggested for the reader to imagine and do not appear on the surface of the page. Emphasis should also be placed on the way in which Simão's madness is "diagnosed": the conclusion is made *verbally*. Withdrawn and casmurrian behavior might suggest misanthropy, but are not sufficient evidence for a diagnosis. It is rather the lacuna in the memoirs and his verbal delirium in the midst of his sermon that form the basis for the verdict: Brother Simão lost his mind.

Recall the passage in question:

> In the friar's manuscript there follows a series of ellipses laid out in eight lines. He himself does not know what happened. But what happened was, having just recognized Helena, the friar went on with his speech. It was something else now: it was an incoherent speech, lacking any subject, a flight of true delirium. General consternation followed. (II, 157)

The evidence for insanity is linguistic in nature: the friar isolates himself from mankind, progressively renouncing even language itself. His memoirs and the memory of his abortive sermon reinforce the idea—"incoherent speech"; "incomplete fragments" (II, 153)—and the pleonasm serves to mark the link between madness and the loss of one's mastery of language.

A similar effect is perfected in "The Alienist," published in several installments in *A Estação* between October 1881 and March 1882 and reproduced the same year in *Loose Papers*. The narrator drops hints as to the growing alienation of another Simão—this one a Bacamarte. The doctor's discourse in general implies his growing dissonance. In an apparently irrefutable definition: "Reason is the perfect equilibrium of all the faculties; outside of this is *insanity, insanity and only insanity*" (Machado de Assis, 2011; italics mine).

The very obsessive repetition of the word demonstrates the absolute disequilibrium progressively overtaking the alienist. The heralding of madness via the linguistic nature of one's understanding of reality was already sketched out back in "Brother Simão."

The story would be even more provocative if it ended here: "It was something else now: it was an incoherent speech, lacking any subject, a flight of true delirium. General consternation followed." Machadinho, however, felt obliged to conclude the story without leaving any lacunae; we are a long way from the author who will come to trust in the act of reading to fill in what the narrative may omit. Two months after the unexpected encounter, "the poor lady fell victim to the commotion" and died (II, 157). The friar's delirium has led to a death. And, reaping what he had sown, Simão's father enters the same order after the death of his wife, occupying the cell that had been his son's, only to (of course) go mad! In the words of the narrator: "It was believed that, in the last years of the old man's life, he was not less mad than Brother Simão de Águeda" (II, 157).

Finally, both the full development of the fictional potential inherent in the game of author-reader as well as the recycling of the model of the author-editor are allowed to flourish in *Esau and Jacob* and *Counselor Ayres' Memorial*. Indeed, the experience of writing *Dom Casmurro* must have been fundamental in Machado's mastery of a special approach to the text. I am referring to the technique of collage-reading.

The Text and Collage-Reading

In the pre-Romantic literary system, one works off the assumption of the existence of a common repertoire, driving the game between producers and receivers. This means that allusions and citations should be recognized easily, intensifying the playful nature of the literary experience. Its structure resembles that of a mental game of chess. By simply shifting one piece on the board of tradition, one can produce potentially infinite variations that may be appreciated depending on one's ability to evaluate the effects of this or that move. In a poem, each word chosen or image employed sets off a chain of associations and parallelisms that constitutes a true invisible oeuvre, a myriad of palimpsests and latent possibilities to be made material in the act of reception.

The technique of collage transforms this latency into a particular act of reading, bringing the radicality of the Machadian form of the novel to the fore.

Ultimately, the advent of romanticism was favored by the progressive loss of a common repertoire. The playful aspect of the technique of *imitatio* hides a social reality that is far from entertaining: knowledge of the literary tradition was restricted to a very limited portion of the population, the lettered elite. To an extent, and perhaps this is overreaching, it recalls the games meant to entertain at court or the pastimes of the salon—admirably sharp-witted, but only when one forgets the structural inequality upon which it rests.

The advent of romanticism, as I was saying, helped to significantly change these circumstances.

On one hand, in place of mastering a true archive of themes and forms, value was placed on one's knowledge of the culture of the homeland. (This is no coincidence: in the writing of literary history, romanticism and nationalism are twin phenomena.) On the other hand, the place reserved for the reader was progressively reduced, girded by the task of understanding the author's intentions—a strategic adjustment, incidentally, and one reproduced in parallel on the level of reading, as one moves from the whole of tradition to the individuality of the artist as creator. In place of the reader-chess player, the role implicit in the technique of *aemulatio*, bit by bit there emerged the figure of the reader-interpreter, a hermeneutist of a limited horizon.

This process leads to the reduction of the cultural repertoire. Nevertheless, the number of inhabitants in the lettered city can be increased, at least in theory. Hence the frankly anachronistic nature of the deliberate return to *aemulatio* in post-Romantic times, principally in slaveholding nineteenth-century Brazil. In the Brazilian context, falling back on emulation was also equivalent to a sort of subtle but acidic political commentary.

In Europe and the United States, mass literacy essentially created a new reading public. Two paths opened up: the Protestant channel, which taught people their first letters so that they might have direct contact with the Gospels, and the Napoleonic current, which considered literacy an indispensable part of fomenting a certain idea of citizenship. No matter the motive—in both cases, the gradual disappearance of the world of *imitatio* and *aemulatio* was tied to the effective emergence of an urban reading public. Without this phenomenon, it is unlikely that the novel as a genre would have attained the prominence it was to enjoy.

In the Brazilian case, devoid of literacy campaigns, the lettered circle—with its solid classical repertoire—faded away, but there appeared no larger public in its stead to avidly consume newspapers, feuilletons, or bound novels. In a crônica from August 15, 1876, commenting on the imperial census, Machado stares down the problem:

> The nation does not know how to read. Only some 30 percent of the individuals residing in this country can read; of them, 9 percent cannot read handwriting. Seventy percent lie in the most profound ignorance. . . . Seventy percent of our citizens vote like they breathe: without knowing why or what they do. They vote like they go to the festivities for Our Lady of Penha—to amuse themselves. (III, 345)

The deceased author's five potential readers may not be so few after all. It all depends on how you count—or where you do it.

Here lies the strength of Machado's oblique political commentary, clarified in the comparison between illiteracy and the faltering exercise of citizenship. A return to emulation in post-Romantic times might suggest that the political and economic structures preserve pre-Romantic elements. In Machado's case, an aesthetic choice may point toward vestiges of the colonial era. The anachronism cuts both ways.

Machado manages to go beyond the model of the reader-interpreter, combining two ways of reading: pre- and post-Romantic. It is as if the text were dropping hints that compromise the semantic stability of what it is saying. Thus, using a recourse that is so simple it is almost imperceptible, the reader-interpreter finds himself on the receiving end of a definitive finger-flick and suddenly finds himself without a function. Just like the deceased author, he must reinvent himself.

In the short stories, that which is declared in one paragraph is cast into doubt in another. In the novels, chapters become traps: this one pulls the rug out from under that one, chapter Y belies that which was promised in chapter X, and so on. Under such circumstances, the reader comes to play a central role in the constitution of meaning, a role that goes beyond a metaphorical sense, as it demands that the reader work to assemble these varied textual manifestations. This is, we might say, the truly Machadian watermark.

Collage-Reading and the Short Story

I would like to propose a rereading of the story "Stuffed-Shirt Theory," published in the *Gazeta de Notícias* on December 18, 1881, and in *Loose Papers* the following year.

The plot is as follows: Janjão, on the eve of his twenty-second birthday, finds that his father's gift to him will be a lesson on how to become a stuffed shirt. The stuffed shirt's prudent posture is useful in all professions, but will be especially so if the young man decides to go into politics. The story may be read as a lighthearted (and extremely well-developed) echo of the advice offered by the flatterer Polonius to his son Laertes, before a journey to begin his studies:

> There—my blessing with thee!
> And these few precepts in thy memory
> Look thou character. Give thy thoughts no tongue,
> Nor any unproportion'd thought his act.
> Be thou familiar, but by no means vulgar:
> . . . .
> Give every man thine ear, but few thy voice;
> Take each man's censure, but reserve thy judgment.
> Costly thy habit as thy purse can buy,
> But not express'd in fancy; rich, not gaudy;
> For the apparel oft proclaims the man. (*Hamlet*, 1.3.57–72, 109–10)

The king's chief counselor, Polonius is characterized by servility so exaggerated that it becomes comic. Nevertheless, in proposing a realistic guide for surviving in the hierarchical society of court, he seeks to save face. Laertes must listen to all those who have more power and prestige than he. He may formulate his own *judgment*, but only as a corollary to the higher order *Give thy thoughts no tongue.*

The Brazilian version abandons all subtlety and provides an explicit take on the counselor's true aims—which fit perfectly into the social relations at play in the world of dependents and patrons. Janjão's father sums up his personal philosophy with a right hook to his son's chin: "never transcend the limits of an enviable vulgarity" (II, 294). The adjective *enviable* reveals that we should consult the noun's etymology: *vulgo*, in the sense of "relating to what is common." The father's advice is an absolute paean to *mediocritas*. Literally placing oneself in the middle is the safest way to proceed amidst the instability of public life, especially if there is practically no difference between liberals and conservatives in terms of their exercise of power—a noted feature of Brazilian political life during the reign of the Braganças (1822–89).

Upon seeing this *enviable vulgarity*, the reader of *Esau and Jacob* may recall the struggles of meek Custódio, owner of the Confeitaria do Império. On the eve of the declaration of the Republic, which would come on November 15, 1889, he decides to order a new signboard for his establishment. Once he gets wind of the latest news, he is quick to move: "He dashed off a note and sent a clerk over to the painter. The note only said: "Stop at the 'd.'" Indeed, it was not necessary to paint the rest, which would be wasted, nor to lose the beginning, which could be used" (Lowe 139). If the Republic were to remain in power, the signboard would proclaim, in tune with these new times, *Confeitaria da República*; but if by chance the monarchy returned, the tea shop's signboard would declare its loyalty to eternal values: *Confeitaria do Império*. The note arrives too late, however, and the Confeitaria's owner is forced to pay up. After all, "revolutions always bring expense" (Lowe 143), expenses, naturally, to be paid by the ranks of Custódios across the history of Brazil.

More cautious than the unfortunate teashop owner, Janjão's father has developed an infallible method for his son to reach political paradise without encountering a rocky path. First of all, he must undertake "a punishing regime, read compendiums of rhetoric, listen to certain speeches, etc." (II, 290)—listen with the diplomatic attention of a Counselor Ayres, not the careless air of dour Bento Santiago. Similarly, Janjão is urged to sprinkle his day-to-day language with clichés, following the example of another Counselor: Acácio, from *Cousin Bazilio*.

Let us examine the formula:

You may employ any number of expressive figures: the Lernaean Hydra, for example, the head of Medusa, the Danaides' sieves, Icaro's wings, and others, which Romantics, classics, and realists employ gracefully, when they need them. Latin proverbs, historical dictums, famous verses, legal adages, or maxims, one is well warned to carry them along for speeches after dinner, of congratulations or of thanks. *Caveant consules* is an excellent ending for a political article; I might say the same of *Si vis pacem para bellum*. (II, 291)

This passage is very important, as it qualifies the overarching dictum that preceded it: to *read compendiums of rhetoric*. In such treatises, the aspiring stuffed shirt may find the complete collection of commonplaces, meaning-less frills, and prefabricated oratorical models, ready for use when custom calls: *Si vis pacem para bellum*.

In a sense, this was truly a discursive war; and the adepts of romanticism prepared themselves for peace by sapping the art of rhetoric of its complexity.

In post-Romantic times, this sapping was evidenced by the semantic turn taken by two key words: *rhetoric* and *commonplace*.

Let us look to the Oxford English Dictionary.

Rhetoric: "the art of using language effectively so as to persuade or influence others."[3]

This is the classical sense. Within its scope, the technique of *aemulatio* assumes the sort of literary chess-playing discussed in chapter 3, providing the foundations for the reading that I am proposing of Machado de Assis's work.

(As the reader will already know by heart and then some, I am proceeding on the assumption of a deliberately anachronistic update of pre-Romantic methods in post-Romantic times.)

The dominant meaning after the Romantic revolution is quite different: "the employment of emphatic and pompous means for persuasion or exhibi-tion; bombastic, emphatic, ornamented, and empty speech."[4]

Ornamented and empty speech: here is the current sense, and the formula proffered by Janjão's father. In this wan register, the stuffed shirt becomes a metonym for the politician, whose discourse is naturally reduced to "pure rhetoric." This semantic metamorphosis was only made possible through the weakening of a fundamental resource.

Back to the dictionary, starting with the definition that is more common today.

Commonplace: "a common or ordinary topic; an opinion or statement generally accepted or taken for granted; a stock theme or subject of research, an every-day saying. Slightingly: a platitude or truism."[5]

A simple cliché, the commonplace has become the Esperanto of received ideas, bringing together Bouvard, Pécuchet, Counselor Acácio, and the countless stuffed shirts of Machado's fiction. From this perspective, the opposite of the commonplace is the creativity of the demiurgic artist, concerned with being the first to say that which has never been said before.

Let us recall, however, the classical sense of the word as associated to the art of rhetoric.

Commonplace: "a passage of general application, such as may serve as the basis of argument; a leading text cited in argument."[6]

General application: the *common purse*, in Machado's terms, as studied in "The Instinct of Nationality." This is tradition itself, the knowledge of which was shared between writers and listeners, or readers. From this treasure trove stems the playful aspect of the literary experience.

This passage—apparently a commonplace in itself, or a simple cliché— implies an unexpected ambiguity, the consequences of which help to clarify what it is that makes Brás Cubas *an author all his own*, in the terms of the preface to the third edition of the *Posthumous Memoirs*.

On one hand, *if the passage is read from the point of view of Janjão's father*, the son must hone his talents in the art of discoursing at length without clarifying what he is thinking. In fact, he does not even need to think. These are the ideal conditions for proffering empty, but inflated speeches; after all, turning to difficult words and well-chosen Latinisms will pave the way to obtaining the longed-for passport to the amusement park of those in power.

On the other hand, *if the passage is read in the opposite sense*, it is a coded bit of praise of the art of rhetoric, suggesting an indirect recognition of the technique of emulation: one has only to read the advice with an inverted hermeneutics. We should recall that the story is a pitiless satire of the mental and political habits of the Brazilian elite; this reading, then, does not seem excessive. In inverting the terms of the equation—or, better yet, restoring the original sense of the terms—Machado entrusts the keen reader with an alternative way to understand his work.

It is all a matter of honing one's ear.

(I have done nothing else, incidentally, throughout this whole essay.)

Here is the paradox that structures the text: "the stuffed-shirt theory," in its most basic form, is destabilized by the very reading of the story "Stuffed-Shirt Theory"! Merely laying out its assumptions, enumerated with all the comic seriousness of a Polonius, makes its application unfeasible. Once the artifice is revealed, the magician is no longer a successful illusionist. Likewise, it is hard to imagine a reader who, upon hearing the advice given to the young man, can avoid "that vague movement at the corner of the mouth, heavy with mystery, invented by some decadent Greek, which infected Lucian, who passed it on to Swift and Voltaire, the very look of the skeptical and the clear-eyed. No. Rather, use a quip" (II, 294). Janjão's father paints irony in suggestive colors but recommends the quip a powerful antidote—since, as the text warns, irony must be avoided at all costs. This care is a part of the treatment: as for ideas of one's own, "best to not have any whatsoever" (II, 290). After all, how to dissociate irony from a quick wit, and a quick wit from one's own thoughts? The quip, meanwhile, is pure exteriority, and goes perfectly with the exercise of *vulgarity*.

An *enviable* one, if possible.

Nevertheless, while the story provokes *that vague movement at the corner of the mouth*, the theory falls apart at the very moment the story is read.

The production of interpretive short-circuits is an effect brought about by the Machadian text, and which calls for the technique of collage-reading.

(The hallmark of his literature.)

As his tricks are exposed, the stuffed shirt becomes a caricature of a society allergic to meritocracy. The curtain rises, but the mask falls. Janjão is made to smile at the ills inherent to his social medium, although his rich repast will depend on them. The practice of the stuffed shirt falls before the clarification of its own theoretical basis: in reading the story we find the mirror of the writing—more precisely, its potential opposite.

This movement favors a truly innovative duality. On one hand there stands writing as a living museum, the reinvention of the library. On the other, we have reading as the antechamber of writing, of the collage of possible books.

The reader reveals herself to be the double of the author, and the latter the future of the former.

Most importantly: at no point does the narrator call attention to the contradiction that structures the story. This is a latent meaning; all its elements may be found laid out on the chessboard of the text, but it is up to the reader to set up the play and assemble the pieces of the puzzle.

However, there is nothing to impede this act of collage from taking place within a very few readers—*perhaps five.* It is likely that the better part of the reading public will remain on the surface of the text, betraying an affinity with the ethic of the stuffed shirt.

The text develops in a palimpsest. On the top layer, the merciless satire of stuffed shirts. Below that, a criticism of all society, including the reader— especially the reader. Machado may have learned this method of writing for a variety of audiences alongside the author of *Hamlet.* This is one of the most fascinating aspects of Shakespeare's theater, and the Machadian leap displays the same ability, associated to an act of reading that evokes the beginning of the collage process.

Collage-Reading and the Novel

Machado's discursive strategy demands a reader able to associate passages in the text that, although far apart from one another, produce an interpretive short-circuit when brought together. The point merits further attention: this effect is not the result of a simple proximity in which, for example, chapter 12 relativizes or contradicts what has been said in chapters 11, 10, or even 9. Rather, the distance between chapters demands a deliberate act on the reader's part. The textual model that encourages collage-reading is above all a sense of latency, something that may only be activated through an autonomous gesture of determining meaning; if this is not the case, collage-reading simply does not come to fruition. In other words, Machado's literature is above all a potentiality.

This technique is at its most vibrant in the sphinxlike novel *Dom Casmurro.*

To offer one example: now I will ask the reader to interrupt his or her reading of this essay in order to undertake a leisurely consultation of chapters 83 and 139, "The Portrait" and "The Photograph," respectively.

Emphasis on the considerable distance between the two occurrences:

they are separated by more than fifty chapters. However, through the use of collage-reading, we may draw their contradictory conclusions together.

Starting with the latter chapter, let us examine the decisive passage:

> Capitu and I, involuntarily, looked at Escobar's photograph, then at each other. This time her confusion became a pure confession. This one was the other; *there must certainly be a photograph of Escobar as a child somewhere that would be our little Ezequiel.* (Gledson 232; italics mine)

The conclusion is made even more drastic because, as is stated at the opening of the chapter, "I give my word that I was on the verge of thinking that I was the victim of a great illusion, the phantasmagoria of a hallucinated man, but the sudden entrance of Ezequiel shouting: 'Mamma! Mamma! It's time for mass!' brought me back to an awareness of reality." Bento Santiago had been on the verge of reconciling with Capitu, stifling his suspicions and recognizing that he lacked irrefutable evidence of her "crime"—the supposed adultery with Escobar, her husband's best friend. This is the key moment of the novel, signaling the definitive break between the couple. The narrator bases his certainty on a hypothesis—*there must certainly be a photograph of Escobar as a child somewhere*—but, as the phrase itself suggests, such a photograph simply does not exist. Unless we consider little Ezequiel a moving photograph of Escobar as a boy!

This conclusion may be placed alongside the situation that unfolds in the chapter "The Portrait." Bentinho, hearing of Sancha's illness, goes to her house. That was his excuse: in truth, he was going to see Capitu. Gurgel, the father of the patient, strikes up a conversation by pointing to a wall "where there hung the portrait of a girl, [and] asked me if I thought Capitu was like the portrait" (Gledson 150). Not one to disagree, Bentinho confirms the likeness without paying much attention to the canvas. Excited by his assent, Gurgel goes on:

> Then he said that it was a portrait of his wife, and that people who had known her said the same thing. He, too, thought that they had similar features, principally the forehead and the eyes. *As for their temperaments, they were identical: like sisters.*
>
> "And to top it all, her friendship with Sanchinha; even her mother

was no closer to her . . . *Life produces these strange resemblances.*" (Gledson
150; italics mine)

The similarity is not merely physical (*principally the forehead and the
eyes*) but above all in terms of their nature (*As for their temperaments, they
were identical: like sisters*). The narrator seems to accept the conclusion
drawn by Sancha's father: *Life produces these strange resemblances.* He does
not contest it, at the very least; and in writing his memoirs he could very well
have done so retrospectively.

Let me recapitulate, as much depends on the form of the chapters in
Machado's novels: when they are taken in through the technique of collage-
reading, a short circuit is created. Now, if what we read in "The Portrait" is
true, the conclusion drawn by the narrator in "The Photograph" can have
little weight: if *these strange resemblances* are allowed to pass, then the similarity between Ezequiel and Escobar can under no circumstances be considered
conclusive proof of Capitu's infidelity.

That said, if the hypothesis laid out in chapter 139 holds water, then the
famous ending to 83 falls apart: the similarity between Escobar and Ezequiel
cannot be a chance one. In this case, the lack of any comment from the casmurrian narrator may simply be a demonstration of his personality: "One
of my habits in life has always been to agree with the probable opinion of
whoever is speaking to me, so long as it doesn't offend or irritate, or otherwise obtrude itself on me. *Before looking to see if Capitu really was or was not
like the portrait, I replied yes*" (Gledson 150; italics mine). Hence, Sancha's
father's conclusion—*Life produces these strange resemblances*—is lost in the
void of Bentinho's overwhelming disinterest. His lack of an answer does not
necessarily mean that Gurgel is right.

What now?

Here lies the challenge of the text that drives collage-reading: the narrator offers no clues, and it is up to the reader to realize that she is adrift. She
can no longer content herself with the role of interpreter of the "truth" of
the text, since the author himself gives no credence to the notion. This is the
radical nature of the Machadian form: the final shaping of the text is partially
transferred to the reader, providing an unexpected and anachronistic *resurrection* of the circuit at the core of *aemulatio*, tempered by a *free form*—both in
terms of appropriation and in terms of the plurality of the acts of reading here.

This semantic disorientation is not recognized by our narrator, and this is the key point. Bento Santiago does not pride himself on his metalinguistic complexity, nor does he admire his own stylistic resources. The narrator seems firmly convinced of Capitu and Escobar's betrayal. The potential collapse of meaning—made possible by the technique of collage-reading—only emerges through a specific act of reading. The reader must compare the chapters and, as in the case of the opening notes to *Esau and Jacob* and *Counselor Ayres' Memorial*, pick out dissonances that only become visible in the act of comparison. Many readers of *Dom Casmurro* remain wrapped up in the question of Capitu's guilt or innocence, preparing laborious lists of proof for or against the hypothesis. In this dispensable, albeit tempting, activity, the potential of the sphinx-text is lost; rather, it remains invisible.

His ability to write for more than one kind of audience and his subtle method for spreading contradictory clues throughout the text allow Machado to return to a pre-Romantic model of writing, thereby favoring an act of reading characteristic of the same historical period. As we have seen, authors, readers, and listeners shared a common repertoire available to them; thus, both production and reception were able to activate the defining framework in this combinatorial art, drawing up virtual palimpsests in their examination of possible variations. And each reader or listener reacted as befitting his or her repertoire and analytic abilities, comprising a diverse audience.

Chess with words: the author begins the game with the white pieces, but the second move is always the reader's.

This is the truly Machadian contribution to the form of the novel, made possible by the deliberately anachronistic return to the techniques of *imitatio* and *aemulatio*.

Aemulatio: To Emend

The technique of collage-reading may help to clarify a relevant element.

In Machado's works from the second phase, we note the constant presence of the word *emendar* (emend, correct). In general, the term's semantic field focuses on the idea of correcting ideas, rectifying procedures, and reforming behaviors, in keeping with the current meaning of the word. However, the verb also appears often in terms of the separate meaning of correcting or rectifying texts or musical scores: these are *emendations* to be made by both the narrator and the reader—especially the reader.

In this context, Machado's twist on Pascal's maxim gains strength. While the idea of man as a "thinking reed" implies a minimum level of stability amid movement, the idea of man as a "thinking erratum" suggests movement as a model of dynamic stability even as it (metaphorically) suggests the possibility of including a new element in the equation: the reader. It is up to him to become an improvised craftsman in an imaginary typographical workshop, set out to *correct* the printed text at his own expense and risk.

The reader will easily recognize the passage in question. It is found in the *Posthumous Memoirs*, chapter 27, "Virgília?" and begins with a typical flick of the finger:

> Ah, how indiscreet! Ah, how ignorant! But it is precisely this that makes us lords of the earth, *this power to restore the past*, to touch on the instability of our impressions and the vanity of our affections. Let Pascal say that man is a thinking reed. No; he is a thinking erratum, that's what he is. Each season of life is an edition which *corrects* the previous one, and which will be *corrected* itself, until the definitive edition, which the editor gives free of charge to the worms. (I, 549; italics mine)

The poetics of emulation, and its deliberate anachronism, is *this power to restore the past*, correcting, insofar as possible, political and cultural asymmetries that lie beyond the author's control. The metaphor returns in chapter 38, "The Fourth Edition," now with a multivalent use of the verb:

> Do you *still* recall my theory of human editions? Well, know that, around this time, I was in my fourth edition, *revised and emended*, but still shot through with oversights and barbarisms; a flaw that I found partly compensated by the typography, which was elegant, and the binding, which was sumptuous. (I, 556–57; italics mine)

The ironic diction in the question recalls the restrained censure of those who did not identify Dinis's imitations *perhaps because they were overlooked*. Few pages lie between instances of the same metaphor. However, a few pages may amount to an eternity for readers in a rush.

In *Quincas Borba*, the use of the word plays with variations on a theme that was particularly dear to Machado. See chapter 168:

> And from there, who knows? repeated Dr. Falcão, the next morning. The night had not snuffed out his distrust. And from there, who knows? Yes, there would be more than morbid sympathy. *Without knowing Shakespeare, he emended Hamlet*: "There are more things between heaven and earth, Horatio, than are dreamt of in your philanthropy." (I, 783–84; italics mine)

Likewise, Bento Santiago, who "had never seen or read" *Othello*, could easily imagine the link between the play and his dilemma: "I only knew the subject, and was pleased at the coincidence" (Gledson 226). In the next chapter in *Quincas Borba*, it seems as if Machado wants to emphasize the idea; the verb appears again.

> In truth, the conclusion did not seem to lie in the premises; but this was cause for another emendation to Hamlet: "There are more things between heaven and earth, Horatio, than are dreamt of in your *dialectics.*" (I, 784)

The reader may wonder as to the purpose of this modest inventory.

The question is fair, and may be answered through an intuition from Raimundo Magalhães Júnior. In an inspiring essay, he opens with a provocative declaration:

> Machado de Assis, disfigurer of quotations . . . Until now, no-one had raised this accusation against the great writer. None, however, would be better founded. *As this is a sin of many*, this is nothing to diminish him. Moreover, *Machado was a prolific quoter.* This was one of his particular pleasures. He liked to parade around his considerable knowledge of foreign literatures, quoting in the original whenever he could, whenever it fit within the limits of his crônicas or stories. This was one of his few points of vanity.[7]

An ancestral vanity, we might note; this being *a sin of many*, it characterizes a typical procedure within the technique of *imitatio*. The essayist proceeds to construct a lovely examination of Machado's *disfigurations*, especially in terms of Molière's works, featuring erudite clarifications of Machado's method: "the fusion of two different elements from two bygone readings" (270). The recycling of a number of sources in the production of new works is the Shakespearean model par excellence, based on the exercise at the core of emulation.

Nevertheless, considering that these omnipresent quotations were a sign of the author's vanity, the essayist cannot escape a disappointing conclusion: "In any case, the hypothesis of a lapse in memory based on confused recollections of one's reading would not be inadmissible or absurd" (269).

Perhaps not, but the hypothesis is simply anachronistic.

Anachronism, pure and simple.

Anachronism in its dictionary state, without the charm of an inside-out anachronism, or the complexity of a two-way anachronism.

Let us accept what Magalhães Júnior has to say: the author of *Resurrection* often disfigures the source that he cites. It would be better to conceive this as the Machadian method desacralizing the source-text, but let us retain Magalhães Júnior's terminology. The greater difficulty is that the essayist does not seem to understand the motive for this disfiguration. It is a sort of gentlemen's agreement—a wink to tradition and to the reader as well, as it is up to him to identify the modifications that have been made. The critic, in this case, did precisely this, reiterating the playful nature of this chess match of words (although such playfulness is made conspicuous by its absence here). An invariably precise quotation would demand the perennial consultation of texts, something one can only reasonably demand within an academic specialization. Meticulous footnotes and interminable squabbles about the best source mark the moment in history in which tradition ceases to be part of daily life, migrating to the realm of academia. Can there be a drier way to address that which was once our common repertoire? Is there any more eloquent medium with which to measure the distance that grows to separate us from texts that were once part of the day-to-day in the lettered city? The subtlety of the classical model emerges in the emendation that every *auctoritas* undergoes. Only the pedant insists on citing word for word, while the true man of letters introduces the *sauce of his own production*, as Machado said of Antônio José's theater. The artisan may be the same, but the glass *bears another wine*, and its *terroir* lies at the root of our deceased author's singularity.

To correct that which is someone else's and make it one's own is the primary modus operandi in *aemulatio*. This procedure plays a central role in memory, and especially in its voluntary lapses. Machado did us the favor of explaining his art, but one must read it with eyes wide open. Recall the story "Um dístico" [A Couplet], published on July 1, 1886, in *A Quinzena* and never reproduced in book form during Machado's life:

> When our Memory is good, *historical, poetical, literary, and political connections fairly pullulate.* One need only walk, see, and listen. Once it so happened that I heard on the street one of our common sayings, at such a time that it suggested a line of the Pentateuch to me and I thought that the latter explained the former, and from the verbal oration I made out its deeper intent. (II, 1063; italics mine)

Such connections do not escape the deceased author in his striking parallel between *The Posthumous Memoirs of Brás Cubas* with, once again, the Pentateuch. This technique is described in the form of one of the dead man's memories of his childhood mischief. Little Cubas, with undisguised glee, reveals the stolen kiss between Dr. Vilaça and D. Eusébia:

> Dona Eusébia raised her handkerchief to her eyes. *The glosser searched his memory for some bit of literature* and turned up this one, which I later confirmed was from one of the Judeu's operas:
> "Don't cry, my dear, lest the day break with two dawns."
> He said this; pulled her to him; she resisted a bit, but let herself go; their faces came together, and I heard the smack, a very light one, of a kiss, the timidest of kisses. (I, 531; italics mine)

Memory freely pillages tradition in search of the right word, phrase, or image for the occasion at hand, a resource that suggests an adaptation of the source. It is also interesting that seductive Dr. Vilaça should turn precisely to the works of Antônio José, an author who had merited a long essay just the year before the publication of *The Posthumous Memoirs of Brás Cubas*, a commentary based on the poetics of emulation.

Magalhães Júnior missed his target, but he pointed his bow in the right direction—which is saying something.

In *Dom Casmurro*, Machado turns the idea of emendations into a structural element.

The first two instances of the verb may be found in the famous chapter 9, "The Opera." First, in the words of Satan: "Here is the score, listen to it, have it played" (Gledson 18). To clarify the context: this is a remarkable dialogue between God, the author of an undoubtedly perfect poem, and Satan, a composer of music that is at times aggressive and likely a bit too long, as would naturally be the case with a Wagnerian devil figure. In spite of this, or because of it, the piece is extraordinarily lively. Shortly thereafter, the leitmotiv returns, marking the tempo for the text:

> The composer's friends assert that such a perfect work is not easily to be found. Some admit to a few blemishes and *the odd thing missing*, but it is probable that, as the opera proceeds, these latter will be filled in or explained, and the blemishes will disappear altogether: the composer has not discarded the idea of *amending* the work wherever he finds that it does not correspond completely to the poet's sublime conception. (Gledson 19; italics mine)

Later on I will return to the matter of these lacunae, the *odd thing missing*, but let me first point out the structural relationship between a lacunar text and the act of emending: these are gestures that inaugurate a new fiction of reading.

Another occurrence of the verb highlights the implicit inclusion of the reader in the potential inversion of what is being stated. The narrator makes an irreverent comparison, concluding with a negative declaration that the reader is obliged to transform into an affirmation. Take another look at chapter 32, "Undertow Eyes":

> The joy of the blessed in heaven must be doubled by knowing the sum of torments their enemies have already suffered in hell; so too the quantity of delights their foes enjoy in heaven must increase the agony of the damned. This particular torture escaped the divine Dante's notice; *but I am not here to correct poets*. (Gledson 63; italics mine)

This emendation or correction may only be made in the act of reading—an implicit suggestion from the narrator, left on the page in a latent form that calls out to the reader's imagination. Collage-reading and the technique of emendation come together in the creation of a textual framework that transfers a large part of the attribution of meaning over to the reader.

(Just imagine what Machado might do if he had lived in the age of hypertext!)

Emending quotations from texts—generally classical ones—is a characteristic procedure in Machado's modus operandi, inserting itself into a long tradition while updating itself with irreverence and irony. The author even incorporates its vocabulary into his personal correspondence, demonstrating how this move filtered into his daily life.

Let us reread a letter sent to José Veríssimo on February 22, 1906:

> I am going on as I can, *to emend* our dear Camões, in that stanza of his:
> My Summer's Pride, to Autumn speed amain . . .
> I sink into the vale of years, and past
> I have put *autumn* where *summer* lies, and *winter* for *autumn*, and this
> itself is vanity, as winter is already here in full. (III, 1076, first italics mine)[8]

Back to the casmurrian narrator.

After recognizing the lapses in his memory, a moment of awareness pregnant with questions for those seeking to reconstruct their life based on their recollections, Bento Santiago finds unexpected consolation:

> Let us hope that it be *forgetfulness* rather than confusion; let me explain
> myself. There is no way of *emending* a confused book, but everything can
> be put into books with omissions. I never get upset when I read one of this
> latter type. What I do, when I get to the end, is shut my eyes and think of
> all the things I didn't find in it. How many delightful ideas occur to me
> then! What profound reflections! The rivers, mountains, churches that I
> didn't see in the pages I have read, all appear to me now with their waters,
> their trees, their altars, and the generals draw the swords that had stayed in
> their scabbards, and the trumpets sound out the notes that were sleeping
> in the metal, and everything proceeds in the most unpredictably lively way.

For everything can be found outside a book with gaps in it, dear reader. *Thus I fill in others' lacunae*: in this way too you can fill in mine. (Gledson 111–12; italics mine)

In confused books, *there is no way of emending* them because they seek to contain everything, especially their own explanations. This is the case of Machado's first four novels in the constant search for the *key to the writing*. Books with omissions, on the contrary, make lacunae into their own structure. The casmurrian narrator's description of his mental attitude—*shut my eyes and think of all the things I didn't see in the pages I have read*—offers a model for the reception of Machado's work.

The reader already knows where I am going with this: Machado turns the impossibility of controlling the ultimate meaning of a text into a literary form, transferring the task to the reader—without reservations or restrictions. It is as if he is amusing himself at the cost of the incomprehension sown by his oblique texts, oblique although on the surface all appears clear, even crystalline. In truly Machadian fiction, the Foucaultian concept of "author function" shifts from center stage, which is now taken by the "reader function"—a notion easily derivable from Machado's literature. In *Esau and Jacob* and *Counselor Ayres' Memorial*, the ultimate organizer of the text is the first reader of the *diary of recollections* by the diplomat—literally, an *Ur-Leser*. Machado develops a literary form in which the author relinquishes his desire to control the "exclusive" authorship of meaning; his technique smirks at this idea, knowing that there can be no "ultimate" meaning.

In that specific sense, *Dom Casmurro* may be considered the ultimate masterpiece of Machadian literature, since the determination of meaning is definitively transferred to the reader. And yet, it is not possible to determine that meaning unequivocally. A similar exercise may be seen both in *The Posthumous Memoirs of Brás Cubas* and in *Quincas Borba*, but the radicality of this experiment reaches its highest point in the prose of the casmurrian narrator. Like a sort of Gorgias on the Rua do Ouvidor, Machado turns the impasse into productivity, the lacuna into structure.

After wishing for his mother's death—in order to free himself from the promise she had made, which obliged him to go into seminary—Bentinho turns to the reader. See chapter 67, "A Sin": "If you find anything similar in this book, *dear reader, let me know, so that I can correct it in the second edition*; there's nothing worse than giving the longest of legs to the shortest of ideas" (Gledson 127; italics mine).

High time I finished up this section, then.

The idea of collage-reading and the act of emendation or correction evoke the contemporary technique of sampling, involving complex questions around the notions of authorship, copies, originals, and plagiarism.

For that matter, can plagiarism be creative?

Plagiarism as Creation?

The textual framework that favors collage-reading and the practice of emendation comprise elements of the formal structure by which the reader is made a part of the constitution of innumerable possibilities of meaning.

Machado will gradually affirm his singularity via the role of a reflexive reader; the text before this figure is the written memory of his imaginary library. Unsurprisingly, we find constant allusions to Shakespeare in his works—no other writer was so important for Machado de Assis as a reader.

This is an elective affinity that defines the journey from Machadinho to Machado.

In chapter 3, we observed the structural relationship between Virgil and Machado.

Shakespeare's importance has already been pointed out by a number of Machado scholars.

For my part, I will underline Shakespeare's link to the technique of emulation, as this is very likely the source of Machado's fascination with the author of *Othello*. In the story "Tempo de crise" [Time of Crisis], published in the *Jornal das Famílias* in April 1873, the character called C. sums up Machado's take: "They say of Shakespeare that, if all humanity were to perish, he alone could comprise it, as he left no fiber of the human heart intact" (II, 784–85).

One can hardly imagine more outright praise.

Of all the canonic authors of Western literature, Shakespeare made the greatest use of *others' spices* in the *sauce of his own production*. According to scholars, of the thirty-seven plays in the First Folio (1623), nothing fewer than thirty-three are the result of the combination of a variety of sources—they are *inventions*, then, not plots *created* by the playwright per se. Only four plays' plots were concocted by Shakespeare himself;[9] even in these cases, he made use of various suggestions for specific scenes or lines.

Shakespeare's sources were multiple and heteroclite in nature: he borrowed not just from the classics, but also from contemporaries. He productively pillaged the comedies of Plautus and Terence, the tragedies of Seneca, tales related by historians from classical antiquity, medieval chronicles, historical episodes, and legends. At the same time, he studied his peers' work, unblushingly lifting some of their better ideas and staging solutions. Likewise, Shakespeare perfected the art of writing for more than one audience, coding messages for a very few listeners in the audience.

Perhaps five?

Or, on the contrary, Stendhal's hundred?

Shakespeare wrote for a variety of audiences, as we may glean from the note appended by John Heminge and Henry Condell, friends of the writer's and the editors of the First Folio: "TO THE GREAT VARIETY OF READERS. From the most able to him that can but spell: there you are number'd."[10]

Machado learned much with Shakespeare: not in terms of topics or plots, but rather a way of approaching tradition and the contemporary world. The Brazilian also intuited the art of writing for a variety of audiences, imagining, below the serene surface of his texts, destabilizing possible readings.

Let us then recall that *Dom Casmurro* constitutes a radical reading of *Othello*, although it goes beyond a rewriting of the Moor's tragedy. And even if we limit our study to the plays of Shakespeare, it will not be a challenge to show how *The Winter's Tale* and *Cymbeline* are also relevant in Machado's shaping of Bento Santiago's memoirs.

(For now, I will simply jot the idea down. Developing it would demand writing another book.)

Helen Caldwell examines the case in *The Brazilian Othello of Machado de Assis: A Study of "Dom Casmurro"*. The tragedy provides the plot for twenty-eight short stories, plays, and articles.[11] Beyond numerical precision, it interests us to observe that Machado's rewriting exposes a productive—and clarifying—contradiction, exposing the political nature of the anachronistic return to *aemulatio* from another angle.

As the intrigue develops, doesn't Othello's insecurity—motivated by his position as a foreigner amid Venice's dominant classes—bear an importance similar to Iago's malice? The instability of this situation is the element that allows the ensign to work his mischief. From this perspective, the Moor's drama is partially reenacted in *Dom Casmurro*, but sans Iago: Othello's dilemma lies less in his jealousy than in his awareness of his condition. The Moor's crown of thorns is another. A son of Mauritania elevated to a position of power and prestige in Venice, the center of the world, the political and economic heart of the Mediterranean, Othello is painfully conscious of the precarious nature of his good fortune.

Before going down this avenue, allow me a succinct summary of Caldwell's reading: Machado's ingenious trick allows him to portray the nature of jealousy as a vicious cycle that, even in the absence of objective evidence, feeds on itself—the firefly and the sun who shine grudgingly but are unable to do otherwise, as we saw in the poem "Vicious Circle." Bento Santiago tries to convince the reader that Capitu and Escobar were lovers. And the longer he presents his case before the jury, the less he seems able to persuade his audience. Without an Iago to blame, how to justify such disproportionate, apparently spontaneous jealousy, unless one turns back to the jealous figure himself and examines the untrustworthy nature of such a biased narrator?

This said, and one need not imagine that these two interpretations are mutually exclusive, Bento Santiago's partial reading of Shakespeare's play introduces a parallelism that ought to be discussed. The Moor and Bento Santiago hail from the same latitude, so to speak: the periphery.

Othello, an indispensable general for the city of Venice *in times of war*, knows very well that, *in times of peace*, he goes back to being just a Moor who is wrongfully taking up a place reserved for others. Especially such a coveted marital bed.

The first act of the tragedy takes place in Venice, on the eve of war with the Turks. At this point, no man is worth more than the Moor. In the Duke's emphatic words: "opinion, a sovereign mistress of effects, throws a more safer voice on you" (1.3.222–23, 87). Who else could face down the foreign threat? Othello is forgiven, despite having married Desdemona without the permission of her father—the powerful senator Brabantio.

The next four acts take place in Cyprus, which will prove a decisive spatial shift. In the very first scene of the second act, we are told of the destruction of the Turkish fleet in a terrible storm; Othello's presence is no longer decisive. At each new scene, the action subtly suggests this. To begin with the delay in his ship's arrival: symptomatically, it is the last to arrive at the island. Finally, in the first scene of the last act, Othello discovers that he has been replaced as the governor of Cyprus.

But this is not all.

In addition to being replaced by Michael Cassio—in a perverse bit of irony, as the Moor believes that the lieutenant is already substituting him in another intimate field—Othello receives news that may be even worse than the alleged betrayal. If we take Iago at his word, after Roderigo's surprise:

> IAGO: Sir, there is especial commission come from Venice to depute Cassio
> in Othello's place.
> RODERIGO: Is that true? why, then Othello and Desdemona return again
> to Venice.
> IAGO: O, no; he goes into Mauritania and takes away with him the fair Des-
> demona, unless his abode be lingered here by some accident: wherein
> none can be so determinate as the removing of Cassio. (4.2.213–20, 171)

Here lies Othello's true defeat.

Back to the starting point: from the center of the world to the center of the periphery, passing through the periphery of the center, the isle of Cyprus. Once again we can make out the triangular relationships at the heart of the shaping of Latin American cultures.

However, the parallel between Bentinho and the Moor demands certain caution. It is no coincidence that Capitu's husband reads Plutarch. Unlike Othello, Bentinho is a child of the economic elite. In this sense, the character most like Othello is Capitu herself. Recall the cruel vision of the casmurrian narrator, staining the memories of young Bentinho:

> I couldn't keep my eyes off this fourteen-year-old girl, tall, strong, and well
> built, in a tight fitting, *somewhat faded cotton frock.* Her thick hair hung
> down her back in two plaits tied together at the ends, as was the fashion at
> the time. She was of a dark complexion, with large, pale eyes, and a long,
> straight nose, a delicate mouth and a broad chin. *Her hands, although used*

to hard household work, were well cared for; they were not scented with fine soaps or toilet water, but she kept them spotless with *water from the well and ordinary soap. She wore strong cloth shoes, flat and old, which she herself kept mended.* (Gledson 27; italics mine)

This is the very picture of the neighbor girl's low social status—much like Simão's cousin Helena, a beautiful orphan without an inheritance. Here Machado returns to the narrative structure with a variety of levels that he had timidly tried out in "Brother Simão," the story from 1864. The casmurrian narrator's prose recalls a triptych: in the middle, Bentinho's memories and his falling in love with Capitu; the two side panels feature Bento Santiago's biased diction in his attempt to convince himself of his love's betrayal, on one side, and the embittered tone of Dom Casmurro, skeptical of everything and everyone, on the other. The fifteen-year-old boy would never tear his eyes away from the figure of teenage Capitu to concentrate on her marks of social inferiority: the cheap cloth and mended shoes. Machado stirs the recollections of the enamored and naive boy together with the perspective of a mature, tormented man.

Hence, although in structurally opposite positions, Othello and Capitu are related characters, both forced to bear up under the consequences of their condition. To some extent both are exiled, although having once known the glories of a temporary ascent.

(Temporariness, let's not forget, rhymes with precariousness: a poor rhyme, I might add.)

Nevertheless, I must highlight the cultural arena, precisely what is implicit in chapter 135, "Othello." A stand-in for an author, a lawyer in appearance only, Bento was familiar with the subject but had never considered reading the Shakespeare play. The narrator's patchwork knowledge comes to fruition in the next chapter, "The Cup of Coffee," in which he finds himself unable to follow the example of Cato's noble suicide—he has no book by Plato to consult—and contents himself instead with "an *abridged volume* of Plutarch" (Gledson 228; italics mine).

The parallel is clearly laughable, as even Bento Santiago's Plutarch is a counterfeit.

It is this laugh, albeit seen from another angle, that comprises the formal novelty of Machado's oeuvre; it is only suggested in the text as a latent possibility awaiting the reader who can follow this logical path and smile to herself alone as she reads, with *that vague movement at the corner of the mouth, heavy with mystery.* I will reproduce the passage in full, as its ironic interaction with the idea of imitation is striking, and engages with the discrepancy between model and appropriation:

My plan was to wait for my coffee, dissolve the drug in it and swallow it. Until then, since I had not completely forgotten my Roman history, I remembered that Cato, before he killed himself, read and reread a book by Plato. I didn't have Plato by me; but an *abridged volume* of Plutarch, in which the life of the famous Roman was told, was enough to occupy that short space of time, and, *so as to imitate him completely*, I stretched out on the sofa. Nor was it merely to *imitate him to this extent*; I needed to instill some of his courage in myself, just as he had needed some of the philosopher's thoughts, to die so fearlessly. One of the disadvantages of being ignorant is that one does not have such remedies to hand at the final hour. There are many people who kill themselves without it, and expire with dignity; but I think that many more people would put an end to their days, if they could find this kind of moral cocaine in good books. Nonetheless, wishing to avoid any suspicion of *imitation*, I remember well that, so that Plutarch's book should not be found next to me, and news of it should not be given out in the papers along with the color of the trousers I was wearing at the time, I decided to put it back in its place before I drank the poison. (Gledson 228; italics mine)

The imitation itself is indisputable; what interests us here is the desire to keep it under wraps. In Bento's eagerness to seem original, the coffee cools while he returns the book to its place and the plan goes down the drain. Perhaps Bento Santiago might have been able to poison himself without turning to Plato. Once the coffee is cold, however, the act itself seems unthinkable.

And we can hardly criticize him.

Emphasis on how close this hews to the parodic vein that defined Lucian's texts and characterizes the mixture of styles perfected by the deceased author.

Cato's noble example becomes Bento Santiago's predictable failure; after all, starting out with an *abridged volume* almost certainly guarantees a ridiculous end. The mismatch between model and copy sets off the comic effect—the result of a simple disproportion, as Bentinho's fumble reveals the superficiality of his cultural appropriation. The problem is not adopting the model, but rather in the low wattage of its assimilation. In Pedro Henríquez Ureña's terms, Bento Santiago is limited to "diffuse imitation"; "systematic imitation" is the province of Machado himself.

This failed attempt at displacement had already appeared as a topic in a short story published in the *Jornal das Famílias* in July and August 1864, and would remain a structural fixture in Machado's work.

I am referring to "Virginius (Narrativa de um advogado)" [Virginius (a Lawyer's Narrative)]. The text offers an idealized image, albeit a contradictory one, of the problem of slavery. Old Pio represents "justice and charity fused into a single person" (II, 738). His slaves love him like a father; he is known as the *Father of them all*. After studying at the court, his son Carlos returns to the farm a changed man, treating the slaves "as if" they were his property. In old Pio's utopia, masters and slaves are brothers: the plantation house and the slave shack are a single harmonious system without hierarchies, much less violence. In this Adamic state of affairs, the trigger for conflict is Elisa—who is, as Julião, her freedman father puts it, "the loveliest little mulatta to be found for ten leagues" (II, 740).

The stage for the predictable drama is set.

Carlos attempts to attack Julião's daughter. In defense of her honor, the father hits upon a tragic solution: he kills Elisa in order to keep her away from the villain. Albeit with a difference of scale, this is the dilemma we see with Estela in *Iaiá Garcia*.

The narrator turns to the parallel with the classical story: "All remember the doleful tragedy of Virginius. Titus Livius, Diodorus Siculus and other ancients speak of it at length" (II, 745). In an attempt to save his daughter from the arbitrary will of Appius Claudius, a magistrate willing to brandish his power to conquer Verginia, her father prefers to kill her. Machado follows his line of reasoning:

Shortly thereafter, the decemviri fell and the republic was restored.

In Julião's case there were neither decemviri to strike down nor

consuls to lift up, but there was outraged virtue and triumphant wicked-
ness. Unfortunately each remains far, the latter from widespread repulsion,
the former from universal respect. (II, 745)

The deceased author turns to a similar technique in articulating his
memoirs. However, in place of the reverence and moralizing tones of the
1864 story, Brás Cubas turns the parallel around, taking the classical model
off its pedestal and winking at local circumstances.

Machado rewrites Terence: nothing human can be alien to derision.

As we have seen, he would take some time to light upon this tone.

To reiterate the idea: Machado's variant on *Othello* is original because it
rearranges preexisting elements.

Once again: the classics come first, but alongside them are recent foreign-language literature and Portuguese-language contemporaries. Precisely
like Shakespeare, who embarked on a shameless rewriting of both the classics
and his peers.

In *Dom Casmurro*, Machado offers yet another remarkable homage
to Shakespeare—as always, problematizing the concept of authorship. In
chapter 9, as already referenced, the narrator recalls the theory put forth by
an old Italian tenor: at the beginning of time, the world was not a dream,
nor a drama, but an opera. Marcolino explains: "God is the poet. The music
is by Satan" (Gledson 18). After his expulsion from Paradise, Satan steals
the manuscript from the Heavenly Father and composes the score—which
God initially refuses to listen to. Buckling beneath the other's insistence,
he decides to put on the opera, creating "a special theater, this planet, and
invented a whole company" (Gledson 19). A few paragraphs later, the reader
comes across a corollary to this theory:

> The element of the grotesque, for example, is not to be found in the poet's
> text: it is an excrescence, put there to imitate *The Merry Wives of Windsor.*
> This point is contested by the satanists, with every appearance of reason.
> They say that, at the time when the young Satan composed his opera, nei-
> ther Shakespeare nor his farce had been born. They go so far as to affirm
> that *the English poet's only genius was to transcribe the words of the opera,*
> with such skill and so faithfully that he seems to be the author of the com-
> position, but of course *he is a plagiarist.* (Gledson 20; italics mine)

This declaration seems a dubious bit of praise. How to say that an author outdoes himself when his work is a *copy* that is, shall we say, *original*? The paradox is only inevitable if we adopt Romantic ideas of authorship, in which the desire for aesthetic primogeniture is contagious and fraught with the jealousy of Othello and Bento Santiago. However, if an author considers his own situation precarious, the confirmation of "influences" may potentially become liberating, because the fact of being "influenced" opens the doors to the whole of literary tradition. The past ceases to be a weight to carry and becomes a mosaic; the recombination of its pieces is the mark of *invention* on the periphery, not in its hegemonic form. What matters is not being influenced *solely* by the latest fashions, but rather by the larger body of tradition—of all traditions, if possible.

This is precisely like Mário de Andrade's ironic reply after an accusation of his having plagiarized Theodor Koch-Grünberg's *Vom Roraima zum Orinoco*. In a good-humored answer to the tiresome allegations of his having plagiarized the German scholar in writing *Macunaíma*, Mário transformed the problem into a source of productivity: "What stuns me and I find sublimely generous is that these scandalmongers have forgotten everything they know, restricting my copying to Koch-Grünberg, *when I copied everyone*."[12] This is not to affirm any hypothetical originality—an inevitably dubious proposal when it comes to inventors from nonhegemonic cultures—but rather to push for maximum intensity in the appropriation of what is not one's own. Put in the same position, Oswald de Andrade releases his "Cannibal Manifesto" in 1928, the same year as *Macunaíma*. In his definitive formulation: "I am only concerned with that which is not mine. Law of man. Law of the cannibal" (47).[13]

On a number of occasions, Machado, the chief cannibal in Brazilian culture, returns to the notion of plagiarism with fresh eyes.

In "Conto alexandrino" [Alexandrian Tale], published in the *Gazeta de Notícias* on May 15, 1883, and collected in *Stories without a Date* (1884), the philosopher Stroibus seeks to convince his friend Pythias of a curious hypothesis: "that rat's blood, given to a man to drink, can make him a *ratter*" (II, 711).[14] With they themselves as the guinea pigs for this innovative experiment, they triumph and are just as soon lost. The two become living proof for the eccentric theory's force, both becoming incurable kleptomaniacs! In the narrator's evaluation:

The ideas of others, precisely because they were not bought on the street corner, *carry a certain common air*; and it is quite natural to start out with them before moving on to borrowed books, chickens, false papers, provinces, etc. The very term for *plagiarism* is an indication that men understand the difficulty in confusing this embryonic thievery with formal thievery. (II, 414; italics mine)

After stealing manuscripts from Ptolemy's Library, the two philosophers are given an exemplary punishment: they are dissected while still alive for the benefit of science.

Meanwhile, in a crônica from November 1893 collected in *Gathered Pages* (1899), the art of pillaging pays dividends, at least in art: "Poetry itself suffers a loss with this; none can deny that the highwayman, in art, is a generous and noble character" (II, 647). Now, as one only steals that which has value, plagiarism is the most sincere form of flattery. A generally anonymous compliment, to be true, but a tribute nonetheless.

To return to the analogy used more than once in this essay: it is as if Machado were linking the process by which one learns literary technique to the method commonly seen in schools of painting. At first the apprentice limits himself to *imitating* paintings by the masters, and then sets himself to *emulating* the tradition in which he was educated.

In a crônica from *A Semana*, published on October 27, 1895, Machado's topic is the short stories of Pedro Rabelo. Here is what he says:

It has been noted that his style is imitative, rather, and one author has been referenced as having a manner that the young writer seeks to assimilate. ... In the flush of youth, it is natural that one should not hit directly upon one's own definitive style, *just as it is to follow one or another*, according to intellectual sympathies or recent impressions. (III, 683–84; italics mine)

Machado turns to the classical method, increasingly evident both in the creative process and in criticism, albeit while imposing changes inspired by the *free form*.

None was more successful in this method than Shakespeare.

Another comparable author would be Lucian.

Or Virgil.

Or Camões.

Or Laurence Sterne.

Machado handpicks his models.

In the post-Romantic mentality, this framework is lost; as I showed in chapter 3, there emerged a decisive rift between the verbs "create" and "invent."

Machado's aesthetic belongs to the register of *invention*, a practice favored by a return to emulation, as a deliberately anachronistic technique.

In this light, we might do well to recall Machado's censure of the aesthetic of creation, as expressed in the 1885 story "The Skillful Man." In this story, the problem is discussed with great vigor, and the pallid fate reserved for João Maria takes shape in his unfortunate refusal: "*Every art has a technique*; he abhorred technique, he was averse to apprenticeship, to learning the rudiments of things" (II, 1051; italics mine). This caricature of spontaneity still yearns for the concept at the core of the Romantic school: "The rest was up to *the artist's genius*, which João Maria supposed himself to possess" (II, 1051; italics mine). Once again, we sense how far this lies from Machadinho's respectful commentary in the reader's note to *Resurrection*: the *law of geniuses* ultimately reveals itself to be an illusion, or even a mistake. After all, without discipline, no talent will be fulfilled. The skillful copier of models never manages to produce *art*; an ignorance of etymology will condemn João Maria to perennially *imitate*, without ever *emulating*, the models that he can only reproduce.

The Machadian reinvention comes when he finds himself to be an inventor of original copies, resuscitating the proper sense that he himself attributes to plagiarism.

Machado's habit of frequenting tradition favors the metamorphosis to a vast and seductive menu, with a list of items to be savored with pure delight. And, to use a metaphor dear to the writer himself, these items are ruminated innumerable times to ensure adequate digestion—drawing up the next text, that is. While his peers sought to keep up with the latest fashions, Machado set himself to rereading the pre-Romantic canon, glimpsing an unmatched alternative that was made current by its anachronism, a return to dusty models—*which by virtue of their age are made new*. Thus there would be no higher compliment than to define a writer as the veritable image of plagiarism: Shakespeare.

For that matter, doesn't the "plagiarist" have to come *after* the historical period of her models?

The political consequences of this observation are decisive.

The plagiarist may never aspire to aesthetic primogeniture. She is in the position of Sarmiento, editor of *El Progreso*. This is why Machado developed a singular framework for addressing authorship and the reading public: here lies the model that may potentially drive an unexpected revitalization of *aemulatio.*

Once again, it is important to reiterate that this hypothesis was born of the reading of Machado's texts. There remains caution, however—note that I always say *potentially.* This is not an inevitable condition, but a deliberately anachronistic decision, the aftermath of which I will discuss in the conclusion.

Time to close out this chapter with one of the most perceptive definitions of Machado's method:

> I discovered by happy accident the turn-of-the-century Brazilian novelist Joaquim Machado de Assis . . . Machado—himself much under the influence of Laurence Sterne's *Tristram Shandy*—taught me something I had not quite learned from Joyce's *Ulysses* and would not likely have learned from Sterne directly, had I happened to have read him: how to combine formal sportiveness with genuine sentiment as well as a fair degree of realism. Sterne is pre-Romantic; Joyce is late or post-Romantic; Machado is both Romantic and romantic: playful, wistful, pessimistic, intellectually exuberant. He was also, like myself, a provincial.[15]

Every provincial is a plagiarist by virtue of his circumstances, but not all provincials are equally peripheral.

Let me explain.

Imagine how unlikely it would be to hear a Latin American author—or a Polish poet, say, or a Danish critic—confess, with similar nonchalance, "I discovered by happy accident the novelists Marcel Proust and Virginia Woolf."

(Need I say more?)

The act of making other cultures one's own favors the critical distance that is fundamental for the pen of mirth. And the perennial awareness of one's place in the republic of letters leads back to the ink of melancholy. In the simple act of recycling tradition in an unconventional fashion, new elements emerge and create the conditions for large-scale formal innovations. Moreover, John Barth links Machado's oeuvre to two opposite historical forms: the deceased author might just as easily be "pre" or "post," independently of the concept associated with his fiction. *The pen of mirth* and *ink of melancholy* occupy center stage—at the same time.

Peripheral, provincial, nonhegemonic. Different names for labeling what Machado truly is: an inventive reader, an original copyist. While certain writers publish more than they write, the plagiarist has read much more than he could ever publish. Machado is not merely a writer aware of being a reader first and foremost, but also an author who has crafted formal techniques that make the reader a potential coauthor of the work.

Jorge Luis Borges imagined Pierre Menard, the writer of an invisible oeuvre. If his project of copying *Don Quixote* had come to fruition, Cervantes would be turned into yet another plagiarist, just as Satan's libretto was contaminated by Shakespeare's work. The Argentine writer would not have disagreed with the plurality of names that may be attributed to Pierre Menard—and always anachronistically, from back to front, with ever-multiplying precursors.

Shakespeare, as the old Italian tenor would have it.

Or: an obsessive reader of *Othello*.

Machado invented a way to transform the dilemma of secondarity into a formal principle, with far-reaching repercussions on the level of cultural politics.

Echoes of Paris?

Of the Western languages, ours is the least well known, and if the countries where it is spoken matter little today, in 1900 they mattered even less in the political game. For this reason, two novelists who wrote in our language and who are the equals of the best then writing remain marginal: Eça de Queirós, well suited to the spirit of naturalism; and Machado de Assis, enigmatic and Janus-headed, looking to the past and the future, hiding a strange and original world under the apparent neutrality of his stories *everyone could read.*

> —Antonio Candido, "An Outline of Machado de Assis"

As he criticized the provincial bent of the rigid literary nationalism preached by romanticism and realism, Machado deemed it necessary for the Brazilian writer, without ceasing to be Brazilian, to be aware that his works belonged to a universal tradition: that of literature.

> —Enylton de Sá Rego, *O calundu e a panaceia*

classicism: in fact, picasso was restoring the classical gesture in the imitation of the ancients, betraying his legacy with utter faithfulness. in a new context emulation was both the same and another, a digested wound, a

master stroke. . . . the result was paintings with a double signature, one
visible, the other half-erased. he did this unabashedly with countless others: poussin, velázquez, van gogh, goya, ingres. it falls to us to reread this
writing on the palimpsest.

—Evando Nascimento, *Retrato desnatural*

Why suppose, even tacitly, that the Brazilian experience is only of local
interest, while the English language, Shakespeare, New Criticism, the
Western tradition, and *tutti quanti*, are universal? If the question is aimed
at masking our shortcomings as an ex-colony, it merits no comment. If its
purpose is to question the universality of the universal, or the localism of
the local, then it is a good starting point.

—Roberto Schwarz, *Martinha* versus *Lucrécia*

Politics of Emulation?

The poetics of emulation is fodder for a potentially political reading.
Potentially, I will note once again.
A reading relative to cultural politics, I might add.
And cultural politics conceived initially within the world of the nineteenth century, the realm of Machado and Eça. I note the time frame in order
to avoid any misinterpretation of the reflection proposed in this essay.
These caveats are important because, in international symbolic relations
and in the day-to-day of cultural life in nonhegemonic contexts, the poetics
of emulation is unlikely to bring about effective changes.
On one hand, the stylistic procedures that comprise it were never the
exclusive province of the peripheral condition. If this were the case, their
use would not call for deliberate anachronism, but would be the natural
result of the essence of the "peripheral being"—the quotation marks mul-
tiply in order to clarify the irony with which this ontological vocabulary is
being used.
I hope it has become sufficiently clear that I am not dealing in essences,
but strategies. The poetics of emulation provides a cheeky angle from which
to behold tradition and the cultural inequalities of the present; this is, however, a potentiality, the revitalization of which calls for a determined effort.

On the other hand, in nonhegemonic contexts, daily life both in literary circles and universities winds up legitimating this structural imbalance, as hegemonic values are adopted without further questioning. At the literary festivals that (happily) are multiplying across Brazil, the stars are (almost) always foreign authors. At research centers, the go-to theoretical models are writers in two languages, three at the most—those of the "great thinking nations." Eça's definition holds true—a disquieting symptom of a permanence of asymmetrical relationships.

Camilo Seabra's reaction, meanwhile, remains disturbingly current. He is the protagonist of "The Blue Parasite," a story published in several installments in the *Jornal das Famílias* between June and September 1872, and reproduced the following year in *Midnight Stories*.

Let us hear what the narrator has to say:

> The commendatary's son had been married for a year when a French traveler appeared on his estate. He carried letters of recommendation from one of his professors in Paris. Camilo received him gaily and asked him for news of *France*, which he still loved, he said, *as his intellectual homeland.* The traveler told him many things, and finally took a stack of newspapers from his suitcase.
>
> It was *Le Figaro.*
>
> "*Figaro!*" exclaimed Camilo, throwing himself on the newspapers.
>
> *They were late, but they were Parisian.* (II, 191; italics mine)

Novelties, however, weren't always slow to arrive. On the contrary, the certainty of the local *backwardness* fueled a collective effort—an inadvertently comic one—to *keep up to date at any cost.* In a dialogue between Jean-Claude Carrière and Umberto Eco about the future of the book, the French writer references, with evident surprise, "an edition of *Les Misérables* that was printed and published in Portuguese, in Rio, in 1862—the same year that it was published in France. Just two months after Paris!"[1]

The dominant rhythm in nineteenth-century texts recalls Tom Jobim and Newton Mendonça's celebrated song "One-Note Samba." It is as if the tempo of culture were beating in perfect time, with its meridian crossing the capitals that defined modernity: Paris and London. It is very difficult to understand the dilemmas and ambitions of authors like Machado and Eça without considering this state of affairs. Both their worldviews and their literary educations spring from this experience.

The poetics of emulation represents a subjective answer to a concrete situation of a massive imbalance in terms of the relations of cultural power. There is a risk of celebrating this asymmetry, however; after all, it favors the emergence of a set of critical procedures with fundamental consequences for art and philosophy.

As an antidote, I might propose the reading of "The Mirror—Sketch for a New Theory of the Human Soul," published in the *Gazeta de Notícias* on December 18, 1881, and reproduced the following year in *Loose Papers*.

In the opening paragraphs, the narrator of the story sets the scene, returning only at the end of the tale and then somewhat enigmatically: "When the others returned to their senses, the narrator had gone down the stairs" (II, 352). This "second" narrator is Sublieutenant Jacobina, the author of the tale, constructed by his recollections of an episode from his youth.

Jacobina begins the story by laying out the theory alluded to in the title: "Each human creature bears two souls: one that looks from the inside out, and another that looks from the outside in" (II, 346). The interior and exterior souls, respectively. The corollary to this hypothesis brings a peculiar philosophy into play. In the sublieutenant's doctrine, man is, "metaphysically speaking, an orange. Having lost one of the halves, one naturally loses one half of one's existence; and there are cases, hardly rare ones, in which the loss of the exterior soul implies the loss of one's entire existence" (II, 1051).

It is inevitably entertaining to read studies of this story that take Sublieutenant Jacobina's theory very seriously. Some analyses are even suggestive and quite intelligent. However, why not recognize the mock-heroic tone of this definition: *metaphysically speaking, an orange.*

An *orange*?

Metaphysically speaking?

The plot is more complex than the theory: a young man without means, Jacobina is named a sublieutenant in the Guarda Nacional at age twenty-five. His family is enchanted by this social ascent: "You can't imagine the event this was in our house. My mother was so proud, so contented!" (II, 347). One aunt, Dona Marcolina, the widow of one Captain Peçanha, invites Jacobina to visit her out at her estate. All demonstrate the due respect: he is no longer the Joãozinho of times past, but the sublieutenant of the present, and the who-knows-what-post of the future. Everything is going swimmingly, and the lad is treated like a real grown-up. Then one of his aunt's daughters falls ill, and she is forced to take a trip.

By now used to being recognized by his rank, Jacobina finds himself alone in the company of the estate's slaves. For a free man of modest means, this is a discomfiting form of solitude in nineteenth-century Brazil. Soon enough he comes to doubt the fact of his own existence, especially so after the slaves take flight. In Machado's incisive formulation: "The sublieutenant eliminated the man" (II, 348). The post eclipses the subject, and the social role reveals itself to be more important than the individual.

Without the mirror provided by the gaze of the other, Jacobina becomes invisible—to his own eyes more than any. He resorts to the most obvious form of therapy: looking at himself in the house's largest mirror, a relic of the days of "King João VI's court" (II, 347). But this comes to naught. His image is "hazy, faded, diffuse, a shadow of a shadow" (II, 350). In desperation, he turns to an infallible method. Jacobina puts on his sublieutenant's uniform and returns to the mirror. Just as the proverb says, the habit makes the monk: "It was me myself, the sublieutenant, who had finally found the exterior soul" (II, 351–52). The construction of the phrase is trickier than it seems at first glance.

The wit of the second narrator helps to tie together the points of my argument.

If the "me myself" is the sublieutenant himself—the uniform, that is to say, or the rank—then the sentence is tautological and even undermines its own meaning. A more logical statement would be to say: "It was me, Jacobina, who had finally found my exterior soul, the sublieutenant." If the "I" is the uniform itself, then what is the role of the interior soul? This "I" is not "an other," as a teenage Rimbaud would have liked. This I is simply "me myself."

Repetition, never difference.

In a previous passage, Jacobina recalls his efforts to survive amid solitude. He tried to sleep, as "fatigue, eliminating the necessity for an exterior soul, let the interior soul act freely" (II, 350). The sublieutenant thus would leave the scene, allowing for the resurrection of Jacobina. The result of this self-medication is as follows: "In the dreams I put on my uniform proudly, amid family and friends who praised my dress, who called me sublieutenant; a friend of the house came and promised me the rank of lieutenant, another promised me that of captain or major; and all this made me live" (II, 350).

Once again, the phrase implies a logical contradiction, reducing the interior soul to the attributes of the exterior. Without a clear difference between the souls, how to sustain the theory described in the story? Before receiving his rank, who was the sublieutenant? Beyond his age, we only know that he is poor. From the perspective of social representation, until he entered the Guarda Nacional, Jacobina spent twenty-five years not existing. The interior soul seems a mirage, a simple formal necessity in order to ensure the visibility of its exterior counterpart. However, if the interior soul is worth so little, the story itself belies the theory of the two souls. A playful reading reveals the mirror image of the writing: if the exterior soul, the uniform, is the central element of the story, how to understand the subtitle, "sketch for a new theory of the human soul"? A similar effect arises from the reading of "Stuffed-Shirt Theory," setting off a short circuit. This is Machado's particular way of turning the technique of *aemulatio* into a specific act of reading, a typically modern act, a sort of *free form* on the level of reception.

This short circuit only deepens, because the mirror is a surface that, in and of itself, is nothing. This is why it can reflect different images, even opposing ones. What can a mirror oriented toward the other reveal? The inventive capacity of fiction; the possibility of producing images that, without the mirror, would be invisible. Here lies Machado's understanding of the power of literature. In this vein, the poetics of emulation is pure invention, allowing the author of "The Immortal" to frequent all time periods and productively overcome the limits of his own condition.

This said, however, the author of *The Hand and the Glove* set this reflection in a handpicked setting: a free, poor man who has ascended socially and, upon finding himself "alone" amid slaves, undergoes a crisis of identity. This is Machado's interpretation of the challenges imposed by Brazil's circumstances. Hence, to dissociate oeuvre from historical experience would be to impoverish this analysis unnecessarily, although my interests have been strictly focused on a journey around the library.

Machado's fiction dialogues with its circumstances and, at the same time, draws up a new way of understanding them. The two gestures are one, and the movement between these two dimensions might well be preserved. I can see no other way of responding in kind to the complexity of the *Machado de Assis literary system*.

Machado learned to deal ironically with his peripheral condition via a model for relating to tradition, based on the productive oscillation between extremes. He announced this model on more than one occasion—albeit, as was his wont, obliquely.

Turn to "The Most Serene Republic," published in the *Gazeta de Notícias* on August 20, 1882, and reproduced the same year in *Loose Papers*. The story transcribes a "lecture by Vargas the canon." With an air of deep conviction, he informs the world of a sweeping scientific discovery: "a species of *araneida* that possesses the power of speech" (II, 341). In addition to satirizing local political habits, Machado throws a bottle into the sea. Here is Vargas's message:

> My discovery is not recent; it dates from the end of the year 1876. I did not divulge it then—and, were it not for the *Globo*, an interesting daily in this capital, I would not have divulged it yet now—for a reason that will find easy entry into your spirits. This work of which I have come to speak lacks finishing touches, verifications, and complementary experiments. But the *Globo* reported that an English scholar discovered the phonic language of insects, and cites a study carried out with flies. *I wrote immediately to Europe and anxiously await answers.* While it is true, however, that by aerial navigation, the invention of Padre Bartolomeu, the foreign name is glorified while that of our compatriot *may hardly be said to be remembered by his countrymen*, I resolved to avoid the fate of the illustrious Flyer by coming to this tribune to proclaim in loud and clear tones, *before the universe*, that far before that scholar, and outside the British Isles, a humble naturalist discovered an identical thing, *and made a superior work with it.* (II, 340; italics mine)

We might assemble an entertaining gallery of Machadian figures who move from the universal scale of an invention to the limited range of their ability to publicize their devices. A new understanding of the problem requires overcoming a predictable resentment—recall the "Queirosian rule of threes."

Machado faces down this situation with the pen of mirth, showing us Vargas the canon and the social organization of arachnids, as well as his desperate search for European recognition. Recall Brás Cubas' idée fixe; his panacea would mean "the invention of a sublime medicine, an antihypochondriacal poultice destined to relieve our melancholy humanity" (I, 515). In the same vein we find Quincas Borbas's philosophical poultice, Humanitism, a sort of slapdash synthesis of the history of ideas. Indeed, Humanitism reveals itself to be a serious jab at the rationalist pretensions of a number of systems of thought, with their insatiable desire for order, inevitably tinged with irrationality. This characteristic also pops up in an equally famous character, Dr. Simão Bacamarte.

Could peripheral attempts at coming up with a universal theory serve as proof of irremediable insanity? But isn't that the aim of every theorist?

The opening paragraph of "The Alienist" derives an irresistibly comic effect from this mismatch between ambition and scale:

> The chronicles of the city of Itaguaí say that, long ago, there lived a certain doctor, Dr. Simão Bacamarte, the son of landed nobility and *the greatest doctor* in all of Brazil, Portugal, and the Spanish Lands. *He had studied at Coimbra and Pádua.* At thirty-four years old, he returned to Brazil, the king not having been able to convince him to stay at Coimbra, conducting the university, or in Lisbon, overseeing matters of state.
>
> "Science," he said to His Majesty, "is my only employment; *Itaguaí is my universe.*" (Rothaus, n.p.; italics mine)

This slide down the scale—Coimbra, Padua . . . Itaguaí, a backwater in the province of Rio de Janeiro—suggests that Simão Bacamarte's eccentricity had shown itself well before the construction of the Casa Verde. Turning out cutting-edge science in this backwoods town, having turned down the most prestigious offers of the time, does not strike the reader as a sensible decision. The phrase unfolds in opposite directions. The first part—refusing prestigious bureaucratic posts in order to dedicate oneself to science—is perfectly reasonable. But the conclusion—declaring Itaguaí ground zero for high-level research—will be the first in a series of false syllogisms, which structure the comic aspect of the narrative.

(Gorgias could hardly do better.)

The poetics of emulation makes it possible to transform the secondarity of the nonhegemonic place into a critical project. Nevertheless, this does not

alter the structural inequality in the circulation—and subsequent legitima-
tion—of knowledge. Isn't it striking that Vargas the canon mentions the
example of the *illustrious Flyer*? A few decades after this story was written,
the problem would come up again in the dispute between the Wright Brothers and Santos Dumont for primacy in the invention of a heavier-than-air
flying machine.

The poetics of emulation is a *potentiality*.

Deep down, one rarely actualized in the cultural history of Latin
America.

Nescafé Civilization?

I will reiterate the structural link between Machado's oeuvre and the poetics
of emulation. In both cases, academic distinctions between text and context,
form and content, pale in importance before the continual elaboration of
acts of reading and forms of writing that tie together the extremes of the
nonhegemonic condition.

Moreover, a simple historical perspective will belie any sort of naïveté in
this case. The usual response to an asymmetrical situation has been the emergence of an anxiety to remain perennially up to date, forcing the writer to set
out in an impossible race for which there is no adequate starting-point. There
is no way to compensate for the distance already covered by writers from
hegemonic countries; the very fact of their writing in a dominant language
gives them a considerable advantage. In this search for lost time, the more
one runs, the later one comes to the finish line. Carlos Fuentes gave a good-
humored diagnosis of this syndrome: "These imitations from the period of
independence outstrip logic: we might be modern instantly, leaving aside the
past and ignoring tradition." Fuentes goes on to emphasize the singularity
of the inventor of Brás Cubas: "Machado's genius was built on precisely the
opposite principle: his oeuvre defends a conviction: there can be no creation
without a tradition to fuel it, just as there will be no tradition without creation to renew it."[2] The reader will identify this modern translation of the
classical pair—*imitatio* and *aemulatio*.

There is an alternative to the mad rush to modernization at any cost; it
was taken by writers who learned to turn the clash of historical perceptions

into a literary project. This method turns the historical precedence of *reading* over *writing*, and of *translation* over the *original*, into a productive feature.

It is as if Machado were bringing a very Latin American experience into the structure of the text: notions of literature in general, and of the novel in particular, were developed through the translation of French and English titles. The first novelists were necessarily keen readers, and at times critical ones, of at least two centuries of European novels. Machado claimed the whole of the Western tradition, without neglecting to study his Portuguese-language peers and recent foreign-language production.

Once again, I will recognize the Achilles' heel of my hypothesis: the gesture of embracing many traditions is common to all literatures, not the exclusive province of those from cultural peripheries. Without this acknowledgment, my argument—even if I were to deny it again and again—could not avoid a basic confusion between strategy and essence.

This point is crucial if we are to avoid a naive paean to "backwardness" identified with nonhegemonic contexts, as if objective inequality mysteriously created some sort of subjective compensation in the form of a particularly keen gaze. Moreover, as the term "backwardness" is controversial, I will explain my reasoning.

First of all, let us read Camilo Seabra's statement against the grain: the newspapers *were late, but they were Parisian*. The Parisian delay is the heat of the moment in the tropics because Paris and London are allowed the privilege of dictating the fashions of the moment. This topos would remain current in the twentieth century, providing the inspiration for Oswald de Andrade's tirade in the "Manifesto of Brazilwood Poetry": "The work of the futurist generation was cyclopean. *To reset the imperial watch of the nation's literature*" (44; italics mine). We might almost think that 1872, the year of "The Blue Parasite," and 1924, the moment when Oswald's manifesto was published, are related dates in terms of the semantic field of "backwardness"; despite their obvious differences, they feature a similar vocabulary that reveals a common set of concerns.

Second, national literatures are made up of loans, appropriations, and dialogues with the broadest imaginable variety of traditions. We already saw the less-than-diplomatic turn of phrase from Pedro Henríquez Ureña: *from imitations, or even thefts*. Likewise, the very idea of a national literature is dated; just as all ideas tend to be. This is a relatively young notion in the larger body of the Western literary experience. Hence, associating "backwardness" to the action of receiving inspiration from literatures other than one's own would reveal a troubling critical naïveté.

That said, naïveté has many faces, and some can even be sophisticated. The circulation of symbolic goods is never neutral. It depends on objective criteria and subjective motivations. Historically, one can find evidence of a hegemonic voice's ability to impose itself, generally represented by the language of the dominant economic and political powers.

I do not intend on turning this essay into a predictable pamphlet—it would be out of place, outmoded, and irrelevant. I would simply like to reinforce my reasoning by linking the reflection on a deliberately anachronistic return to *aemulatio* to Ricardo Piglia's question: *What happens when one belongs to a secondary culture? What happens when one writes in a marginal language?* Deep down, ignoring that objective conditions of the production and circulation of academic knowledge and artistic invention obey the economy of political power is just as naive as believing that the nonhegemonic condition provides some sort of innate cognitive advantage.

We must find some compromise between an undoubtedly foolish paean to backwardness and the equally fatuous negation of asymmetry in international symbolic exchanges.

Here lies Machado's leap, made possible by the discovery of the poetics of emulation.

Time to stop beating around the bush: a Brazilian author's evaluation of his own work tends to consider the limited circulation of Portuguese, which directly influences the recognition he may garner. If the critic is examining the nineteenth-century context, there is no way of getting around the myriad of texts on this very dilemma. On more than one occasion, I recalled the implacable Queirosian rule of threes, and we have seen how it has held up: "*Faute de l'Abbé Mouret* must be to *The Crime of Father Amaro* as France is to Portugal. Little effort was required to turn up the following unknown quantity: PLAGIARISM!"

One would be hard-pressed to find a clearer instance of the structural imbalance in symbolic exchanges.

In the nineteenth century, and even in the first decades of the century that followed, the echoes of Paris and London were omnipresent, haunting authors from a stunning variety of latitudes: from Georg Brandes to Eça de

Queirós, from Domingo Faustino Sarmiento to Machado de Assis, not to leave out Richard Wagner.

Ecos de Paris [Echoes of Paris] is the title of a posthumous book of Eça's, published in 1905 and comprising crônicas published in the Brazilian newspaper *Gazeta de Notícias*. His texts were highlighted features, and wielded considerable influence on the intellectual life of the time. In an article from 1880, the author of *A Capital* [The Capital] describes the impasse as follows:

> And so for the human mob, which is more impressionable than critical, the world appears to be a piece of decoration set up around Paris and London, a scenographical curiosity that one gazes on for a moment and quickly fixes all one's attention on the social tragi-comedy *palpitating at the center*. . . .
> Whatever *the humanity of the provinces* does, says, suffers, or enjoys— they are indifferent. . . . The multitudes clearly recognize only one society—that of Paris and London.[3]

Queirós's vocabulary here is suggestive. Paris and London are the palpitating center of cultural and political life, while the other countries are wrapped up into a revealing unit: *the humanity of the provinces*.

Even more emphatically, and in a passage frequently discussed in Brazilian cultural history, Joaquim Nabuco once said nearly the same thing:

> I do not mean that there are *two humanities, a high and a low*, and that we are of the latter; perhaps humanity will renew itself one day *through its American branches*; but, in the century in which we live, the *human spirit*, which is singular and terribly centralist, lies on the other side of the Atlantic; the New World, in terms of all aesthetic or historical imagination, *is true solitude*.[4]

Once again, London and Paris absorb the *human spirit* as the "simple" result of their *centralist* vocation. Beyond this center, there is only the bitterness of *true solitude*, expressed metonymically through the *American branches*—a suggestive representation of the province, the periphery of the world-system.

I could string together a necklace of similar quotations; but I will simply note the obvious: one cannot evaluate the better part of Latin America's cultural manifestations, at least up to the Second World War, without considering the fact that, for the actors in this process, the center of attention was situated in *another* place.

A place with a proper name: Paris.

And a headquarters: London.

From this perspective, Machado's singularity may be understood more clearly in terms of his "return-trip" mentality, opposed in every sense to the dazzling fascination of the parvenu. Counselor Ayres describes this habit precisely: "tired of hearing and speaking the French language, I found new and original life in my own tongue, and now I wish to die with it in my mouth and my ears" (I, 1182).

This should not be confused with a symptom of senile nationalism. The Counselor can only find a radically new diction in his own language because he first set himself to the task of mastering a foreign tongue and culture.

The French language and culture, in this case.

He might as well have mastered English and its literature.

Plus a basic knowledge of German and Greek, simply in order to sample the pleasure of reading texts with the surprise of a reader who deciphers them bit by bit.

The most important thing is to never stop broadening one's repertoire. In order to incorporate one's own culture as well, thus finding in it *new and original life*.

Why not? Believing oneself so cosmopolitan as to scorn what is being done here and now is the most melancholy variety of provincialism.

The extreme opposite, however, should also be avoided at all costs.

Hence Machado's ironic criticism of the project concocted by "Sr. Dr. Castro Lopes, the illustrious Brazilian Latinist [who] created a series of neologisms, which struck him as indispensable in order to do away with French words and phrases" (III, 517). The conclusion of this crônica, published in the series *Bons Dias* on March 7, 1889, is of a delicious *boutade*:

> I am not joking. I have never eaten *croquettes*, as delicious as I am told they are, simply because of the French name. I have eaten and will continue to eat *filet de boeuf*, but with the mental restriction of eating *sirloin*. Not everything, however, can be subject to such restrictions; I could not do the

same with the *bouchées de dames*, for example, as *mouthfuls of ladies* gives the impression of cannibalism, given the misnomer. (III, 517)

The utopia of linguistic purity is the target of the cronista's derision; an oscillation between what does and does not belong to one is the bread and butter of the poetics of emulation. The phenomenon was never exclusively Latin American. We saw the eclipse that Georg Brandes believed himself to be living under in his far-flung Denmark: "We in recent days have been buried under repugnant snows; *separated from Europe*" (88; italics mine).

Richard Wagner also succumbed to the siren song of the echoes of Paris. But who could resist, in the nineteenth century?

Or even in the twentieth century, if we consider the so-called *lost generation* of Americans who faithfully carried out the ritual pilgrimage to the City of Light; or the Latin American artists who "discovered" their own countries in Paris, London, or New York. Oswald de Andrade, Tarsila do Amaral, and Anita Malfatti would all be included on the eclectic list, alongside Alejo Carpentier, Xul Solar, and Jorge Luis Borges, among so many others.

Wagner went a bit beyond them.

Not only did he go into debt, trusting in a Parisian smash hit that would ideally translate into generous profits; the willful composer also made serious aesthetic concessions, modifying the opening of *Tannhäuser*—the opera with which he hoped to conquer Paris. His efforts, however, found no reward. Wagner's style disoriented audiences—with the notable exception of Baudelaire, who was dazzled by the composer from the start.

(I offered up this brief fable to those who smile at the naïveté of those who, *like me*, still think in terms of center and periphery—that is to say, in terms of hegemonic and nonhegemonic circumstances.)

Poetics of Emulation

Machado did not appear indifferent to the subject. We have seen his letter to Joaquim Nabuco, in which he considered it *indispensable to claim a rightful place for our language*. On July 10, 1902, when the first translation of the *Posthumous Memoirs* was released—a Spanish-language version, in Uruguay—he wrote to Luís Guimarães Filho: "I could only read the translation in full now, and I tell you that I found it as faithful as it was elegant, with Júlio Piquet meriting my thanks *even more for that*" (III, 1060; italics mine). There had been a previous ill-fated attempt to publish Machado's books in the language of one of the "great thinking nations," as we may glean from a letter sent to Alfredo Elis on June 10, 1899: "I have just written to Paris, to Sr. H. Garnier, asking him to directly authorize the lady, of whom you spoke in your note, to translate my books into German" (III, 1047). The authorization was never given, but Machado's effort is what matters.

Even more for that: Machado gives thanks for the translator's diligence, but the more crucial recognition is warranted for the simple fact of disseminating his works. A meritorious task, albeit one with uncertain results: after all, who would be interested in the literature of a Brazilian, in the thick of the nineteenth-century concert of nations?

This is not a resentful question, nor a rhetorical one.

Let us turn to another text from *Echoes of Paris*. All signs seem to indicate that Eça was concerned with the events of the Revolta da Armada, when parts of the Brazilian navy, led by Admiral Custódio de Melo, rose up against the government of Marshal Floriano Peixoto. The Portuguese writer, however, was unable to accompany the rebellion as it unfolded:

> In vain, one may look now for any news, even false ones, about Brazil. Nothing! It is as if Admiral Melo and his dreadnoughts had disappeared forever in the Atlantic mists. What am I saying? *It is as if Brazil had disappeared*—or rather entered into that joyful era, classically known, in which *the peoples of the world cease to have history.* (127; italics mine)

In the nineteenth-century mentality, without history meant unwritten: how, then, to expect news about *Brazilian literature*?

Echoes of Paris: you already know.

Or of London.

Echoes—in both cases.

Machado's singularity is clarified in contrast. The author of *Gathered Pages* understood that if an author from nonhegemonic contexts can rarely manage to be considered "original," then literary tradition should be appropriated with irreverence. The combination of several centuries of tradition and a variety of literary genres—and, above all, the recovery of pre-Romantic acts of reading and writing—favored the rupture of the *Posthumous Memoirs.* Carlos Fuentes observes:

> Latin American hunger, the desire to embrace everything, to appropriate all traditions and cultures, even the aberrations; the utopian drive to create *a new atmosphere in which all spaces and times are simultaneous,* appears brilliantly in the *Posthumous Memoirs of Brás Cubas* as a surprising vision of the first Aleph, prior to the celebrated one imagined by Borges. Yes: this is the Aleph of Machado de Assis. (24; italics mine)

It is as if Machado were transforming the notion of "backwardness," which accompanies the process of peripheral modernization, into a critical project. He turns the game around with a simple question: since aesthetic primogeniture is off the table, why not allow the writer to become a malicious reader and, at the same time, an irreverent author, playing with cultural hierarchies and literary glories?

The poetics of emulation makes it possible to elaborate on peripheral circumstances, *potentially* converting scantiness into a productive stimulus; scarcity into incisiveness; lacuna into structure itself.

An art of a few.

And for a few.

Perhaps five.

The reader who has followed the path proposed in this essay may have appreciated this thick description of the *Machado de Assis literary system.*

The result I have to offer is the discovery of the semantic field of emulation, the procedure that structures Machado's turnaround.

If my study has made this semantic field visible, I may consider this essay finished. Or nearly finished. There remains one last matter to be addressed; briefly, as its complete development must wait for a new book.[5]

Structural Intensity

I took the care to underscore (to the point of exhaustion) the deliberate nature of the anachronism that facilitates the return to pre-Romantic literary practices in a post-Romantic setting. Likewise, I considered the political consequences of this extemporaneous recovery.

John Barth understood this issue perfectly in his observation of how Machado develops his own way of being simultaneously *Romantic and romantic*—in my terms, "pre-Romantic" and "post-Romantic" at the same time.

I thus sought to emphasize the strategic, not the essentialist, side of the poetics of emulation.

It could not be otherwise: the technique's methods may *potentially* belong to authors at any latitude. It would be absurd, from the point of view of the most basic understanding of literary history, to limit the elements studied in chapter 3 to those operating on the periphery.

To recall those elements: the phenomenon of the compression of historical periods and hence the exercise of deliberate anachronism; the primacy of invention over creation, and thus the centrality of translation; the precedence of reading in place of writing, and from that, a very particular notion of authorship.

In isolation, such elements may be found in any context, and in the works of any variety of authors. The strength that I attribute to the anachronistic nature of the poetics of emulation depends on the simultaneous articulation of all these procedures.

In chapter 2, I suggested this point when I recalled T. S. Eliot's essay "Tradition and the Individual Talent," published in 1919. Indeed, many of the mechanisms of the poetics of emulation are perfectly described by the poet-critic.

In his words:

> Tradition is a matter of much wider significance. It cannot be inherited, and if you want if you must obtain it by great labour. . . .
>
> No poet, no artist of any art, has his complete meaning alone. His significance, his appreciation is the appreciation of his relation to the dead poets and artists. You cannot value him alone; you must set him, for contrast and comparison, among the dead. I mean this as a principle of aesthetic, not merely historical, criticism. The necessity that he shall conform, that he shall cohere, is not onesided; what happens when a new work of art is created is something that happens simultaneously to all the works of art which preceded it. . . .

But the difference between the present and the past is that the conscious present is an awareness of the past in a way and to an extent which the past's awareness of itself cannot show.[6]

My hypothesis's Achilles' heel is threatening to become a compound fracture. And I could easily provide a number of similar quotations. All would reiterate what I have said: in isolation, the procedures behind the poetics of emulation do not demand any *terroir*. Hence, they do not belong to a specific territory.

That said, I propose that we reserve the concept of the *poetics of emulation* for the sense of the *simultaneous* updating of the elements described in chapter 3. This simultaneity is the decisive element, favoring the production of a critical synthesis that generates its own intensity in the recycling of pre-Romantic procedures. As we saw in the past two chapters, this voltage will define Machado's second phase. And all this was addressed by the deceased author: "The work of a late man. I wrote it with the pen of mirth and the ink of melancholy, and it is not difficult to predict what may come out of this mixture" (I, 513).

A mixture that seems lacking, for example, in Eliot's very essay. We can detect the perspective (both reduced and reductive) at work in this key reflection:

Whoever has approved this idea of order, *of the form of European, of English literature* will not find it preposterous that the past should be altered by the present as much as the present is directed by the past. (15; italics mine)

As is generally the case with authors from hegemonic contexts, Eliot seems to place *this idea of order, of the form of European, of English literature*, alongside the essence of literature itself. Not merely *English literature*, but rather a specific image of Western literature, ultimately circumscribed by the limits of the "great thinking nations." Hence the surprising confidence with which Eliot draws his borders.

This same confidence allows for literatures produced outside hegemonic contexts to be ignored—which ends up impoverishing one's critical perspective.

By way of a conclusion, I might recall the distinction proposed by Ernesto Sábato: "Europeans aren't Europeists; they're simply European."[7]

The Europeist—that is, someone not from Europe but who has mastered a European language—grapples with codes from a culture that will forever remain a foreign land. It is this status as foreigner that allows the Europeist to keep up the necessary level of irreverence with which to poke fun at the arrogance of hegemonic values. In order to be a Europeist, one must learn at least one second language, and then a new culture and literature—Counselor Ayres's method, let me add.

In a good-humored translation, one may imagine that the distance between the typical European and the irreverent Europeist lies in the size of one's library. The Europeist has to master at least two traditions: the European, and her own. This is not a matter of how many books there are on the shelf, but rather the necessity of establishing a link between them, concocting critical criteria for one's reading—the broader, the greater the structural intensity that characterizes the *poetics* of emulation. The difference is thus not one of nature, but of degree. *Latin American hunger*, as identified by Carlos Fuentes, favors a particular approach to the assimilation of foreign ideas. The notion of structural intensity is tied to this demand.

Such a notion, I recognize, seems excessively vague—a concept we cling to when we do not know exactly what to say.

Or how to conclude a book.

Well, then.

Back to the dialogue between Jean-Claude Carrière and Umberto Eco. The mediator at the colloquium, Jean-Philippe de Tonnac, posed an apparently anodyne question. Eco's and Carrière's answers, however, serve as a definitive clarification of the idea of structural intensity.

A backward definition.

I will quote the passage in full; it is long, but indispensable:

> JPT: *That brings us to another question: is it conceivable that an unknown masterpiece might still be discovered?*
>
> UE: An Italian aphorist once wrote that there is no such thing as a great Bulgarian poet. This may seem a little racist. What he probably meant was one of two things (and he could have chosen any small country instead of Bulgaria), or perhaps both: firstly, even if this great poet had existed, his language wouldn't have been widely enough known for us to have ever come across his work. So if "great" means famous, he might

be a very good poet, but not famous. When I visited Georgia, they told
me that their national poem, Shota Rustaveli's *The Knight in the Pan-
ther's Skin*, was a great masterpiece. I agree, but he's hardly caused the
same stir as Shakespeare.

Secondly, a country must have endured the great events of history
if it is to produce a mind capable of thinking in a universal way.

JCC: How many Hemingways were born in Paraguay? When they were
born they may have had the potential to produce a work of great originality and power, but they didn't do it. They couldn't. Either they didn't
know how to write, or there weren't any editors to support their work,
or perhaps they didn't even know that they could write, that they could
be "an author." (155–56)

I hope that the reader will not expect indignant comments on my part,
nor clarifications as to the naïveté of the discussion among these interlocu-
tors—otherwise quite sophisticated intellectuals. Why bother bringing up
the name of Augusto Roa Bastos and invoke the importance of *Yo, el supremo*
as one of the definitive novels of the twentieth century in any language?

Is it worth it to point out the basic contradictions in Umberto Eco's
words? Perhaps, although without pushing too hard.

The masterpiece by the Bulgarian poet will not pass into the Western
canon, because *his language is not well known enough and therefore we will
never have the opportunity to cross paths with him*. After all, the idea of studying the languages of nations set apart from *the great events of universal history*
seems purely absurd. The easy tautology goes unnoticed.

The vicious circle of this reasoning is so elementary that simply transcribing their dialogue is enough to identify the crucial phenomenon: the
naturalization of one's own place, the effect being a considerable reduction in
one's cultural repertoire. This naturalization limits the intensity of one's use
of the defining procedures at work in the poetics of emulation.

The Europeist, on the other hand, is driven to broaden her references,
languages, literatures, and cultures, and processing all of this demands a high
voltage. This energy lies at the core of the structural intensity that I have
associated, *potentially*, to nonhegemonic conditions.

This is what I have to offer: beyond the discovery of the semantic field of emulation in the deep structures of Machado's work, the postulation of structural intensity as a hallmark of the poetics of emulation.

◆ ◆ ◆

To some, the result will seem insufficient.

However, in the arithmetic of scarcity, Brás Cubas found reason to celebrate his *small balance.*

This is little, many will say. And they are right.

But a small balance is not the same as nothing.

(At least it is a beginning.)

Notes

Preface

1. John Golding, "Introduction," *Matisse Picasso*, ed. Elizabeth Cowling, Anne Baldassari, John Elderfield, John Golding, Isabelle Monod-Fontaine, and Kirk Varnedoe (London: Tate Publishing, 2002), 13.

2. René Girard, *Deceit, Desire and the Novel: Self and Other in Literary Structure,* trans. Yvonne Freccero (Baltimore: Johns Hopkins University Press, 1990), 2. Girard further develops the notion: "The triangle is no *Gestalt.* The real structures are intersubjective. They cannot be localized anywhere; the triangle has no reality whatsoever; it is a systematic metaphor, systematically pursued." In future instances, I will simply cite by page number.

3. Golding, "Introduction," 24. In future instances, I will simply cite by page number.

4. Anne Baldassari, "La peinture de la peinture," in *Picasso et les maîtres,* ed. Anne Baldassari and Marie-Laure Bernadac (Paris: Éditions de la Réunion des musées nationaux, 2008), 21.

5. Marie-Laure Bernadac, "Picasso Cannibale: Deconstruction-Reconstruction des Maîtres," in *Picasso et les maîtres,* ed. Anne Baldassari and Marie-Laure Bernadac (Paris: Éditions de la Réunion des musées nationaux, 2008), 37.

6. Giuseppe Fornari has a sharp-eyed take on this point. See Fornari, *Fra Dioniso e Cristo. La sapienza sacrificale greca e la civiltà occidentale* (Bologna: Pitagora Editrice, 2001), 14, 22–23, 163–67. In René Girard's words: "Giuseppe Fornari has a more positive view. According to his idea of good internal mediation, he sees art as an instrument to unfold positive internal mediation." René Girard, *Evolution and Conversion: Dialogues on the Origins of Culture,* with Pierpaolo Antonello and João Cezar de Castro Rocha (London: Continuum International Publishing, 2007), 174.

7. Laurence Madeline. "Picasso / Manet: La partie carré," in *Picasso / Manet: Le déjeuner sur l'herbe,*

ed. Laurence Madeline (Paris: Musée d'Orsay, 2008), 20. In future instances, I will simply cite by page number.

8. According to Bate there is no better way to understand "the whole of the English poetry during the last three centuries—or for that matter the modern history of the arts in general—than by exploring the effects of this accumulating anxiety and the question it so directly presents to the poet or artist: *what is there left to do?*" W. Jackson Bate, *The Burden of the Past and the English Poet* (New York: The Norton Library, 1970), 3.

9. In the critic's eloquent words: "My concern is only with strong poets, major figures with the persistence to wrestle with their strong precursors, even to the death." Harold Bloom, *The Anxiety of Influence: A Theory of Poetry,* 2nd ed. (Oxford: Oxford University Press, 1997), 5.

10. David Solkin, "Education and Emulation," in *Turner and the Masters,* ed. David Solkin (London: Tate Publishing, 2009), 101.

11. Kathleen Nicholson, "Turner, Claude and the Essence of Landscape," in *Turner and the Masters,* ed. David Solkin (London: Tate Publishing, 2009), 58. In future instances, I will simply cite by page number.

12. In Kathleen Nicholson's opinion, the English painter was quite successful: "Claude's art takes us back to a crystalline moment locked in a distant past, albeit a past and a moment refreshed by the image of the natural world into which it has been set. Turner, on the other hand, summons up that past from the recesses of his and our collective memory, and then leaves us in a very present state of awareness—of nature, of art and of our encounter with the essence of both" (71).

13. Frederick Ilchman, "Venetian Painting in an Age of Rivals," in *Titian, Tintoretto, Veronese: Rivals in Renaissance Venice* (Boston: Museum of Fine Arts, 2009), 21.

14. William Shakespeare, *Othello,* ed. Norman Sanders (Cambridge: Cambridge University Press, 2003), 71.

15. John H. Elliott, "El Greco's Mediterranean: The Encounter of Civilisations," in *El Greco* (London: National Gallery, 2003), 19.

Introduction. The Paradox of the Ur-Author

1. Translator's Note: the word *crónica* designates a mode of writing with a rich history in the Brazilian tradition, often translated with a surfeit of Latin pomp as a "chronicle," but closer in spirit to an essay or a newspaper column—short first-person pieces generally published in dailies, necessarily concise. Within this broad designation lies everything from political texts to fervent paeans to football to poetic reflections.

2. Translator's Note: the other instrument in this duet is not a large knife, but a precursor of the petite, four-stringed *cavaquinho.*

3. José Gaos, *Historia de nuestra idea del mundo,* ed. Andrés Lira, vol. 14 of *Obras completas* (Mexico City: Universidad Nacional Autónoma de México, 1994), 17.

4. As I clarify in the first chapter, the author was called this even after age thirty.

5. I will cite the works of Machado de Assis in the three-volume Nova Aguilar edition—hence, indicating simply the number of the volume and page of the edition. Translator's Note: whenever the Nova Aguilar edition is cited without comment, this is my translation. In other cases, the specific edition will be cited.

6. "By 'modernity' I mean the ephemeral, the fugitive, the contingent, the half of art whose other half is the eternal and the immutable. Every old master has had his own modernity; the great majority of fine portraits that have come down to us from former generations are clothed in the costume of their own period." Charles Baudelaire, *The Painter of Modern Life*, ed. and tr. Jonathan Mayne (London: Phaidon, 1964), 13.

7. Translator's Note: the *agregado*, to borrow John Gledson's definition from his notes to *Dom Casmurro*, is "literally . . . an addition, an adjunct" (xiv) to the Brazilian family of the time, a figure living under the auspices of the family unit, but pointedly not a part of it: neither kin nor servant, in the uncomfortable space between.

8. This story is not reproduced in the Nova Aguilar edition. Hence, I will reference the John Gledson edition, *Contos: Uma antologia*, citing by volume and page number.

9. Clifford Geertz, "Thick Description: Toward an Interpretive Theory of Culture," in *The Interpretation of Cultures: Selected Essays* (New York: Basic Books, 1973), 3–30, especially 5–10.

Chapter 1. The Shipwreck of Illusions

1. An essay such as this would not be possible without the indispensable work of José Galante de Sousa, the *Bibliografia de Machado de Assis*. I recommend consulting the "Quadro demonstrativo da obra de Machado de Assis." José Galante de Sousa, *Bibliografia de Machado de Assis* (Rio de Janeiro: Instituto Nacional do Livro, 1955), 37–38.

2. In 1910, Mário de Alencar collected Machado's literary criticism. In the note to the reader, he reflected: "After reading this book, the reader will naturally ask why the author of these excellent works of criticism did not continue with the diligence with which he cultivated another literary genre." The editor clarifies the apparent mystery: "The critic's profession is thus, in our circles, one of the most arduous, thankless, and perilous." Mário de Alencar, "Advertência da edição de 1910," in *Crítica Literária* (São Paulo: Mérito, 1959), 7 and 9.

3. "Two great forces that were triumphantly emerging, at times conjoined in one: the college graduate and the mulatto." Gilberto Freyre, *The Mansions and the Shanties*, tr. Harriet de Onis (New York: Knopf, 1966), 354.

4. As I demonstrate in chapter 5, this textual model is intrinsically related to the *poetics of emulation*, in the form of a piece of writing that structurally stimulates the act of what I will call "collage-reading."

5. I refer to chapter 71, "The Defect of This Book," the first paragraph of which reprimands the reader: "I begin to regret this book. Not that it tires me; I have nothing to do, and, indeed, dispatching a few lean chapters into this world is always a task that distracts a little from eternity. But the book is tedious, it smells of the sepulcher, it bears a certain cadaverous rictus; a grave vice, and an insignificant one at that, because *the greatest defect of this book is you, reader*. You are rushing to grow old, and the book moves slowly; you love straightforward, robust narratives, regular and flowing style, and *this book and my style are like drunkards*, they swerve right and left, go and stop, grumble, howl, cackle, threaten the heavens, slip and fall" (I, 538; italics mine)

6. Translator's Note: Another way to conceive of the "casmurrian narrator" (*narrador casmurro*, in the original) is as an incarnation of some aspects of Wayne Booth called the "unreliable narrator."

7. William Shakespeare, *Hamlet*, ed. Philip Edwards (Cambridge: Cambridge University Press, 2003), 177. In future instances, I will simply cite by page number.

8. "adultery, n." *OED Online*. Oxford University Press, September 2014.

9. "jealousy, n." *OED Online*. Oxford University Press, September 2014.

10. William Shakespeare, *Othello*, ed. Norman Sanders (Cambridge: Cambridge University Press, 2003), 139. In future instances, I will simply cite by page number.

11. In chapter 4, I return to an analysis of *Dom Casmurro*, associating Machadian processes to the structural principles of the poetics of emulation. It is important for the reader to associate these two moments in my argument, so that she may assemble the jigsaw.

12. "Tame sense with a dash of sugar, / stroke your reader's cheek / while you box his ears: / Then everyone reads you." Horace, *The Art of Poetry*, tr. Burton Raffel (Albany: State University of New York Press, 1974), 24.

13. Eça de Queirós, *Alves & Co. and Other Stories*, tr. Margaret Jull Costa (Sawtry, Cambs: Dedalus, 2012), 101.

14. Translator's Note: Machado himself, in introducing this word at the start of the eponymous novel, warns the reader that the meaning of *casmurro* as he is using it can't be found in the dictionary. The casmurro is a person who is self-absorbed without being self-centered, so immersed in himself that he barely deigns to interact with others. The word has a dash of terse arrogance, a bit of navel-gazing, and considerable aloofness. Translators have been happy to dodge a direct translation by preserving the original *Dom Casmurro*, with the exception of Robert L. Scott-Buccleuch's rendering as *Lord Taciturn*. The decision made here has been neither to reproduce this move nor to opt for a near substitute, but begin an attempt to bring *casmurro*, the aloof and self-absorbed term that has never deigned to get along with other languages, into English. The noun, from the original Portuguese, is *casmurro* (n.), the person characterized by this trait; in order to distinguish other uses, we are introducing the barbaric but useful coinages *casmurrian* (adj.) and *casmurrism* (n.).

Chapter 2. In the Middle of the Way There Was an Author

1. Jane Austen, *Northanger Abbey* (London: Richard Bentley, 1833), 60.

2. "The problem of expression is staked out by Kafka not in an abstract and universal fashion but in relation to those literature that are considered minor, for example, the Jewish literature of Warsaw and Prague. A minor literature doesn't come from a minor language; it is rather that which a minority constructs within a major language. But the first characteristic of minor literature in any case is that in it language is affected with a high coefficient of deterritorialization." Gilles Deleuze and Félix Guattari, *Kafka: Toward a Minor Literature*, tr. Dana Polan (Minneapolis: University of Minnesota Press, 1986), 16.

3. Georg Brandes, *Nietzsche: Un ensayo sobre el radicalismo aristocrático* (Mexico City: Sexto Piso, 2008), 77; italics mine. In future instances, I will simply note the page number.

4. Czeslaw Milosz, *The Witness of Poetry* (Cambridge, MA: Harvard University Press, 1984), 3–4; italics mine.

5. Pereira da Silva, "Os romances modernos e sua influência." Published by Marcus Vinicius Nogueira Soares in *Matraga, Revista do Programa de Pós-graduação em Letras da UERJ*, year 10, no. 15 (Rio de Janeiro: Caetés, 2003), 43. In future instances, I will simply reference the page number.

6. Eça de Queirós, "Idealismo e realismo," in *Cartas inéditas de Fradique Mendes e mais páginas esquecidas* (Porto: Lelo & Irmão, 1929), 171. In future instances, I will simply reference the page number.

7. Oswald de Andrade, "Manifesto da Poesia Pau-Brasil," in *A utopia antropofágica*, vol. 6 of *Obras Completas*, 2nd ed. (São Paulo: Globo, 1995), 44.

8. The passage is quoted in full in chapter 4.

9. Eça de Queirós, *O crime do padre Amaro (Cenas da vida devota)*, vol. 1 of *Obras de Eça de Queirós* (Porto: Lello & Irmãos, n.d.), 8; italics mine. Henceforth, I will simply indicate the volume and page number of the passage.

10. Alberto Machado da Rosa, *Eça, discípulo de Machado?*, 2nd ed. (Lisbon: Editorial Presença, 1979), 227; italics mine. I will henceforth quote Eça's letter from this edition; in later instances, I will cite it by the relevant page number. In the fourth chapter I return to the analysis of the ill-fated relationship between the two authors, taking up this letter once again.

11. In *Dom Casmurro* this idea is refined and takes on its definitive form in the famous characterization: "Capitu was Capitu, that is, a very particular person, *more of a woman than I was a man*" (Gledson 59; italics mine).

12. José Carlos Rodrigues, "Um romance fluminense," in *Machado de Assis: Roteiro de consagração (crítica em vida do autor)*, ed. Ubiratan Machado (Rio de Janeiro: Eduerj, 2003), 91.

13. Eça de Queirós, *Cousin Bazilio*, tr. Margaret Jull Costa (Sawtry, Cambs: Dedalus, 2003), 304.

14. The chapter closes as follows, insinuating the perfect union between the lovers in the absolute symmetry of the punctuation:

    Brás Cubas
    . . . . !
    Virgília
    . . . . !

15. Eça de Queirós, *O primo Basílio: Episódio doméstico*, 3rd ed. (São Paulo: Ateliê Editorial, 2004), 48. In future instances, I will simply reference the page number.

16. The same stuffed shirts of one of Machado's most acclaimed short stories, "Stuffed-Shirt Theory."

17. Here, I am citing the essential work by José Leonardo do Nascimento: *O Primo Basílio na imprensa brasileira do século XIX: Estética e história* (São Paulo: Editora da Unesp, 2007), 221. In subsequent citations from authors of the period, I will simply refer to the page number. Machado used the pen name "Eleazar" for his articles—hence this reply's title.

18. Augusto Meyer, "De Machadinho a Brás Cubas," *Revista Teresa* 6–7 (2006): 409. From here on, I will simply quote by page number. Augusto Meyer's essay was originally published in the *Revista do Livro* in 1958.

19. The passage that Machado refers to goes as follows:

    "Did you know that he was Luísa's childhood sweetheart?" asked Sebastião softly, as if frightened by the gravity of this confidence.
    And then, responding immediately to the look of surprise in Julião's eyes:
    "Well, he was. No one knows about it. Not even Jorge. I only found out a short while ago. They were going to be married. When his father went bankrupt, he went to Brazil and wrote to her from there breaking off their engagement."
    Julião smiled and leaned his head back against the wall. "This is like something out of *Eugénie Grandet*, Sebastião! What you're telling me is straight out of a Balzac novel. It is, it's *Eugénie Grandet*!" (Jull Costa 127).

20. Jorge Luis Borges, *Obras completas*, vol. 4, *1975–1988* (Buenos Aires: Emecé, 1996), 460. Alberto

Machado da Rosa is skeptical of this famous anecdote: "During Eça's lifetime, only *The Mandarin* was translated into French (but never published), and none of his works was translated to Italian. What could Zola have made of all of Eça's works in Portuguese?" *Eça, discípulo de Machado? Um estudo sobre Eça de Queirós*, 2nd ed. (Lisbon: Presença, 1979), 68. A skepticism that evokes the "translation imperative." In future instances, I will simply refer to the page number.

21. Gustave Flaubert, *Madame Bovary*, tr. Margaret Cohen (New York: Norton, 2005), 32. In future instances, I will simply reference the page number.

22. I might as well go ahead and expose the Achilles heel of my hypothesis: considering the irreverent appropriation of tradition as the natural consequence of a nonhegemonic origin is pure foolishness—as if literary techniques were determined by a given latitude! This, incidentally, is clarified by the reference to the essay by T. S. Eliot. I will return to this subject at the end of chapter 5, and principally at the conclusion, but let me reiterate now that I am not seeking to define essences, but rather identify strategies.

Chapter 3. Toward a Poetics of Emulation

1. José Basílio da Gama, *The Uruguay (A Historical Romance of South America)*, tr. Sir Richard Burton (Berkeley: University of California Press, 1982), 87.

2. "I don't believe in the theory of catharsis. As for criticism, it is one of the modern forms of the autobiography. A person writes about his life in the moment in which he believes he is writing about his readings. Isn't this the opposite of the *Quijote*? The critic is the figure who reconstructs his life within the texts that he reads. Criticism is a post-Freudian form of autobiography." Ricardo Piglia, "La lectura de la ficción," in *Crítica y ficción* (Barcelona: Anagrama, 2001), 13.

3. "Repeating Aristotle, Emanuele Tesauro defines 'emulation' in *Il Cannocchiale Aristotélico*: "I therefore call imitation a type of wisdom whereby you propose to yourself a metaphor or some other flower of human ingenuity; then you attentively consider its roots; and transplanting it into different categories as though into well-ploughed and fertile soil, you cause other flowers of the same species to be generated, but not the same individuals." João Adolfo Hansen, "Introdução: Notas sobre o gênero épico," in *Épicos*, 20, in *Italy in the Baroque: Selected Readings*, ed. and tr. Brendan Dooley (New York: Garland, 1995), 468.

4. Lucian of Samosata. "Zeuxis and Antiochus," in *The Works of Lucian of Samosata*, vol. 2, tr. H. W. Fowler and F. G. Fowler (Oxford: Clarendon, 1905), 94. For later citations, I will simply note the page number.

5. I am quoting from the translation by H. E. Butler: *The Instituto Oratoria of Quintilian* (London: Heinemann; New York: G.P. Putnam's Sons, 1921), 285; italics mine. For later occurrences, I will simply note the page number.

6. Antonio Vieira, "Sermão da Sexagésima," in *Sermões*, vol. 1 (São Paulo: Loyola, 2009), 22.

7. As the sermon continues, Vieira argues for a different guiding principle for the art of preaching. I will note the point here, but my focus is the analogy between the game of chess and *aemulatio*. Vieira clarifies his position: "Is it not enough that we shall not find two words at peace in the whole of a sermon? Must all be eternally bordering their opposites? Let us learn from the sky the style of disposition, and of words as well. The stars are very distinct and very bright. So must be the style of preaching; very distinct and very bright" (22).

8. This project should be developed shortly: an essay dedicated exclusively to the relevance of music in Machado de Assis's literature and worldview. Carlos Wehrs has written a key book on the topic: *Machado de Assis e a magia da música* (Rio de Janeiro: Sete Letras, 1997).

9. Luis de Camões, *The Lusiads*, tr. Geoffrey Bullough (Carbondale: Southern Illinois University Press, 1963), 59. For future references, I will simply cite by page number.

10. Oswald de Andrade, "Manifesto Antropófago," in *A utopia antropofágica*, vol. 6 of *Obras Completas*, 2nd ed. (São Paulo: Globo, 1995), 48; italics mine. In future instances, I will simply reference the page number.

11. "Problems of the Novel?" by Gabriel García Márquez, qtd. in *Gabriel García Márquez: A Life*, by Gerald Martin (London: Bloomsbury, 2008), 138.

12. Alejo Carpentier, "América ante la joven literatura europea," in *Los pasos recobrados: Ensayos de teoría y crítica literaria* (Havana: Unión, 2003), 165.

13. Pedro Henríquez Ureña, "Herencia e imitación," in *La utopia de América* (Caracas: Biblioteca Ayacucho, 1989), 52. In later citations, I will simply reference by page number.

14. Domingo Faustino Sarmiento, "Nuestro folletín," in *Obras completas*, vol. 2 (Santiago de Chile: Imprensa Gutenberg, 1885), 3; italics mine. I owe this quotation to Jens Andermann.

15. Ricardo Piglia, "La novela polaca," in *Formas breves* (Barcelona: Editorial Anagrama, 2000), 72; italics mine. In future instances, I will simply reference the page number.

16. Milton Hatoum, "Encontros na península," in *A cidade ilhada: Contos* (São Paulo: Companhia das Letras, 2009), 104. In future instances, I will simply reference the page number.

17. Marie-Laure Bernadac, "Picasso cannibale: Deconstruction-reconstruction des maîtres," in *Picasso et les maîtres* (Paris: Éditions de la Réunion de musées nationaux, 2008), 49.

18. Bernadac, "Picasso cannibale," 48.

19. Jorge Luis Borges, *Collected Fictions*, tr. Andrew Hurley (New York: Penguin, 1998), 95.

20. Roberto Fernández Retamar, "¿Y Fernández?," in *Versos* (Havana: Letras Cubanas, 1999), 182. Poem originally published in *Juana y otros poemas personales (1975–1979)*.

Chapter 4. The Decisive Years

1. In *Poets of Brazil: A Bilingual Selection*, tr. Frederick G. Williams (New York: Luso-Brazilian Books; Provo: Brigham Young University Studies; Salvador: Editora da Universidade Federal da Bahia, 2004), 143.

2. Luisa López Grigera, *Anotações de Quevedo à "Retórica" de Aristóteles* (Campinas: Editora Unicamp, 2008), 182. In future instances, I will simply reference the page number.

3. Aristotle, *The Rhetoric of Aristotle: A Translation*, tr. Sir Richard Claverhouse Jebb (Cambridge: University Press, 1909), 97. In future instances, I will simply reference the page number.

4. Information compiled in Arnaldo Faro's *Eça e o Brasil* (São Paulo: Companhia Editora Nacional, 1977), 205–13.

5. His reaction is wrenching:

> "You came to love him!" he exclaimed. "You did not detest him? You loved one another? And I'm only hearing of it now . . . Well, I declare; you are a beast. You have no care for my old age, nor did you ever . . . He is so good! So noble! And if he died for you? Would you have no remorse? Wouldn't your heart ache when you found out that such a well-born young man, who cared for you . . . Yes, he cared for you; and you as well . . . and I'm only hearing today!"

Estela closed her eyes so as not to see her father. Even this support would be denied her, in her solitude. She understood that she could only rely on herself, and faced the future with serenity. She left; her father, wracked with desperation, bid her farewell. This time the pain was selfless and pure. Jorge soon consoled her. There would be no break in their living situation, and Sr. Antunes would continue to find the same protection and cordiality as always. (I, 508)

6. To recall José Galante de Sousa's clarification on this score: in publishing fragments of "O Almada" in the *Revista Brasileira* in October 1879, Machado added a note in which he mentioned his predecessor: "Alencar wrote about this same episode in one of his last novels, *O Garatuja*" (514).

7. Victor Hugo, *Notre-Dame de Paris*, tr. Alban Krailsheimer (Oxford: Oxford University Press, 1993), 190.

8. "Oh, Funes, god of the intimidations of memory! Oh for the mania of the catalog, goddess of the boundlessness of indemonstrable knowledge! Oh for the sleepless nights spent without reading in order to draw up lists of fundamental readings! . . . Now that my genealogical tree as a reader and writer has been shown, in deference to a ritual long naturalized in countries previously (as now) considered peripheral, I shall note my education, whatever it may be." Carlos Monsiváis, *Las alusiones perdidas* (Barcelona: Anagrama, 2007), 30.

9. The dominance of the novel is intimately interwoven with a progressive downturn in the social relevance of the art of rhetoric. I will address this subject in the next chapter.

10. This is the 119th stanza of the third canto of *The Lusiads*: "Thou, only Thou (pure Love) with bended bow, / Against whose Force no brest whate're can hold, / As if thy perjur'd Subject, or Sworn Foe, / Did'st cause her death whom all the World condol'd. / If Tears (which from a troubled Fountain flow) / Quench not thy Thirst, as hath been said of old; / It is, that such is thy tyrannick mood, / Thou lov'st thy Altars should be bath'd in blood" (144).

11. Eça de Queirós, *The Mandarin and Other Stories*, tr. Margaret Jull Costa (Gardena, CA: Dedalus, 2009), 57.

12. *The Inferno of Dante*, tr. Robert Pinsky (New York: Farrar, Straus and Giroux, 1994), 39.

13. Henry Fielding, *Tom Jones* (Oxford: Oxford University Press, 1996), 67. For future citations I will simply reference by page number.

14. Laurence Sterne, *The Life and Opinions of Tristram Shandy, Gentleman*, ed. Howard Anderson (New York: Norton, 1980), 74.

15. Here is how that chapter from *Tom Jones* begins: "As truth distinguishes our writings from those idle romances which are filled with monsters, the productions, not of nature, but of distempered brains; and which have been therefore recommended by an eminent critic to the sole use of the pastry-cook . . ." (131). With *idle romances* Fielding is making reference to Romanesque stories, the very sort he wishes to distance himself from.

Chapter 5. Forms of Emulation

1. The novel opens with an "Author's Preface," in which we are told: "It is true, that the original of this Story is put into new Words, and the Stile of the famous Lady we here speak of is a little alter'd, particularly she is made to tell her own Tale in modester Words than she told it at first; the Copy which came first to Hand, having been written in Language more like one still in Newgate, than one grown Penitent and Humble, as she afterwards pretends to be." Daniel Defoe, *Moll Flanders*, ed. Edward Kelly (New York: Norton, 1973), 3.

2. Recall the opening of the "Foreword by the Author of the Memoirs of a Man of Quality": "Although I could have included the *Adventures of the Chevalier Des Grieux* among my memoirs, I decided that, there being no necessary connection between the two works, the reader would derive more pleasure from seeing them presented separately. An account of such length would have interrupted for too long the thread of my own history." Abbé Prévost, *Manon Lescaut* tr. Angela Scholar (Oxford: Oxford University Press, 2008), 3. Later on, the narrator goes into greater detail as to the circumstances under which he was writing: "I should here inform my readers that I wrote his story down almost immediately on hearing it, and that in consequence they can be sure that nothing is more accurate and more faithful than the narrative that follows" (11).

3. "rhetoric, n." *OED Online*. Oxford University Press, September 2014.

4. "rhetoric, n." *OED Online*. Oxford University Press, September 2014.

5. "commonplace, n." *OED Online*. Oxford University Press, September 2014.

6. "commonplace, n." *OED Online*. Oxford University Press, September 2014.

7. Raimundo Magalhães Júnior, "O deturpador de citações," in *Machado de Assis desconhecido*, 3rd ed. (Rio de Janeiro: Civilização Brasileira, 1957), 257; italics mine. In future instances, I will simply reference the page number.

8. Machado is referring to the ninth stanza of the tenth canto of *The Lusiads*, but, as is common with his quotations, he disfigures the source; in this case, he alters the order of the verses: "I sink into the Vale of years; and, past / My Summer's pride, to Autumn speed amain. / And my Wit (more than *years*) MISFORTUNES blast; / Which *Wit* I own not *now*, nor boast my *Vein*. / *Sighs* blow me to that *Port*, where all must cast / The *Anchor* never to be *weigh'd* again. / Yet, great *Queen* of the MUSES, grant that *I* / May close my NATION's *Poem* e're I dye." (300)

9. According to specialists, they are the following, in chronological order: *Love's Labour's Lost, A Midsummer Night's Dream, The Merry Wives of Windsor*, and *The Tempest*.

10. What follows is priceless: "We had you were weigh'd; especially when the fate of all books depends on your capacities; and not of your heads alone, but of your purses. Well, it is now public; and you will stand for your privileges, we know—to read and censure. Do so, but buy it first." John Heminge and Henry Condell, "TO THE GREAT VARIETY OF READERS," in *The Complete Works of William Shakespeare* (Hertfordshire: Wordsworth, 1994), vii.

11. Helen Caldwell, *The Brazilian Othello of Machado de Assis: A Study of "Dom Casmurro"* (Berkeley: University of California Press, 1960), 1. In future instances, I will simply reference the page number.

12. Mário de Andrade, "A Raimundo de Moraes," in *Macunaíma: O herói sem nenhum caráter*, ed. Telê Porto Ancona Lopez (Paris: UNESCO; São Paulo: EdUSP, 1996), 525; italics mine.

13. Recall Machado's insight regarding cannibalism.

14. *Ratoneiro*, or "ratter," is a slang term denoting a petty thief.

15. John Barth, foreword to *The Floating Opera and The End of the Road* (New York: Doubleday, 1988), vi–vii.

Conclusion. Echoes of Paris?

1. Jean-Claude Carrière and Umberto Eco, *This Is Not the End of the Book*, tr. Polly McLean (London: Harvill Secker, 2011), 48. In future instances, I will simply cite by page number.

2. Carlos Fuentes, *Machado de la Mancha* (Mexico City: Fondo de Cultura Económica, 2001), 10. In future instances, I will simply reference the page number.

3. Eça de Queirós, *Ecos de Paris* (Porto: Livraria Lello & Irmãos, 1945), 6 and 8; italics mine. In subsequent citations, I will simply quote by page number.

4. Joaquim Nabuco, *Minha formação* (Rio de Janeiro: Topbooks, 1999), 50; italics mine.

5. I am starting to draw up *Toward a Poetics of Emulation*, a book in which I seek to develop theoretically the method presented in this essay.

6. T. S. Eliot. "Tradition and the Individual Talent" (London: Faber & Faber, 1932), 14–16. In future instances, I will simply reference the page number.

7. Ernesto Sábato, *La cultura en la encrucijada nacional* (Buenos Aires: Crisis, 1972), 27.

Bibliography

Andrade, Mário de. "A Raimundo de Moraes." In *Macunaíma: O herói sem nenhum caráter.* Edited by Telê Porto Ancona Lopez. Paris: UNESCO; São Paulo: EdUSP, 1996.

Andrade, Oswald de. "Manifesto da Poesia Pau-Brasil." In *A utopia antropofágica*, vol. 6 of *Obras Completas.* 2nd ed. São Paulo: Globo, 1995.

———. "Manifesto Antropófago." In *A utopia antropofágica*, vol. 6 of *Obras Completas.* 2nd edition. São Paulo: Globo, 1995.

Austen, Jane. *Northanger Abbey.* London: Richard Bentley, 1833.

Baldassari, Anne. "La peinture de la peinture." In *Picasso et les maîtres,* edited by Anne Baldassari and Marie-Laure Bernadac. Paris: Éditions de la Réunion des musées nationaux, 2008.

Bandeira, Manuel. "O poeta." In *Obra completa*, by Joaquim Maria Machado de Assis, vol. 3. Rio de Janeiro: Nova Aguilar, 1986.

Baptista, Abel Barros. *Em nome do apelo do nome: Duas interrogações sobre Machado de Assis.* Lisbon: Litoral Edições, 1991.

Barbieri, Ivo. "O lapso ou uma psicoterapia de humor." In *A biblioteca de Machado de Assis*, edited by José Luís Jobim. Rio de Janerio: Academia Brasileira de Letras / Topbooks Editora, 2001.

Barth, John. Foreword. In *The Floating Opera and The End of the Road.* New York: Anchor, 1989.

Bate, W. Jackson. *The Burden of the Past and the English Poet.* New York: The Norton Library, 1970.

Baudelaire, Charles. *The Painter of Modern Life.* Edited and translated by Jonathan Mayne. London: Phaidon, 1964.

Bernadac, Marie-Laure. "Picasso cannibale: Deconstruction-reconstruction des maîtres." In *Picasso et les maîtres*, edited by Anne Baldassari and Marie-Laure Bernadac. Paris: Éditions de la Réunion de musées nationaux, 2008.

Bloom, Harold. *The Anxiety of Influence: A Theory of Poetry*. 2nd ed. Oxford: Oxford University Press, 1997.

Borges, Jorge Luis. "Pierre Menard, Author of the *Quixote*." In *Collected Fictions*, translated by Andrew Hurley. New York: Penguin, 1998.

———. "Prólogo." In *El mandarín*, by José Maria Eça de Queirós. In *Obras completas*, vol. 4, *1975–1988*. Buenos Aires: Emecé, 1996.

Bosi, Alfredo. "Brás Cubas em três versões." In *Brás Cubas em três versões: Estudos machadianos*. São Paulo: Companhia das Letras, 2006.

Brandes, Georg. *Nietzsche: Un ensayo sobre el radicalismo aristocrático*. Mexico City: Sexto Piso, 2008.

Caldwell, Helen. *The Brazilian Othello of Machado de Assis: A Study of "Dom Casmurro"*. Berkeley: University of California Press, 1960.

Camões, Luís de. *The Lusiads*. Translated by Geoffrey Bullough. Carbondale: Southern Illinois University Press, 1963.

Candido, Antonio. "Eça de Queirós, passado e presente." In *O albatroz e o chinês*. Rio de Janeiro: Ouro sobre Azul, 2004.

———. "An Outline of Machado de Assis." In *On Literature and Society*, translated by Howard Becker. Princeton: Princeton University Press, 2014.

Carpentier, Alejo. "América ante la joven literatura europea." In *Los pasos recobrados: Ensayos de teoría y crítica literaria*. Havana: Ediciones Unión, 2003.

Cruz, Dilson Ferreira da. *O éthos dos romances de Machado de Assis*. São Paulo: Nankin Editorial / EdUSP, 2009.

Dante Alighieri. *The Inferno of Dante*. Translated by Robert Pinsky. New York: Farrar, Straus and Giroux, 1994.

Defoe, Daniel. *Moll Flanders*. Edited by Edward Kelly. New York: Norton, 1973.

Deleuze, Gilles, and Félix Guattari. *Kafka: Toward a Minor Literature*. Translated by Dana Polan. Minneapolis: University of Minnesota Press, 1986.

Domínguez Michael, Christopher. "Eçalatría." In *El XIX en el XXI: Ensayos*. Mexico City: Universidad del Claustro de Sor Juana / Sexto Piso, 2010.

Eco, Umberto, and Jean-Claude Carrière. *This Is Not the End of the Book*. Translated by Polly McLean. London: Harvill Secker, 2011.

Eliot, T. S. "Tradition and the Individual Talent." In *Essays*. London: Faber & Faber, 1932.

Elliott, John H. "El Greco's Mediterranean: The Encounter of Civilisations." In *El Greco*. London: National Gallery, 2003.

Faro, Arnaldo. *Eça e o Brasil*. São Paulo: Companhia Editora Nacional, 1977.

Fernández Retamar, Roberto. "¿Y Fernández?" *Versos*. Havana: Letras Cubanas, 1999.

Fielding, Henry. *Tom Jones*. Oxford: Oxford University Press, 1996.

Flaubert, Gustave. *Madame Bovary*. Translated by Margaret Cohen. New York: Norton, 2005.

Fornari, Giuseppe. *Fra Dioniso e Cristo: La sapienza sacrificale greca e la civiltà occidentale.* Bologna: Pitagora Editrice, 2001.

Freyre, Gilberto. *The Mansions and the Shanties.* Translated by Harriet de Onis. New York: Knopf, 1966.

Fuentes, Carlos. *Machado de la Mancha.* Mexico City: Fondo de Cultura Económica, 2001.

Gaos, José. *Historia de nuestra idea del mundo.* In *Obras completas*, vol. 14, edited by Andrés Lira. Mexico City: Universidad Nacional Autónoma de México, 1994.

García Márquez, Gabriel. "¿Problemas de la novela?" In *Obra periodística*, vol. 1, *Textos costeños (1948–1952).* Mexico City: Editorial Diana, 2010.

Geertz, Clifford. *The Interpretation of Cultures: Selected Essays.* New York: Basic Books, 1973.

Girard, René. *Deceit, Desire and the Novel: Self and Other in Literary Structure,* trans. Yvonne Freccero. Baltimore: Johns Hopkins University Press, 1990.

Girard, René. *Evolution and Conversion: Dialogues on the Origins of Culture.* With Pierpaolo Antonello and João Cezar de Castro Rocha. London: Continuum International Publishing, 2007.

Gledson, John. *Por um novo Machado de Assis.* São Paulo: Companhia das Letras, 2006.

Golding, John. "Introduction." In *Matisse Picasso*, edited by Elizabeth Cowling, Anne Baldassari, John Elderfield, John Golding, Isabelle Monod-Fontaine, and Kirk Varnedoe. London: Tate Publishing, 2002.

Grammont, Guiomar de. *Aleijadinho e o aeroplano.* Rio de Janeiro: Civilização Brasileira, 2008.

Grigera, Luisa López. *Anotações de Quevedo à "Retórica" de Aristóteles.* Campinas: Editora UNICAMP, 2008.

Guimarães, Hélio de Seixas. *Os leitores de Machado de Assis: O romance machadiano e o público de literatura no século 19.* São Paulo: Nankin Editorial / EdUSP, 2004.

Hansen, João Adolfo. "Introdução: Notas sobre o gênero épico." In *Épicos*, edited by Ivan Teixeira. São Paulo: EdUSP, 2008.

Hatoum, Milton. "Encontros na península." In *A cidade ilhada: Contos.* São Paulo: Companhia das Letras, 2009.

Heminge, John, and Henry Condell. "To the Great Variety of Readers." In *The Complete Works of William Shakespeare.* Hertfordshire: Wordsworth Editions, 1994.

Henríquez Ureña, Pedro. "Herencia e imitación." In *La utopía de América.* Caracas: Biblioteca Ayacucho, 1989.

Horace. *The Art of Poetry.* Translated by Burton Raffel. Albany: State University of New York Press, 1974.

Hugo, Victor. *Notre-Dame de Paris.* Translated by Alban Krailsheimer. Oxford: Oxford University Press, 1993.

Ilchman, Frederick. "Venetian Painting in an Age of Rivals." In *Titian, Tintoretto, Veronese: Rivals in Renaissance Venice* (Boston: Museum of Fine Arts, 2009)

Lucian of Samosata. "Zeuxis and Antiochus." In *The Works of Lucian of Samosata*, vol. 2. Translated by H. W. Fowler and F. G. Fowler. Oxford: Clarendon Press, 1905.

Machado de Assis, Joaquim Maria. *Contos: Uma antologia*. Edited by John Gledson. 2 vols. São Paulo: Companhia das Letras, 1998.

———. *Crítica Literária*. São Paulo: Editora Mérito, 1959.

———. *Dom Casmurro*. Translated by John Gledson. Oxford: Oxford University Press, 1997.

———. *Esau and Jacob*. Translated by Elizabeth Lowe. Oxford: Oxford University Press, 2000.

———. *Helena*. Translated by Helen Caldwell. Berkeley: University of California Press, 1970.

———. "The Alienist." In "Madness in Translation: Language, Laughter, and Loucura in 'O Alienista,'" translated by Philip Rothaus. Undergraduate senior thesis, unpublished, Princeton University, 2011.

———. *Obra completa*. 3 vols. Rio de Janeiro: Nova Aguilar, 1986.

Madeline, Laurence. "Picasso / Manet: La partie carré." In *Picasso / Manet: Le déjeuner sur l'herbe*, edited by Laurence Madeline. Paris: Musée d'Orsay, 2008.

Magalhães Júnior, Raimundo. "O deturpador de citações." In *Machado de Assis desconhecido*. 3rd ed. Rio de Janeiro: Civilização Brasileira, 1957.

Marques, Luiz. "Apresentação." In *A fabricação do antigo*. Campinas: Editora da UNICAMP, 2008.

Martin, Gerald. *Gabriel García Márquez: A Life*. London: Bloomsbury, 2008.

Massa, Jean-Michel. *A juventude de Machado de Assis, 1839–1870: Ensaio de biografia intelectual*. Translated by Marco Aurélio de Moura Matos. Rio de Janeiro: Editora Civilização Brasileira, 1971.

Merquior, José Guilherme. "Gênero e estilo das *Memórias póstumas de Brás Cubas*." *Colóquio Letras* 8, Lisbon, 1972.

Meyer, Augusto. "De Machadinho a Brás Cubas." *Teresa: Revista de Literatura Brasileira* 6–7 (2004).

Milosz, Czeslaw. *The Witness of Poetry*. Cambridge, MA: Harvard University Press, 1983.

Monsiváis, Carlos. *Las alusiones perdidas*. Barcelona: Anagrama, 2007.

Nabuco, Joaquim. *Minha formação*. Rio de Janeiro: Topbooks, 1999.

Nascimento, Evando. *Retrato desnatural*. Rio de Janeiro: Editora Record, 2008.

Nascimento, José Leonardo do. *O Primo Basílio na imprensa brasileira do século XIX: Estética e história*. São Paulo: Editora da UNESP, 2007.

Nicholson, Kathleen. "Turner, Claude and the Essence of Landscape." In *Turner and the Masters*, ed. David Solkin. London: Tate Publishing, 2009.

Passos, José Luiz. *Machado de Assis: O romance com pessoas*. São Paulo: Nankin Editorial / EdUSP, 2007.

Pereira, Lúcia Miguel. *Machado de Assis: Estudo biográfico e crítico*. São Paulo: Companhia Editora Nacional, 1936.

Piglia, Ricardo. "La lectura de la ficción." In *Crítica y ficción*. Barcelona: Editorial Anagrama, 2001.

———. "La novela polaca." *Formas breves*. Barcelona: Editorial Anagrama, 2000.

Prévost, Antoine François. *Manon Lescaut*. Translated by Angela Scholar. Oxford: Oxford University Press, 2008.

Pujol, Alfredo. *Machado de Assis*. Rio de Janeiro: Academia Brasileira de Letras / Imprensa Oficial, 2007.

Queirós, Eça de. *Alves & Co. and Other Stories*. Translated by Margaret Jull Costa. Sawtry, Cambs: Dedalus, 2012.

———. *Cousin Bazilio*. Translated by Margaret Jull Costa. Sawtry, Cambs: Dedalus, 2003.

———. *Ecos de Paris*. Porto: Livraria Lello & Irmãos, 1945.

———. "Idealismo e Realismo." *Cartas inéditas de Fradique Mendes e mais páginas esquecidas*. Porto: Lelo & Irmão, 1929.

———. *The Mandarin and Other Stories*. Translated by Margaret Jull Costa. Dedalus: Gardens, CA, 2009.

Quintilian. *The Instituto Oratoria of Quintilian*. Translated by H. E. Butler. London: Heinemann; New York: G.P. Putnam's Sons, 1921.

Riedel, Dirce Côrtes. *Metáfora, o espelho de Machado de Assis*. São Paulo: Livaria Francisco Alves Editora, 1979.

Rodrigues, José Carlos. "Um romance fluminense." In *Machado de Assis: Roteiro de consagração (crítica em vida do autor)*, edited by Ubiratan Machado. Rio de Janeiro: EdUERJ, 2003.

Rosa, Alberto Machado da. *Eça, discípulo de Machado? Um estudo sobre Eça de Queirós*. 2nd ed. Lisbon: Editorial Presença, 1979.

Rouanet, Sérgio Paulo. *Riso e melancolia*. São Paulo: Companhia das Letras, 2007.

Sá Rego, Enylton de. *O calundu e a panaceia*. Rio de Janeiro: Forense Universitária, 1989.

Sábato, Ernesto. *La cultura en la encrucijada nacional*. Buenos Aires: Crisis, 1972.

Sabino, Fernando. *Amor de Capitu*. São Paulo: Editora Ática, 2006.

Santiago, Silviano. "The Rhetoric of Verisimilitude." In *The Space in-between: Essays on Latin American Culture*. Edited by Ana Lúcia Gazzola. Translated by Tom Burns, Ana Lúcia Gazzola, and Gareth Williams. Durham, NC: Duke University Press, 2001.

Sarmiento, Domingo Faustino. "Nuestro folletín." In *Obras completas*, vol. 2. Santiago de Chile: Imprensa Gutenberg, 1885.

Schwarz, Roberto. *Martinha* versus *Lucrécia: Ensaios e entrevistas*. São Paulo: Companhia das Letras, 2012.

———. *A Master on the Periphery of Capitalism: Machado de Assis*. Translated by John Gledson. Durham, NC: Duke University Press, 2001.

Sena, Jorge de. "Machado de Assis e o seu Quinteto Carioca." In *Estudos de cultura e literatura brasileira*. Lisbon: Edições 70, 1988.

Shakespeare, William. *Hamlet*. Edited by Philip Edwards. Cambridge: Cambridge University Press, 2003.

———. *Othello*. Edited by Norman Sanders. Cambridge: Cambridge University Press, 2003.

Silva, Pereira da. "Os romances modernos e sua influência." *Jornal de Debates* 32 (September 23, 1837). In *Matraga: Revista do Programa de Pós-graduação em Letras da UERJ*, year 10, no. 15. Rio de Janeiro: Caetés, 2003.

Solkin, David. "Education and Emulation." In *Turner and the Masters,* edited by David Solkin. London: Tate Publishing, 2009.

Sousa, José Galante de. *Bibliografia de Machado de Assis.* Rio de Janeiro: Instituto Nacional do Livro, 1955.

Sterne, Laurence. *The Life and Opinions of Tristram Shandy, Gentleman.* Edited by Howard Anderson. New York: Norton, 1980.

Teixeira, Ivan. *Apresentação de Machado de Assis.* São Paulo: Editora Martins Fontes, 1987.

Vasconcellos, Paulo Sérgio de. *Efeitos intertextuais na "Eneida" de Virgílio.* São Paulo: Humanitas/ FFLCH/USP, 2001.

Vasconcelos, Beatriz Avila. *Ciência do bem dizer: A concepção de retórica em Quintiliano em "Institutio Oratoria", II, 11–21.* São Paulo: Humanitas, 2005.

Vieira, Antônio. "Sermão da Sexagésima." In *Sermões*, vol. 1. São Paulo: Edições Loyola, 2009.

Wehrs, Carlos. *Machado de Assis e a magia da música.* Rio de Janeiro: Sette Letras, 1997.

Wey, Valquiria. "Reflexiones sobre una crisis: 1878 en la obra de Machado de Assis." In *Anuario de studios latinoamericanos.* Mexico City: UNAM, 2001.

Wisnik, José Miguel. "Machado maxixe." In *Sem receita*: Ensaios e canções. São Paulo: PubliFolha, 2004.

Index